WILDERNESS RIVERS *of* MANITOBA

JOURNEY BY CANOE THROUGH *the* LAND WHERE THE SPIRIT LIVES

This edition is dedicated to the new wave of Manitoba eco-warriors
whose concerted efforts to preserve these rivers
serve to bring awareness to this precious Canadian resource.

A BOSTON MILLS PRESS BOOK

Published by Boston Mills Press, 2003
132 Main Street, Erin, Ontario N0B 1T0
Tel: 519-833-2407 Fax: 519-833-2195
e-mail: books@bostonmillspress.com
www.bostonmillspress.com

In Canada:
Distributed by Firefly Books Ltd.
66 Leek Crescent
Richmond Hill, Ontario, Canada L4B 1H1

In the United States:
Distributed by Firefly Books (U.S.) Inc.
P.O. Box 1338, Ellicott Station
Buffalo, New York 14205

National Library of Canada Cataloguing in Publication

Wilson, Hap, 1951-
Wilderness rivers of Manitoba : journey by canoe through the land where the spirit lives /
compiled and illustrated by Hap Wilson & Stephanie Aykroyd.

Includes bibliographical references.
ISBN 1-55046-440-X

1. Canoes and canoeing—Manitoba—Guidebooks. 2. Wild and scenic rivers—
Manitoba—Guidebooks. 3. Manitoba—Guidebooks. 4. Manitoba—Description and travel.
5. Wilson, Hap, 1951- —Travel—Manitoba. 6. Aykroyd, Stephanie, 1970- —Travel—Manitoba.
I. Aykroyd, Stephanie, 1970- II. Canadian Recreational Canoeing Association. III. Title.

GV776.15.M36W54 2004   797.1'22'097127   C2004-900047-0
U.S. CIP data available upon request.

The publisher acknowledges the financial support of the Government of Canada
through the Book Publishing Industry Development Program (BPIDP) for its publishing efforts.

Cover photos: Hap Wilson
Photography, maps, illustrations by Hap Wilson & Stephanie Aykroyd
Cover design by Gillian Stead

Printed in Canada

WILDERNESS RIVERS
of
MANITOBA

JOURNEY BY CANOE THROUGH
the
LAND WHERE THE SPIRIT LIVES

Compiled and Illustrated by

HAP WILSON & STEPHANIE AYKROYD

The BOSTON
MILLS PRESS

Northwest

River

Nueltin
Lake

Territories

Thlewiaza

East R.

Caribou

River

Cochrane

River

Lac Brochet

Tadoule
Lake

SEAL

RIVER

Churchill

HUDSON

Brochet

Reindeer
Lake

MANITOBA

York Factory

BAY

Lynn Lake

Ontario

THOMPSON

HAYES

RIVER

Flin Flon

GRASS

RIVER

Oxford House

Norway House

LAKE WINNIPEG

Saskatchewan

Berens
River

Little Grand
Rapids

BERENS

PIGEON

R.

R.

Bloodvein

Leyond R.

BLOODVEIN

RIVER

N

CAMMON

RIVER

Manigotagan

Manigotagan R.

Y

SWIFT

W

E

WINNIPEG

S

UNITED STATES

100   0   200   300   400

km.

Wild Rivers
of
MANITOBA

Illustrating Canoe Journeys by the Authors 1994-97

"Few pleasures equal the genuine enjoyment of a vacation spent amidst the beauties of Nature with its pure air, inspiring scenery and health-giving qualities, and the opportunity it gives us to forget the hustle, bustle and drive of our modern competitive life, and commune for a while in peace and quiet with the Things That Are, the Things That Have Always Been and, let us hope, Always Will Be."

Grey Owl, 1937

FOREWORDS

Manitoba is a canoeist's paradise with rivers traversing rolling prairie, woodlands, boreal forests, delta marshlands, rugged Precambrian shield and northern tundra. Through an ever-changing landscape with more than 100,000 lakes flow countless rivers waiting to share their history, wildlife and wilderness with new adventurers who will follow the routes of explorers and traders of days gone by.

Hap Wilson and Stephanie Aykroyd's book, *Wilderness Rivers of Manitoba*, will unlock the mysteries of navigating Manitoba rivers to both the regional and international canoe enthusiast. It contains extensive information on historical activities along selected river systems. The authors' firsthand knowledge of the geography, archaeology, and essential canoe route know-how will help the novice and expert alike to meet the challenge and experience the adventure of a lifetime. The Department of Industry, Trade and Tourism's contribution to this publication has been made in the interest of marketing and stimulating the growth of wilderness canoeing activities throughout the province.

Manitoba Department of Industry, Trade & Tourism

When Hap first approached me, as Senior Advisor to the CHRS, proposing a guidebook to Manitoba Rivers, I was excited. I'd known Hap's work for years as the standard remote wilderness touring guidebooks against which all others were judged. But more than that, his books had a spiritual quality about them which I admired; and they were comprehensive in addressing not only the trip, but also the natural and cultural aspects of the rivers themselves, giving them a much more personal dimension far beyond the physical challenge. In short, they provided a perfect fit with the type of series I had in mind for all Canadian Heritage Rivers. Who better to design a Manitoba prototype, especially following on the immense success of the 1996 international award-winning book *Voyages* edited by Lynn Noel, illustrated and written in part by Hap, and sponsored by the CHRS.

The result, as you will see herein, is what you would expect from Hap. The persistent support of Manitoba Tourism specialist Jan Collins in getting the project off the ground, and the illustrative beauty created throughout by Hap's partner Stephanie Aykroyd, have enabled Hap, through his "Wilderness Rivers of Manitoba", to realize my dream to create a prototype for a series on Canadian rivers for use by the CHRS or other Canada-wide groups interested in promoting and protecting Canada's world-renowned river heritage.

By supporting Hap's efforts, Manitoba has taken a solid step forward. But much remains to be done both in Manitoba and across Canada. Manitobans must encourage their government leaders, first, to implement those measures which must be taken now to ensure proper protection and management of the river resources in their home province, and then having done so, to stand as leaders encouraging their colleagues across Canada to do the same.

Michael E. Greco
President, Canadian River
Management Society, and Patron of
The Bennett Smith Heritage Foundation
of Windsor, Nova Scotia

The first edition of *Wilderness Rivers of Manitoba* offered a unique and unprecedented invitation to explore some the world's last truly unspoiled wilderness highways. More than just river guides, Hap Wilson and Stephanie Aykroyd introduced us to the history, culture and ecosystems of Manitoba's rivers and ensured that these rivers, if not travelled, would at least be visited by readers through the authors' words. Although the focus of the book was Manitoba, rivers such as the Hayes have a historical significance for all Canadians, one which transcends provincial boundaries.

As our society struggles to avert the dangers caused by increased consumption of resources and consequent climate change, the power harnessed from our rivers becomes increasingly attractive as a source of "clean" energy. But no development is without a cost to our wilderness environment. Books such as *Wilderness Rivers of Manitoba* offer us the opportunity to explore this environment before it is threatened with further alteration in the name of development. We can better protect that which we know and have experienced for ourselves.

Paddle Manitoba is proud to continue its long association with Hap and Stephanie. We hope that our rivers will survive to provide them with the inspiration for many more editions. So grab a coffee, settle into the big chair by the fire, and join us for a journey of discovery.

Paddle Manitoba/MRCA

ACKNOWLEDGEMENTS

If it were not for the assistance of several individuals we would not have entertained the thought of writing another guidebook. While a project of this magnitude may keep us in the canoe for the longest period of time, there are the obvious shortcomings to our extended life on the trail – like paying bills for instance. Although rolling quarters to cover rent is a somewhat humbling necessity, peculiar in that we are seldom at home anyway, we do manage to pull ourselves from the abyss of financial distress in more unconventional ways. The indulgence in adventure and the opiate of experience in the great wilderness of Canada supersedes all else; the wallet and the state of the exchequer lie buried at the bottom of the pack until we decide to come out. Wealth is a condition of mind and being, marked by the amount of time one can free oneself from the superfluity of a feckless "system". Wealth and harmony then, could be considered in terms of the number and quantity of exotic spices you carry in your kitchen wannigan, or gauged by the number of rainless days out on the trail, or, the pecuniary ability not to pay bills on time!

The inspiration and driving force behind the Manitoba book came in many forms: The vivid scene of two young canoeists who had drowned at a waterfall in Ontario because a cartographer's mistake on a topographic map placed the portage on the wrong side of the river, in itself is enough reason to correct and update seriously deficient navigational resources – improved field-friendly information is paramount if provincial governments continue to sell wilderness as a commodity. And, on this note we would like to extend our thanks to Jan Collins of Travel Manitoba, Industry, Trade & Tourism, for his concerted effort, along with Henry Goy and Collette Fontaine, whose support and encouragement made this book a reality which in turn will create a safer venue for wilderness travel.

I personally would like to introduce to the readers a very special person, my paddling partner, best friend and wife – Stephanie Aykroyd. Stephanie has added a personal touch to the book through her talents as a fine artist, photographer and mapmaker; without her devotion and hard work, both on and off the trail, this guidebook and my life would not be so enriched. It's not easy finding someone who will carry a heavy wannigan for two kilometers over spongy tundra and wield an art pen tirelessly and with such finesse when in the studio.

Heartfelt appreciation goes to our good friend and confidant, Mike Greco of the Canadian River Management System/ Heritage River Board, whose immortal presence and indefatigable encouragement kept us moving in the right direction. Mike was our motivational spare paddle – he was there whenever we needed a dose of hope and faith when we needed to find a channel through the bureaucratic morass.

Gratitude goes to our good friends and tripping cohorts from CITY-TV, Toronto; Stephen Hurlbut, Bob Hunter who flashed his agile wit around as often as his can of bear spray, and Todd Southgate, who captured the beauty of the Manitoba wilderness on video so that others may share in the adventure.

I commend *Men's Journal Magazine* for sponsoring our first Manitoba expedition on the Seal; also thanks to Mary and Allan Code of Tree-Line Productions, and the Dene people of Tadoule for their hospitality and for welcoming us to the sweat-lodge ceremony.

Enid and Hugh Carlson of Viking Air in Red Lake deserve a special thanks, not just for their hospitality but also for introducing us to Walter and Jöri Von BallMoos from Switzerland whose comradeship made the long trek across the barrens possible, enduring hardships without complaint and never without wit and humour, often required to diffuse several moments of tension and mild despair.

Thanks to the Ontario Ministry of Natural Resources fire-control centre and Woodland Caribou Park staff in Red Lake for their assistance; the Klassens of Sasaginigak Lodge for their hospitality and stories; and to Rick Wilson of the Manitoba Natural Resources for arranging some of the shuttles and for supplying topographical maps for all of the rivers researched. We also appreciate the services of WamAir, Webber's Lodges and Skyward Aviation for getting us in and out safely; and many thanks to both Knee Lake and Nueltin Lodge for giving us lunch and a cold beer; Tony and Susan Brew of Wekusko Falls Lodge on the Grass, and Garth Duncan and Karin Aldringer of Raven Eye Outfitters in Lynn Lake; the Mystery Lake Hotel in Thompson, our home away from home for the past few years (sorry for the spilled rice on the carpet and the pot-black in the bathtub), and, thanks to Natural Resources conservation officer Chuck Young who found us a cheaper place to pitch our tent in Thompson; and, thanks to friendly Earl W. Simmons for the shuttle on the Grass River.

The assistance of the various First Nations was appreciated, so too was the additional information supplied by the Manitoba Recreational Canoeing Association. Thanks to Randy Todd of the Water Survey of Canada in Thompson. Our thanks also to the original team of people who helped with the production of the first edition of this book.

Finally, our indebtedness goes to Manitoba, *Land Where the Spirit Lives*, for sharing some of its secrets and allowing our hearts to sing.

CORPORATE SPONSORS

**211 King Street
London, Ontario, Canada
N6A 1C9**

A TRADITION OF QUALITY SINCE 1900.
58 Middle Street Old Town, ME USA 04468

PO Box 1500
319 Roddy Lane
Harriman, TN 37748

Without the generous assistance of the following sponsors, the Manitoba Wilderness River survey would have been ill-equipped, to say the least, certainly less colourful had I been forced to bring my aging cedar/canvas canoe and other antiquated gear out of retirement. I believe every piece of outdoor equipment that we actually own is either forest green or earth tan, implicating an era when one tried to blend with nature.

Outdoor impedimenta has come a long way in the last three decades; some of it I must admit, if not ablaze in Day-Glo brilliance, is actually quite serviceable. The goodwill of sponsors not only helped keep the overall cost of research down, but continually introduced a steady stream of technical achievements in the adventure industry.

Consider that during our travels, over the span of but one canoeing season alone, we put to the extreme test each piece of equipment equal to 8-10 years hard service by any mere mortal. Our sponsors donated most of the canoes and gear knowing full well that resale was a poor option.

First, Stephanie and I would like to thank Sandi and Paul Caplan and Terry Needham and the rest of our friends at **Novacks**, London's finest outdoor and adventure travel store, for their continued generosity, encouragement and friendship. Thanks also to **Swift Canoe & Kayak** for the use of three canoes; the Winisk 17', the Dumoine 16', and the Yukon 17'. The Dumoine clearly championed 15 of the total rivers and is still going strong.

Wolverine Paddles/Kijik Canoe supplied some outstanding blades, one of which is still floating somewhere on the Caribou; while Jim Stevens and Ron Thompson of **Eureka** and **Camp Trails** made sure that we were well stocked with tents and packs.

Thanks to Steve Krautkremer and his predecessor, Jo Moon, of **Old Town Canoe Co.**, for supplying 17' Trippers and an Appalachian 16' – the expedition workhorse and the spunky light touring boat that never needed a spray deck regardless of conditions. And finally, thanks to **Dagger Canoe** for letting us try out the Venture 17' – the Mercedes of serious expedition canoes.

Other sponsors include: Rockwater Designs who supplied tents, Turtle Paddleworks, *Men's Journal Magazine* who sponsored our Seal River expedition, and Harvest Foodworks for donating dehydrated foods for the initial survey.

CONTENTS

INTRODUCTION

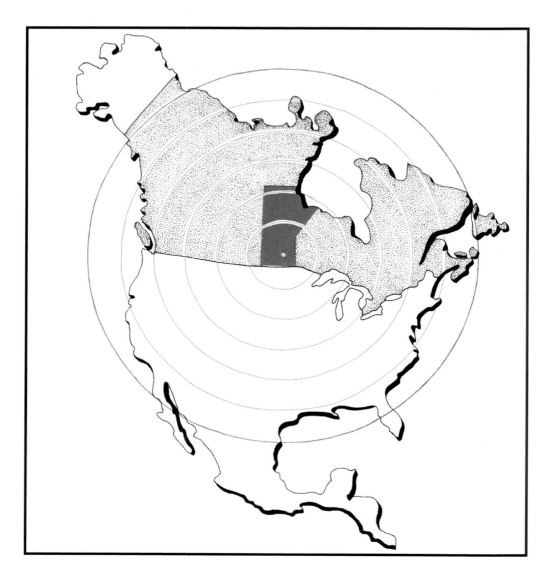

It might be said that the spirit and personality emanate from the heart. The Cree and Ojibway people referred to Manitou-ba as the "Land Where the Spirit Lives," derived from the provocative and often impetuous character of Lake Winnipeg, vibrant and full of life, yet dangerous and steeped in mystery.

Manitoba is the geographic heart of Canada; it also best represents the distinctive wild nature of this country through its earth-science and human history. Nowhere else on this continent can the stalwart explorer stand on an aspen bluff in the southwest and view an endless sea of prairie grass, or trek across the open reaches of the northern tundra on the edge of the Arctic ocean. So diverse is the landscape of Manitoba that it continually provokes that impulse to explore, and believe me, a mere taste is just not enough!

The province boasts of having over 100,000 lakes and innumerable rivers and streams. A vast territory five times the size of England yet with only 1/50th the population — and the majority of people live within the greater Winnipeg area. To the gallant adventurer, this means wilderness like no other place on earth and Manitoba has it.

The rivers highlighted in this book have been chosen for their austere and wild nature; they have also been selected for their ability to taunt and tantalize the greatest variety of adventure seekers of various levels of skill and tastes. From novice to expert there is something to stir the blood of each individual. As the centre of this enormous country, adventure starts right here — in the Land Where the Spirit Lives!

PREFACE

Undertaking a book project that consumes five years of your life is likely to leave an indelible impression on your psyche. It may be insidious in nature, at least until you have had the opportunity to reminisce — to catch your breath so to speak, and to use that "inward eye" as Wordsworth puts it, in order to fully evaluate the impact that a particular pilgrimage has had on one's spirit.

In retrospect, when I first paddled the Seal River in 1994 for *Men's Journal Magazine*, I had no idea that this *baptism* to Manitoba rivers would have ever led to a provincial canoeing guidebook. Itemizing the multitude of reasons for not writing another travel journal was based on the premise that funding or subsidies for such a venture would be scant. That alone has all kinds of repercussions, knowing well that my life would be in total chaos and financial exhaustion until the book was complete and out of my hands. And then there was that other inexorable dilemma that confronts many outdoor writers, that being moral conscience. The question whether or not secret and often sacred places be revealed to the throngs of Gore-Tex-clad adventure seekers is an enigma faced by those destined to fall upon their own swords. One has hope that the wilderness code of ethics will prevail, and that those explorers who may be inspired by the published word will be respectful of the harmony of place and leave it as beautiful for others as they themselves lay witness to.

Manitoba, like any other province, has its fair share of environmental concerns...the salient offspring of ambitious corporate and government maneuverings, and the pressure to ensure employment and a comfortable standard of living — quite often at the cost of sustaining the quality of life through the loss of wilderness.

At the rate in which we lose wilderness across Canada, for the aforesaid reasons, and out of sheer ignorance of the overall benefits of the economics of aesthetics, it is paramount that we make a critical "leap of faith" — to do what one can in order to protect the remaining vestiges of wild places. From the perspective of extraction-based industry, for us to say nothing is an apathetic compliance to the views and whims of the developers. We make the loudest statement by keeping silent.

The elite genre of paddler who cares to see absolutely no one else on a particular river will complain vehemently to me that our guidebook is exploiting wilderness; yet, will this same coterie take the initiative to investigate the upcoming plans for riverside clear-cut logging? Or, would they complain about Hydro's intention of diverting a whole river into another? Or, might they even be concerned that several new roads and proposed bridge crossings will allow unregulated access by the mechanized sportsman? Likely not.

The paradox of nature writing dictates drastic measures when relating wise use of a particular ecozone to the general public. Use it or lose it. It's as simple as that. The reality that ecotourism is an economic contributor to provincial coffers is finally hitting home; and in some cases, it may be the only sustainable option for development of a natural resource. It's good business in long-term yields, and the impact on the environment is minimal.

As a somewhat seasoned environmentalist I do have my own agenda. Personally, I would rather bump gunnels with a few like-minded canoeists paddling a river than have to portage around a hydro dam, or listen to skidders and chainsaws and watch helplessly as the skyline of spruce gets loaded onto the back of a hauler.

Administrators tend to look at the ready, known, tangible uses of public lands in a purely pragmatic way. Self-propelled adventure tourism is not the invisible industry as once thought. As a major component of the fast growing eco-travel trade it generates millions annually into tertiary economies and offers unlimited entrepreneurial opportunities for those interested in this facet of tourism. Governments are coming around, slowly, realizing that setting aside tracts of wilderness is protecting a commodity that is fast disappearing. And, as a commodity becomes scarce, it also becomes more valuable; spiritually, it represents a template or guide-post for all aspects of personal well-being. Rivers then, are an important resource, and to save them we must get out and paddle them; not to usurp them unwisely but to bask in the primal richness of place and proffer due respect for such linear galleries of earthly treasures.

My first taste of Manitoba wilderness ignited that deep core, essential urge to explore further. Here was a place, I thought, that resonated with the voices of early travellers both white and native, and a landscape so discreet and multifarious as to beguile the senses. Even Manitobans have been fooled by the typecast provincial image of wheat-fields and roaming bison herds. It was obvious that the only eyes cast upon this vast wilderness were those of the resource developers save for a few dispersed inquisitors who sought solitude and adventure instead of quick profit.

And so, *Wilderness Rivers of Manitoba* was born out of a passion for soulful exploration and the need to preserve some of the finest rivers in Canada. Not that this book will present itself as the panacea for all ill-will projected against river environments, but it is our way of doing something about river conservation through eco-tourism. Vainglorious as it may seem to some, we aspire to encourage others to make the journey; to taste, smell, and touch the alluring vibrancy of the Manitoba hinterland.

Without the inspiration of Mike Greco of the Canadian Heritage Rivers Board, and the support and faith of Jan Collins and the Travel Manitoba team, this book could not have been possible. A further boost came when my wife Stephanie shared the work load, in the field and in the studio, starting in the summer of '96, working diligently to produce a quality guidebook with her own particular flair for detail.

To be succinct, *Wilderness Rivers of Manitoba* is not a "how-to" book, although we have included chapters that briefly cover worthy areas of interest; there are other current publications that are aptly suited which expand on all facets of wilderness travel. Instead, this is a book of maps. Over 300 hand-drawn and labelled maps to be more specific. People love maps, and cartography done in the old style is a lost art. People have been inspired by maps since time immemorial; in fact mapmaking is one of the world's oldest professions (not prostitution as one is led to believe).

Maps relate the story of the river; each meander, riffle and fall is plotted with the utmost care and accuracy using data accrued in the field. Portage trails indicate the necessity to carry around an abrupt or dangerous drop in the elevation, and the location of campsites make daily planning easier. Even the armchair outdoor enthusiast will find fancy in tracing the course of each river from head pond to point of egress.

Singularly, each river could have easily produced whole volumes of text, maps, sketches and photographs. Our task to condense the collected material into one volume that included 17 rivers was not a simple one. Route maps were drawn to the 1:250,000 scale; this required fewer overall maps but many more detailed drawings of particularly difficult or confusing sections of river. We made the decision not to use computer digitized maps for two reasons; neither of us like them because of the techno-look and electro-magnetic radiation, and specifically because we wanted to maintain that "old-world" charm and hand-drawn tradition of mapmaking.

After four years of exhausting field expeditions that traced more than 4,000 kilometres of Manitoba wilderness rivers onto the pages of this book, it may be interesting for the reader to know that it actually took longer to draw the maps than it did to paddle the rivers. It is our hope that those who peruse this book will look at each map as a work of art, and maybe appreciate better the time that went into producing them.

And as for the Manitoba wilderness, the poignant emotions transfixed to the memories of places we have been, are woven deeply into the fabric and convolutions of our souls, and we have only an impatient longing to go back there. And if I were asked what it was about Manitoba that affected me the most, I know well that simple words and metaphors could only betray my answer. It is truly the Land Where the Spirit Lives and that time has forgotten; of chromatic tundra sunsets and crisp Arctic nights when the stars dance tauntingly within reach; it is an old grave atop a sandy esker, marked with a ring of stones and an old sheath knife; or perhaps the broken bowl of a voyageur's clay pipe found at Trout Falls on the Hayes River, or a rusted cannonball half buried on the beach at York Factory; or the mystery of native rock-paintings, etched in red-ochre or were they actually painted with the blood of the Memegwishiwok who dwell behind the face of granite?; the terrible awe of an all-consuming boreal fire and having to wrap wet bandanas around our faces so that we could breathe the acrid smoke-filled air; a sudden confrontation with a wolf, a cow moose protecting a calf and a curious polar bear; or maybe sailing down the Hudson Bay coast in the middle of the night and getting stranded on the tidal flats for 6 hours waiting for the tide to come in; and the dynamic primitive energy of a Dene hand-game and the smile of a child's face as it rides in the back of a pick-up truck on a dirt road that goes nowhere. Manitoba is all of this and more. There were good times and there were hard times, there were blistered hands and swollen feet, of being cold, wet and fly-bitten, and riding the backs of dangerous rapids crashing through the very bones of Mother Earth, and long treks across the lonely tundra looking for water to float the canoes...but there were no bad times. After all, this is the stuff of true adventure and if it is adventure and entertainment you seek then you will find it here, in Manitoba and within the pages of this book. Listen carefully and you can hear the clicking of caribou hooves on a gravel esker behind your tent, or the sonic whispers of beluga whales as they swim alongside your canoe, feel the heartbeat of a Dene drum and allow your soul to be whisked away. This is Manitoba and you will be surprised.

Hap Wilson
September 1998

SECTION I

THE SPIRIT OF PLACE

Helpful Information

"Wherever we go in the wilderness, we find more than we seek."

John Muir

Caribou antlers, Wolverine River

THE SPIRIT OF PLACE

GENERAL INFORMATION ABOUT MANITOBA

The water that tumbles recklessly through the chasms and channels of the wilderness is just passing through, like us, on a voyage of discovery. For those individuals who seek only the excitement of water in its transitory state, they will find rapids enough to quell the passion for the adrenaline rush of river over boulder. But it's the boldness of the land itself and the environment through which the river descends that blesses the water with character and vitality.

The desire to know the land in which you travel is a show of respect for the individuality of the spirit of place, not to mention that it gives freely of its bounty to those willing enough to place nature, and the river, above the need for self-adulation or the "quest" to vanquish its disposition. Water is water, different perhaps in terms of turbidity and flow, but its distinction as a river comes from the geography and history around it. For the adventurer with a soul for exploration and discovery, Manitoba offers one of the most diverse landscapes in North America; from prairie grassland and the transitional forests of the time-worn and glacially sculptured Precambrian Shield, to one of the most austere and harsh seacoasts in all of Canada; you can find prickly-pear cactus in the south, Arctic tundra in the north. It's a land of variety, of moods, of contrasts and uniqueness.

Bison roam the prairie-aspen southern plains while polar bears range along an Arctic coast that is also home to one of the largest populations of beluga whales in the world. What better way to see it all than in a canoe.

This book may only skim the surface of a myriad of adventure possibilities and potential discoveries to be made. In brief we have illustrated some basic information that the reader/explorer may find of particular interest and help in deciding where to go.

NATURAL VEGETATION – MAP #1

This map indicates a rather broad or basic look at regional distinctions noting that there may be an overlapping of species; for example, certain prairie grasses and ferns found in site "E" may also be found within zone "D", etc.

ZONE "A" – ARCTIC TUNDRA

Found north of the tree-line, this vast plain is carpeted with sedge, grass hummocks, lichens and saxifrage. Over 900 species of flowering plants can be found but few trees other than scattered stands of stunted black spruce growing in depressions. Lichens are an important food source for barrenland caribou, as are the variety of mosses and grass. The Caribou and Seal River canoe routes pass through this zone.

ZONE "B" - NORTHERN TRANSITION

Black spruce is the predominant species throughout with tamarack occurring on poorly-drained, lowland areas. White spruce, balsam fir, trembling aspen, balsam poplar, alder and a variety of willows can be found along the river valleys (specifically along the Hayes, Cochrane and upper Thlewiaza). Scattered jackpine and white birch favour areas that have been recently burned over. As one proceeds closer to the tundra, stands of spruce become less dense and stunted. Riverbanks may support wild rose, aster, fireweed and goldenrod, interspersed with a feathermoss and lichen ground cover while backshores often change to semi-open spruce bogs.

ZONE "C" - NORTHERN CONIFEROUS FOREST

This zone supports a continuous forest of spruce, jackpine and fir, with jackpine, aspen and birch habitating areas of recent fire. River valleys tend to nourish a variety of shore willows and alder while backshores support typical fen and bog communities. Wild rice is found in various locations, most notably along the Bloodvein watershed.

ZONE "D" – MIXED FOREST

The only river that shares some of the floral species found in this region is the Manigotagan. Here, mixed stands of broadleaf hardwoods such as burr oak and maple mingle with conifers. Frequent meadows can be found bordering the prairie region to the south.

ZONE "E" – WOODED GRASSLAND

This is an open to treed prairie grassland with scattered patches of willows and aspen breaking an otherwise sweeping vista. There are no representative rivers in this region.

AVERAGE PRECIPITATION (MAY - SEPT.) – MAP #2

The chief indicator here is the decrease in summer rainfall as one travels north. It does not mean that you will encounter more hours of sunshine – just less rain. As you travel north the climate is generally drier, the days longer with prevailing winds from the north and northeast. The Arctic influence is felt upon nearing Hudson Bay. Prevailing winds in south and central Manitoba are generally from the southwest to northwest.

JULY MEAN DAILY TEMPERATURE – MAP #3

These are not daily highs, but an average temperature between night minimums and day maximums. There is a 6–7°C. (10-12° F.) difference in temperature from southern Manitoba (Winnipeg) to that in the north (Churchill). You can usually add 5-10°C. (15-20°F.) to mean temperatures in order to find normal daily highs. Water temperatures in the far north remain quite cold throughout the summer; there is often ice on Nueltin Lake in early July and canoeists paddling this area, or descending the Caribou or Seal, are encouraged to don wet suits while running any whitewater. Summer water temperatures south of York Factory (57°) are generally warm enough for swimming through July and August.

PROGLACIAL LAKES – MAP #4

This map indicates the two major glacial lakes that were impounded during the Pleistocene epoch, marked by several glacial and interglacial episodes. Lake sediments or deposits are defined by glacial "strandlines" and outflow channels – the Nelson River basin being the most prominent channel cut by meltwater escaping from glacial lakes.

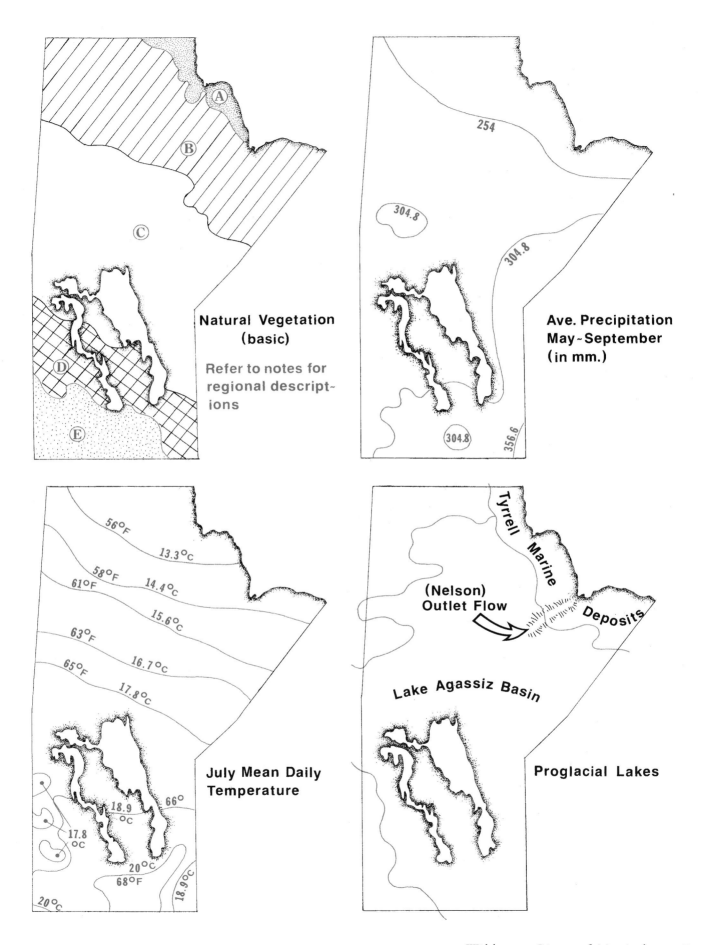

Natural Vegetation (basic)

Refer to notes for regional descriptions

(A)
(B)
(C)
(D)
(E)

Ave. Precipitation May~September (in mm.)

254

304.8

304.8

304.8

356.6

July Mean Daily Temperature

56°F   13.3°C
58°F   14.4°C
61°F
63°F   15.6°C
65°F   16.7°C
17.8°C
66°
18.9°C
17.8°C
20°C
68°F   18.9°C
20°C

Proglacial Lakes

Tyrrell Marine

(Nelson) Outlet Flow   Deposits

Lake Agassiz Basin

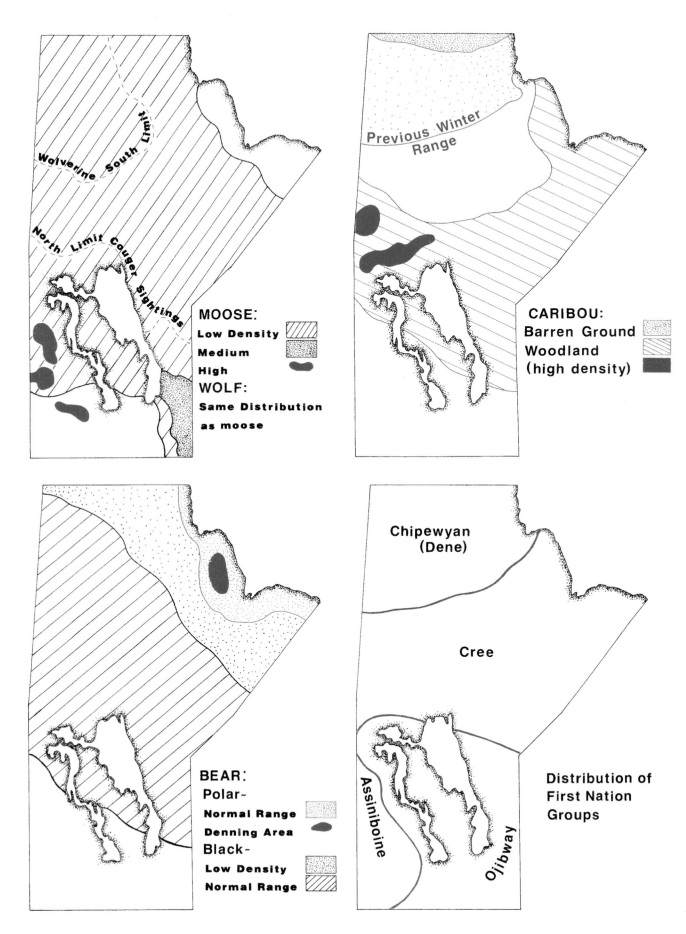

MOOSE:
Low Density
Medium
High
WOLF:
Same Distribution as moose

Wolverine South Limit

North Limit Cougar Sightings

CARIBOU:
Barren Ground
Woodland
(high density)

Previous Winter Range

BEAR:
Polar-
Normal Range
Denning Area
Black-
Low Density
Normal Range

Chipewyan
(Dene)

Cree

Assiniboine

Ojibway

Distribution of
First Nation
Groups

DISTRIBUTION OF MOOSE & WOLF – MAP #5

Because of the vastness of Manitoba and the generally harsh climate and limited vegetation in some regions, the moose population is widespread and elusive. We experienced more sightings within Woodland Caribou Park in Ontario and along the Gammon and Manigotagan Rivers in Manitoba than anywhere else in the province. The Leyond River environment was also prime habitat for moose.

Timber wolf sightings seemed to correspond with the frequency of moose activity throughout Atikaki Park, and the movement of caribou near the Grass River (Woodland caribou). Wolves were often noted travelling along or near eskers in the barrens adjacent to caribou trails.

DISTRIBUTION OF CARIBOU – MAP #6

The chance of sighting Woodland caribou is remote as there are only several hundred animals remaining adjacent to any of the rivers below 57° latitude. Woodland caribou can be distinguished from barrenland caribou by its larger body and smaller antler display; the two seldom share the same territory. Barrenland caribou, on the other hand, are still well established in large numbers in the area indicated on the map. Although their wintering grounds have retracted further to the north and the overall population has been much reduced, canoeists still have the opportunity to see the Kaminuriak herd as it moves south in late July through August, north and east of Nejanalini Lake and along the entire Caribou River. Those travelling the Seal may not encounter caribou unless travelling in late August and early September.

DISTRIBUTION OF BEAR – MAP #7

POLAR BEAR: After feasting on seal throughout the winter, living offshore on the ice mass of Hudson Bay, polar bears come ashore in the spring and undergo a type of "walking hibernation." This is a time when bears fast and females retreat to inland dens by September, give birth in midwinter and return with the cubs to the ice by spring. Wapusk National Park, the seventh largest in Canada, now protects one of the largest polar bear denning sites in the world (as indicated on the map). Polar bears can be a nuisance while camp-ing along the Hudson Bay coast; it is a wonderful experience to actually see one, but caution should be taken while walking alone or paddling near the coast. Polar bears can swim at a speed of 10 k.p.h. (6 m.p.h.) and run up to 30 k.p.h. (18 m.p.h.). Canoeists travelling near the coast should refer to the CRCA book listing on bears.

BLACK BEAR: Black bears are often seen roaming the shorelines and scavenging through the semi-open boreal regions. Populations are widespread, thinning out towards Hudson Bay and the area normally patrolled by polar bear. Outside of roadside provincial campgrounds black bears are not a problem; however, keeping a clean campsite will discourage unwanted encounters.

DISTRIBUTION OF FIRST NATIONS – MAP #8

There are four distinct First Nations groups as indicated by the map. You may notice a close similarity to the division of geographic zones as they relate to homeland territory: the Dene inhabiting areas of barrenland and Hudson Bay coast; the Swampy Cree residing in the northern boreal reaches; the Ojibway keeping much to the mixed transitional forest southeast of Lake Winnipeg (Saulteaux Ojibway are the western limit of that Nation); and the Assiniboine representing the grassy plains Nation west of Lake Winnipeg. Representative Nations as depicted within the geography of this book are the Dene, Swampy Cree, and the Saulteaux Ojibway; territories also coincide with the three travel zones – Land of Little Sticks, the Middle Track, and Atikaki.

GENERAL OBSERVATIONS CONCERNING FIRST NATIONS

Most activities are concentrated at or near reserves although there is some trapping and fishing that are carried out along the rivers with most of the travel done by motorboat and snowmachine usually within 30 km. of home base. Hunting and wild rice harvesting also play a part in the economic and social dynamic of each band. Several First Nations groups have taken steps to improve social conditions and an active role in developing tourism strategies.

Seal River wildfires

SECTION II

BEING PREPARED

Things You Should Know

"Our lives improve only when we take chances and the first and most difficult task we can take is to be honest with ourselves."

Walter Anderson

Overboard on the Pigeon

No Trace Camping

INTRODUCTION

The tedium of our social niche and the pursuit of status therein has, in a visual sense, manipulated the outdoor adventure psyche to the point where proficiency is gauged by appearance. We look good, therefore we are good. Industry floods the hungry market with day-glo outer wear and necessary gadgetry and we, the ravenous consumers, devour it.

It wasn't long ago when blending with nature (green army-surplus clothing, green tents, green canoes) was symbolic of our desire to be inconspicuous and alone – a symmetry between self and forest, where upon meeting someone along a portage trail you exchanged a plug of tobacco for advice on where to set your fishing line. Taking water in your canoe (cedar/canvas vintage) or hitting a rock in a rapids was tantamount to the worst heinous trail crime imaginable.

Portaging was revered as a welcome change from paddling and an opportunity to jaw with other members of your canoe party.

Today, portages resemble fashion-show catwalks and the river rapids are deluged with bath-tub shaped playboats – canoes designed specifically to compensate for lack of finesse... built to endure the punishment inflicted upon them by the bones of the earth, and making portages unessential except in the most severe instances.

We love to play. We thrive on the exhilaration of the whitewater and are willing to pay dearly for the façade of appearing to know how to do it safely.

The price and consequence of our naïveté in the least could jeopardize the lives of those travelling with us. In terms of outdoor sensibility, commercial enterprise is good as long as our ability exceeds that of the value of the product. Buying an expensive compass doesn't mean that we automatically know how to use it more proficiently than the cheap one we replaced. While purchasing a $2,000 whitewater canoe may improve the boat's chance of survival on a difficult run, the risk to the unskilled canoeist remains the same.

There exists an element of risk, regardless of equipment or canoeing savvy; the character of the river seldom reveals all its cards, but you can be certain that if anyone is carrying the joker in their hand it will be the canoeist who displays overconfidence over common sense.

The river is a regal master, a dedicated tutor, patient and tolerant of our weaknesses (that we should admit to our limitations as paddlers undeniably makes us better canoeists). Knowledge of self, of the equipment we use, and of our place on the river administers a profound sense of security that only experience can give us. Good equipment can certainly make life more pleasurable as we wend our way down the river, but it will never compensate for lack of competence. Learn first and then go out and buy a good whitewater boat but remember...experience without instruction only tempers bad habits. Technical whitewater skills are not hard to develop in a few days; more importantly, it is the science of "reading" moving water that may take years to evolve.

And what about the selection of canoes and equipment? Well, if you take river tripping seriously, then stick with serious gear. There are already enough department-store canoes littering the rapids – the choice is simple...compromise anything but your own safety. A successful river expedition also depends on how well you pack to keep things dry, knowing what to do in case of emergencies and generally anticipating anything that could possibly go wrong.

This is not a "how-to" book. We've simply isolated important topics of discussion concerning equipment recommendations best suited for a Manitoba adventure.

Whitewater canoeing requires specialized gear. Many established whitewater schools teach "aggressive" or "competition" skills but do not cover expedition skills such as "lining or tracking," or running rapids with a fully loaded canoe.

For those without such experience, this chapter may at least profile the necessary skills required to safely navigate the wilderness rivers of Manitoba. It is up to the individual to ensure that all aspects of river paddling are fully understood and practiced.

NO TRACE CAMPING

In the attempt to quell whatever primitive urge compels us to seek the sanctity of the river, there will always be those neophytes who disregard ethical, moral, and environmental responsibilities by despoiling our wilderness trails.

It is our nature to create garbage...and our weakness not to know where to put it.

As soon as we step across that civilized threshold and climb into our canoes, or walk that forest trail, we have an individual responsibility to uphold the unwritten laws and ethical codes of the wilderness. The degenerate slobs who abuse these rules, at our expense, should be subject to some form of mediaeval "trial by ordeal" – a public flogging perhaps.

Canadian rivers provide us with the last vestiges of wild landscape – should we

"Bearproofing your pack."

decide
to desecrate them with our obscene lack of reverence and consideration, then we shall have no place else to enjoy that pristine sense of "connection" with an unmolested environment. At the rate we are losing wilderness in this country, we should do our best to protect what's left. It is up to the canoeist to practice conscientious camping habits that transcend the parameters of their own existence while on the

trail. And that may signify doing the little extras that undoubtedly benefit all, such as picking up someone else's garbage left behind, or clearing that deadfall tree on the portage that everyone seems to be stumbling over. Besides, who else is going to pick up after us? To preserve the integrity of our wild places we will, without options, be required to manage the river environment with the same diligence and dedication as we would apply to the grooming of our own backyard.

NO TRACE CAMPING is just that: leaving no trace of your passing so that the party travelling behind you should see no evidence of your being there. In some wilderness areas it is illegal to light campfires, move or arrange firepit stones, or alter the environment in any way. The carrying of bottles and cans may also be banned, and although not enforced, common sense should invent alternative methods of preparation and packing. Manitoba wilderness binds itself to most of these rules except for the option of using the campfire as a source of warmth or cooking, or for the sheer enjoyment as a still acceptable element of canoe trip dynamics. The "Canoeist's Code" of ethics developed by the Canadian Recreational Canoeing Association (CRCA) offers a good guide-line for no trace camping and is available upon request.

GARBAGE

ALL refuse should be packed out; chiefly, anything that is not safe or environmentally acceptable to burn in your campfire. Cans and bottles should be avoided (food packed in plastic nalgene bottles as an alternative); however, if you do bring them along, cans should be burned, flattened, and packed in the heavy-duty, double-lined garbage bag you conveniently brought along. Note: the burning of tins, rinsing of plastics and bottles will eliminate smells that may attract bears or skunks to the campsite.

Plastics should not be burned in the campfire!

Foodstuffs should either be completely incinerated in the fire, or buried far back of the campsite in the same manner that you would use to cover up your own fecal dump. There is nothing more disgusting than arriving at a nice campsite and finding the fire pit littered with globs of half-burnt oatmeal, melted shoes or socks (perched too close to the fire to dry) and shards of greasy tin foil; and tent sites left decorated with whatever slid out of tents when they were shaken out before being rolled up...like wads of kleenex, gum wrappers and used condoms.

Final campsite inspection should be done with conviction and garbage bag in hand – every day! Beaches, shorelines, lunch spots, portage trails should show no evidence of your travels. Seasoned campers and responsible canoeists often pick up garbage left behind by the more unrefined adventurer, displaying an obvious philosophy of "leaving the river cleaner than they found it".

CAMPFIRES

The campfire represents a primordial dependence on basic, essential, and life-giving elements – to warm our bodies and to cook our food, and also to give us pleasure in a communal, ritualistic sense. We orbit around the evening campfire like planets around the sun, and as we stare into the dancing flames, our brain waves mesh with the spears of light and heat, and our thoughts are spirited away as we slip deeper into a meditative trance.

While the new-age, high-tech canoeist may shun the practice of building fires, employing the use of the pack-stove exclusively (in true conservation methodology), the traditional camper requires a campfire in order to fulfill complete canoe-quest bliss. And there are rules. Unwritten codes, of course, but still, considerations for the environment and those that travel after you have gone. Considerations such as the following: fire pit rocks should remain on bedrock or mineral soil (sand/gravel) and away from forest duff. This tinder can burn, unseen, for days and spring up somewhere else. Avoid lunch fires and keep your campfire small to conserve wood. Don't use grates or grills that sit too high off the ground. Attend your fire at all times and make sure it's completely extinguished before you leave camp.

Firewood can be picked up along the shore in advance of your intended campsite. Abandoned beaver lodges are a great source of sun-dried poplar and birch hardwood.

You should carry an axe and saw – the only way to get dry firewood after a three-day rain is to split it. A small quantity of firewood should be left behind for the next party, a token of consideration for others.

Firewood becomes scarce as you enter the treeless heath of the tundra on both the Seal and Caribou rivers. Please consider the exclusive use of stoves when entering this ecozone.

LATRINES

Vanity is sacred to us. How we look in front of others denotes the meticulous grooming and tending we contribute to whatever level of "appeal" we may aspire to. And we extend that to our visible surroundings – our home, gardens, interior decor...we'll even stoop to bag "Muffy's" rude little dump on the sidewalk with indifference. Within our fabricated, controlled and regulated urban environment we either respect rules or we suffer administerial repercussions. Compliance to the social framework makes us responsible citizens.

Why, then, when it comes to taking a shit in the woods, do we lower ourselves to the debased creatures we really are by our inability to do it with finesse? Animals crap in the woods and you wouldn't know it. When humans answer the call they make sure that everyone gets a good view of it. Trees and bushes decorated with garlands of used toilet paper, trails and tent sites start to resemble stockyard cattle pens and there are more plastic tampon applicators scattered about than spent cartridges at a military firing range! And the abandoned underwear – scads of it – do people just forget to put it back on or is this some kind of satanic ritual and sacrifice?

Fear often compels us to do contrary things. Campers are afraid to take a dump at night more than a few metres away from the tent, as if some slithering beast will snatch them up at the most vulnerable moment. There is an obvious mind-block or deep psychosis and primordial turbulence in our brain-wave patterns during this biological function to make it impossible for us to scrape a tiny hole in the ground and bury our stool. We have

become too accustomed to flushing ourselves down a toilet. Some also believe that nature will look after this stuff for us – *like it's going to dissolve right before our eyes or something.*

Doing it Right! Latrines should be established far back of the tenting area or shore (no less than 100 metres). (Toilet paper can also be burned in the fire pit.) Shallow holes should be scraped or dug and filled in when finished – covering toilet paper too! Grey or dishwater too should be dumped well back in the bush. Avoid using several-ply or colour T.P. or try sphagnum moss for a change like the anishnabeg once did – it works great!

OTHER CODES

• Be a considerate camper, leave the campsite cleaner than when you found it.
• Trees should not be defaced or cut or stripped of bark or denuded of branches for bedding purposes.
• Latrines should not be established on small island campsites. It is customary to paddle to the mainland for such purposes if feasible to do so.
• Allow faster or more organized canoe parties to pass you on a portage and don't leave your gear directly on the trail or canoes beached, obstructing clear passage.
• Allow larger groups to occupy the bigger campsites, particularly if there are several small sites nearby.
• Respect the need for others to enjoy the quietude of the surroundings – leave your radio at home and keep the noise level to a bare minimum.
• You are required, by law, to assist those in need of assistance or medical aid. Being properly prepared reduces the risk to your own party and allows safer assistance while executing rescue manoeuvres on other paddlers. Rescuers often become victims if equipment and procedure methods are not well thought out.
• When travelling within provincial parks (Atikaki, Nopoming & Grass), canoeists are generally restricted to using only the prescribed, established campsites where a proper fire pit area has been safely established. Remember, this is a high risk fire region – if you use any other campsite please make sure that the fire is established in a safe location.
• While travelling in the tundra please try and minimize the impact on sensitive

heath flora by camping on beaches and bedrock outcrops only, AND DO NOT MOVE OR ALTER ANY OTHER ROCK OR STONE THAT MAY BE REGARDED AS ARCHAEOLOGICAL LANDMARKS!

A WORD ABOUT POLAR BEARS

Polar bears range along the coastal regions of Hudson Bay. While paddling the Hayes, Seal or Caribou rivers, care should be taken while performing the daily dump once you reach the last several kilometres near the Bay (although polar bears have been reported as far inland as Oxford House!). DO NOT wander the tundra alone, particularly where visibility may be obscured by boulders and deep sedge.

CANOES

The type of canoe you decide on usually reflects the kind of canoeing you intend to practice. It may be a cliché, but you are what you paddle. If you resort to assembling a department-store canoe on your back porch, just be prepared to watch it willingly disassemble itself on the first rock you bash in the rapids. Some styles and brands of canoes are best kept behind the boathouse at the cottage.

River paddling comes in two apparent varieties: the "traditional," where specialized equipment is minimal; and "aggressive play," where serious modifications are imposed upon both craft design and paddler psyche.

TRADITIONAL

We have seen "stripper" canoes survive low-water bump and grinds only because their owners knew when to portage or line. For wood, wood/canvas, fiberglass or kevlar canoes the owner requires a good repair kit and an affinity for portaging.

Traditional canoes have recognizable hull designs and are shipped from the factory with just enough flotation to keep the craft from sinking. Hull specifications can be compromised to add or diminish speed, agility, initial or mobile stability. Faster canoes have less rocker which may significantly affect both response capability and capacity to displace bow waves; whereas a severely rockered canoe will dance around rocks and bob in the waves, but paddle like the Titanic in open flat water.

A good tandem whitewater canoe will have "modest" lines, falling somewhere in the categories indicated below. Before you purchase or rent a canoe, test paddle it to make sure it is what you want.

Recreational, touring, or expedition canoes under the traditional category generally have a deep, high-volume capacity and run more efficiently under a moderate load.

For larger, more difficult rivers, or rivers experiencing above volume flow, canoeists paddling tandem should consider using 17' "touring class" expedition canoes (37" at the beam/center thwart, and at least 15" deep with slight rocker); or use 16' canoes with the appropriate spray cover.

CANOE MATERIALS

Royalex – Still the preferred choice of whitewater enthusiasts, using a thermo-molded hull consisting of a foam core sandwiched between layers of ABS sheathing and then covered in a vinyl skin.

RPF – Rotomolded polyethylene and foam as heavy as Royalex but much cheaper to purchase. Hull is a triple "dump" of polyethylene powder, resin and foam, "shaken, not stirred" in a heated mold.

Aluminum – Stretch-formed hull halves are riveted to a stiff keel and ribs are spot-welded. Once the favourite for whitewater because all you needed for repairs was a rubber hammer and a tube of liquid steel. The aluminum canoe seems to be making a bit of a comeback but still ranks low as a choice alternative.

SAFETY OPTIONS

Foam-core seats add extra flotation and vinyl/aluminum gunwales are more impact-resistant than wood trim. Added flotation is highly recommended, particularly if you travel alone. Kevlar "skid plates" should be added to each lower stem to ease abrasion and add extra life to your canoe. *Spray Covers:* Spray covers or decks are not only great for displacing water on the bigger rapids but keep passengers and gear dry during rain showers, not to mention warmer in cold weather. If using a spray cover it is essential that you are familiar with extrication procedures in the event of an upset. For quick and safe escape from an overturned canoe, spray covers should have "quick-release" skirts for both bow and stern paddlers, fastened

with velcro to the body of the cover and complete with an escape grab loop.

Rescue Throw Bags: Each canoe should have one: a 50 to 75-foot cable of floating rope coiled inside a weighted nylon bag. If you don't know what they're useful for then you shouldn't be on the river. Throw bags can also be used as handy painters for lining. Bow and stern lines should be accessible at all times.

P.F.D. (Personal Flotation Device): They should be approved and quality-constructed, allowing free arm movement. An additional head support system bumps a P.F.D. up to an actual life-saving garment.

Helmets: Since most P.F.D.'s will not keep an unconscious person from drowning, it is wise counsel to at least wear an approved safety helmet for all whitewater running. Hockey helmets can be substituted for helmets specifically designed for whitewater paddling.

AGGRESSIVE PLAY

These are primarily performance canoes that are designed for optimum maneuverability and are most popular with solo paddlers. The use of full flotation (at least 50% of hull space) replaces the necessity of a spray skirt by limiting the amount of water the canoe can take in. Whitewater hardware usually includes a fully adjustable seat or pedestal, thigh straps, affixed knee pads and...yes, a helmet.

Flotation: Vinyl or nylon air bags can be added to the canoe to lessen the chance of broaching a rock in the event of an upset. By displacing water, the "swamped" canoe will ride higher and facilitate an easier rescue. A 60-inch commercial inflatable centre bag is functional but makes portaging difficult, whereas two 30-inch tandem bags placed fore and aft remain fixed and unobtrusive.

Knee Pads: Hit a rock once and you quickly realize that the full impact is on your knees. Cupped knee pads are best because they eliminate that lateral slide, but for optimal performance it is far better to have something permanently fixed to the hull. This is an easy do-it-yourself project requiring some closed-cell foam (1/2") and waterproof contact cement.

Thigh Straps: These allow better motion or body weight transfer (while still remaining in the canoe). Practical for the more daring and dramatic water play for solo performers but can be installed in kit form in tandem canoes.

PADDLES

Each paddler should be equipped with 2 paddles (each canoe should have at least one spare paddle attached to the canoe thwarts by bungee cords). On rivers where there is considerable flat-water, you may consider bringing along a light cruising paddle such as the ottertail-style. ABS and aluminum paddles are durable, as are the laminate with reinforced kevlar-tipped paddles. RIM (Reaction Injection Moulding) Cross-linked polyurethane composed of 16 various chemicals is shot into a mould forming a blade that is tightly bonded to an aluminum shaft; some even come with a Shock Absorbing System (SAS) — a dense foam outer coating on the blade which reduces shock to the joints. AMT (Advanced Moulding Technology) is a controlled volume of nitrogen, an inert gas, which is injected into the blade after molten plastic has been added; carbon fibres can be added as well to make a super-light paddle of great strength. RIM & AMT paddles are recommended for serious whitewater expeditions. Paddles should be the right weight and proper length with a comfortable grip...just in case, take along a pair of gel-palmed bicycle gloves.

WATERPROOFING

"A small leak will sink a great ship." Benjamin Franklin

A canoe capsizing in the middle of a rapids need not be the traumatic misadventure responsible for ruining an otherwise perfect canoe trip. Let's face it...river paddling is exciting, exhilarating, sometimes tenuous, potentially dangerous and often stressful; but one thing we can all agree upon is that it is almost always WET! We are constantly in and out of the canoe, wading, lining, running, dumping, and the stuff just gets wetter.

CANOE DESIGNS:

Level of "rocker"

17' Lake Touring   17' Expedition Whitewater   14' Whitewater Playboat

But next to attitude, skill and canoe, the waterproofness of your personal gear is the determining factor to the success or failure of your expedition.

Without taking the appropriate precautions, running whitewater is synonymous to living in a house without a roof on. The technique which you employ to keep your duffle dry is a matter of personal choice; again, like the canoe, if it works for you...fine, but for those who are prone to reversing the polarity of their canoes and getting their gear wet – these tips are for you:

1. Packs that are waterproofed and air-tight will float. Don't lash your packs in tight — it will make canoe extrication/rescue difficult. Instead, use a four to six-metre "tether" line fastened to each major pack. This is important when running sections of continuous rapids – for short drops it is not necessary to tie gear in (also make sure all loose items are well packed and cameras are in their cases – small "thwart" bags can remain attached to the canoe while running.) In the event of an upset, packs can be picked up in the eddy below AFTER persons and canoe have been rescued.

2. *Poorman's Pack:* You can portion your food and double-pack it into heavy-duty zip-loc bags and insert them into hardier cloth or nylon "ditty" bags. Heavy cardboard boxes can be glazed with waterproof varnish and lined with industrial-gauge garbage bags, or liberate some waterproof restaurant food pails from your local eatery. Outfitters often carry the popular olive barrel for under $20 each – two of these fit comfortably into a standard Deluth canoe pack with room on top to spare. If you are using an old pack, make sure the straps are going to last the duration of the trip. Take a leather punch and heavy waxed cord for repairs.

3. *Yuppie Gear:* There is a whole industry devoted to supplying ingenious outdoor contrivances to a ready market of adventure seekers. Some of this stuff is actually useful, if not colourful – river bags that are completely waterproof come in two basic formats: float bags that insert into larger, not necessarily waterproof packs; or, larger portageable packs in which you place smaller items, not necessarily waterproofed. Shapes and sizes vary for both formats and can accommodate anything from sleeping bag to kitchen sink.

4. *Backpacking:* Avoid external "backpack" type frame-packs and don't tie a lot of junk on the outside, instead keep day items in a small day pack or thwart bag. Stick with internal frame or standard Deluth canoe pack designs, or the barrel-style with shoulder harness.

5. *Avoid Over-Packing:* The first time you grab the shoulder strap of a cheap pack it'll likely rip off. When picking up packs, make sure you lever the weight from more than one shoulder strap contact point – your pack will last longer.

6. *Waterproofing:* Anything you carry that could be damaged or altered by becoming wet should be waterproofed.

7. *Fishing Gear:* DO NOT attempt to run rapids with fishing gear/hooks loose in the canoe (try doing a canoe over canoe rescue with fishing line and lures tangled in everything!)

8. *Packing:* Take the time each morning to pack your gear with care – waterproof packs only work if they are closed properly.

9. *Colour:* Day-glo orange packs are easiest to pick out of the rapids or eddies.

EMERGENCY REPAIR KIT

- 1 roll of 5 cm (2") duct tape
- needlenose pliers
- multihead screwdriver
- bolts/self-tapping screws
  (canoe/gunnel repair)
- leather punch or awl
- heavy-gauge waxed cord (or nylon)
- tube of epoxy (waterproof)

CANOE SAILING

Canoe sailing isn't something that's taught at paddling clinics, and like "lining" and running whitewater with a full canoe load, we are coerced by necessity and circumstance to learn the more recondite canoeing skills on our own – unless we are fortunate enough to have signed up with a reputable tour company that still practices the more exotic maneouvers (like "poling").

The sailing part is fundamental...you lean back, put your feet up on the gunnels and just steer with the wind; it's the actual rigging of the canoe that must be done with scrutiny or you'll suffer more anguish than you bargained for. It could be dangerous.

Not many years ago, a party of four American canoeists had just completed the Albany River and were resting over at Fort Albany, located some distance up the James Bay coast from Moosonee. Local O.P.P. had warned them of high winds on James Bay but the canoeists shunned the recommended services of a native guide who could have motor-shuttled them safely down the coast to Moosonee where they intended to catch the train south.

They were experienced canoeists, still on the high from coming off the Albany. They would simply lash the two canoes together and sail down the coast and save the extra shuttle expense (figuring the locals were probably exaggerating the dangers just to bilk them for a shuttle). This was a decision that cost them their lives – they were never seen again after heading out from Fort Albany into the Bay. There was an intense search, an inquest, newspaper headlines, but all that was recovered were scattered bits of gear...no bodies were ever found.

And we can only speculate what may have happened; we do know that the party had experienced extreme conditions when they set out down the coast. Offshore mud flats, exposed at low tide, would have forced the canoeists out into deep water several kilometres from the mainland...the shore horizon would become a scant thin line with indistinct navigational reference points. They may have rigged their canoes wrongly, or possibly taken on water and swamped in the heavy wind and waves that plagued the final days of their journey down the coast...falling victim to hypothermia in the cold Arctic waters. A lonely and needless death.

Canoes are not sailboats; they are not manufactured for sailing, but...by making compensations for design and functional shortcomings (while under the influence of sail and wind), a canoe can be transmogrified into the best damned sailing yacht that ever bucked a wave.

I remember quite vividly my first attempt at canoe sailing, exiting a protected bay and coming into contact with a fierce tailwind and metre-high whitecaps. Why not, I thought...so we pulled the canoe over to shore and rigged a couple of poles and attached a huge 10' x 12' canvas tarp to a crosspole, shoved off into the full force of the wind and hoisted the sail.

Canoes aren't meant to fly either; people camped on shore claimed we had cleared the water by about four feet before nosediving back into the lake; sail, poles, rigging, packs and occupants dumped unceremoniously out of the canoe. Luckily we were right over a shoal where it was only a metre deep, and our gear was waterproofed and the water tepid, but it could have been much worse under different circumstances.

There is a correct way to rig up a sail, and a wrong way to do it that could actually be quite dangerous. If the waves are breaking then you must use a spray cover and always keep two large bailers in each canoe. Here are a few pointers that I've managed to glean from my own travels over the years:

*Paddle Stabilizer for single canoe
(deep water only)*

SOLO RIGGING (ONE CANOE)

DON'T rig solo when the wind is strong enough to cap the waves – it's too dangerous...unless you use a spray cover and employ the use of a "dagger-board" system – lashing a spare paddle as indicated in the diagram.

It's tedious for the bow paddler to hold on to two paddles used as sail supports, and although it'll do in a pinch, any longer than ten minutes stops being fun.

I like to carry a couple of poles with me if there are no portages, and use them for quick tie-in masts. Whether paddling alone or with a partner I normally reverse the canoe, stern-forward and lash the two 8-foot mast poles to the seat, secure it further with a 5-foot cross-brace with carabiners attached to the ends as line guides; and sometimes when it is particularly rough I'll add a short brace from the base of the "V" masts to the deck handle. The "V" mast displaces wind shifts and gusts more equally than any other method I've installed and gives better stability overall. If you move gear forward your partner can move back to midship and handle the sail painters (make lunch, fish, sleep...whatever). You just have to steer. Easy, huh? Wind adjustment, unfortunately, is minimal – you have about 90° for wind direction compensation to play with.

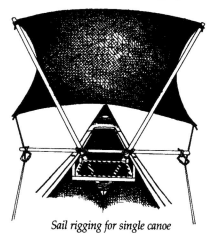

Sail rigging for single canoe

TANDEM RIGGING
(TWO CANOES OR MORE)

I've had up to four canoes rigged for sailing; great for socializing but too unwieldy in tight places. For river work two canoes are certainly easier to handle...you don't want to get hung up in strong current, and that means keeping an eye out for deep channels.

There are a number of variations for field rigging tandem canoes – I've tried them all... here's what I believe may be one of the best methods, as shown in the illustration.

Canoes must be separated by at least two feet at mid-thwart; if you don't, a great

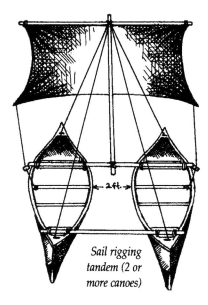

*Sail rigging
tandem (2 or
more canoes)*

flume of water will fill both canoes in less than a minute. Brace-poles are lashed behind both bow and stern seats, making sure both canoe ends are at equal distances. A centre mast may be attached to front crossbrace, notched and lashed securely. The sail hanging beam, sail and bow and stern mast-support lines should all be attached to the top of the mast before securing it to the crossbrace. The hanging beam should not be secured too tightly, allowing it to swivel about 45° each way. Mast lines should then be tied to bow and stern handle grips and adjustment painters secured to the bottom corners of the sail. Now you're set to go!

Tandem canoes, with spray covers attached, can manage turbulent seas but it is always wise to carry two bailing buckets in each canoe – just in case. You have to monitor the wave surge between the two canoes – rough water and speed will create heavier centre splash so you should be aware of the potential problem of swamping if you don't create some system of deflecting water midship. Unlike actual sailing yachts, a canoe-rig has a very high final velocity – just make sure your Tilley hat doesn't fly off your head.

CLOTHING & FOOTWEAR

Avoid fashionable tightness, subcribing to a "layered" wardrobe of loose-fitting duds, lots of T's and socks, and extra clothing for cold-weather paddling (fleece, long underwear, light parka, paddling gloves and hat). Northern Manitoba experiences very unpredictable weather, particularly close to Hudson Bay where the Arctic influence is clearly experienced even in mid-summer.

It is essential to have a 2-piece Gore-Tex rain outfit, preferably with armpit vents and a hood with retractable "periphery-view" straps.

Boots are a matter of personal preference; nonetheless, they should be "broken-in," comfortable, with good ankle support and removable insoles.

Avoid sandals for anything but campsite lounging, and consider neoprene "booties" for easier river work in the canoe. The most practical river boot that we've found is the L.L. Bean "Marine Hunting Shoe" or "gumboot" with rubber bottoms and high leather tops, first designed in 1912 by Leon Leonwood Bean.

WATER QUALITY AND PERSONAL HYGIENE

The risk of contracting illness due to giardia, cysts, viruses and bacteria is present regardless of how pure river water may seem. Boiling water is sometimes inconvenient but necessary if you don't carry a water purifier or water treatment tablets. There are several commercial quality "pumps" available that effectively remove the microorganisms that cause sickness.

It is also important that canoeists practice clean habits. One of the most prevalent contributing factors to the spread of certain viruses and parasites is through poor hygiene (such as the "communal" gorp bag lunge; reaching in with dirty hands). Before preparing or handling food, hands should be washed thoroughly with soap and water; food distribution from a single package should be "poured" into the hands, or make sure everyone has their own private stash.

When obtaining drinking water it is better to fill your container in deep, still water as giardia cysts are carried near the surface in moving water. It is important to note that these "natural" microorganisms do not render a waterway dirty or contaminated. Manitoba rivers are remarkably pristine; however, precautions still should be taken in active wildlife and human communities where water quality might be questionable.

HYPOTHERMIA AND COLD WATER IMMERSION

Death by hypothermia is common – and preventable. Water temperatures outside of the summer months drop rapidly, adding to the overall risk of paddling. Because humans have evolved from tropical climates, moving later to colder, northern reaches after the dissipation of the great ice-fields, we have not developed the ability to control body heat loss without adequate external protection. Heat loss by CONVECTION (wind-chill factor increases risk) or through CONDUCTION during cold water immersion, contributing to hypothermia reaction, should be fully understood by all members of your expedition.

Water conducts heat 240 times better than air, hence the increased risk during a capsize in cold water. Hypothermia can occur in water temperatures of up to 21°C (70°F) but more commonly in water below 16°C (60°F).

Without protection (P.F.D./wet or dry suit), through panic and struggling – hypothermic reaction is accelerated.

SYMPTOMS AND EFFECTS OF IMMERSION

1. Hyperventilation — possibility of aspirating water in turbulent water increases, victims cannot "catch their breath".
2. Heart Dysfunction — possible lethal cardiac abnormalities in people with weak hearts.
3. Muscle Contraction — ability to swim or tread water terminates within 10-15 minutes in 10°C (50°F) water, or as little as five minutes in ice water. Victim will not be able to latch on to a throw bag line or climb up.

The core body temperature of hypothermic victims generally does not begin its steady drop for about 15-20 minutes after initial immersion. That is why it is imperative to move quickly before the body reaches the state of profound hypothermia (which is difficult to treat in the field).

Most victims of cold water immersion are extricated within minutes of an upset and may display symptoms of mild hypothermia (uncontrolled shivering, disorientation, slurred speech, muscle constriction). Removing wet clothing is essential to stop further heat loss. Giving the victim warm liquids to drink will only offer a psychological lift, whereas gentle warming by external means (second or third person in a sleeping bag(s), or building a reflector fire) works more effectively.

For severe or profound hypothermic victims it is important to keep the person inactive. If the victim has been in the water for a long period of time, it is critical that the rescuers "lift" and move the immersion victim as gently as possible. Rapid "rewarming" or movement may induce shock and ventricular fibrillation – CPR and/or mouth-to-mouth resuscitation may be futile or even cause death.

The victim can actually remain in this metabolic state (without further heat loss) for up to a few days. If evacuation from the river is not possible within a short time, DO NOT add additional external heat unless further core temperature continues to decrease. Gentle application of heat to the key heat loss areas may be beneficial. Ground insulation, removal of wet clothing, warm covers and a reflector fire (gentle heat only) are important remedial steps to take in aiding the victim.

DO NOT GIVE ALCOHOL.

Plans for evacuation should be made quickly.

Prevention: Vest-type P.F.D.'s worn snugly against the chest will give some thermal protection; however, if you paddle in extreme conditions (spring or fall) when

Fringe season paddling – not for the unprepared

water temperatures are below 16°C (60°F), each paddler should be wearing a wet or dry suit that adequately protects the major heat loss areas. Canoeists should practice rescue procedures (canoe over canoe/throw bag rescue, etc.) early on in their trip. Avoiding the more difficult rapids is also wise practice.

STRANDING

During the initial few minutes of an upset in rapids, paddlers sometimes find themselves stranded in the middle of the river, particularly when their canoe folds around a prominent boulder. Heat loss from convection is accelerated and the paddler is reluctant to re-enter the river and "free-float" to the bottom to be rescued. This is understandable where there may be a dangerous chute or falls. The rescuers then must get a rescue line out to the victims as quickly as possible. If they are beyond the throw-bag reach, the next procedure involves accessing the opposite shore above the rapids and moving the line back downstream to the victim. The line is secured and the strandee removed either under their own power or by assistance. It is important that rescuers enter cold water gradually to lesson immersion shock. They should also "attach" themselves to the secured rescue line with a carabiner (all persons should be carrying one attached to their P.F.D., along with an extrication knife). Victims should also be attached to the line because by this time they may have lost the ability to function on their own.

SUGGESTED READING

Hypothermia, Frostbite, and Other Cold Injuries. James A. Wilkerson, M.D., Douglas & McIntyre, 1986.

Medicine for Mountaineering. James A. Wilkerson, M.D., Douglas & McIntyre, 1985.

There are several books on canoe safety and rescue available through the Canadian Recreational Canoeing Association (CRCA) (613) 269-2910.

EMERGENCY LOCATING TRANSMITTERS (E.L.T.'S)

The popularity of wilderness travel in remote places, and the need to remain in contact in case of emergencies make the E.L.T. a valuable piece of safety equipment. At one time, locating transmitters, when set off, could not be distinguished from downed aircraft or troubled canoeists; now the P.L.B., or Personal Locator Beacon, when triggered, makes that distinction clear. The transmission is sent directly to a satellite, which relays the message to a Rescue Coordination Centre. Aircraft and/or helicopters are dispatched to the scene at first light.

P.L.B.'s are compact, hand-held devices costing under $1,000 and do not require licensing. Their use should be limited to cases of dire or life-threatening circumstances; for example, an accident in which the victim cannot be moved without causing further injury; profound hypothermia, cardiac arrest, etc. – not to be used for non life-threatening conditions. E.L.T.'s or P.L.B.'s should be used in conjunction with some form of ground-to-air signal, such as three smokey fires in a triangle, an orange tarp, or flares.

If possible, the location should allow the landing of an aircraft, or float-equipped helicopter.

GLOBAL POSITIONING SYSTEMS

GPS (Global Positioning System) is a network of 25 orbiting satellites that send signals to earth. With the use of hand-held receivers you can determine your ground position to within 15-100 metres, depending upon the quality of the unit, and the number of satellites you are locked onto. They are invaluable for locating your position where visual reference points are confusing (large lakes with many islands), or static (Arctic tundra and Hudson Bay coast). A GPS should be backed up with a good compass and two sets of topographical maps.

TOPOGRAPHICAL MAPS

This book requires the use of the standard 1:50,000 topographic series maps, as indicated on each route description. It must be understood by the canoeist that these maps were not designed for field use by canoeists or hikers and that mistakes are quite common. The purpose of this field guide is to make the appropriate corrections but it is still up to the individual to properly transfer the book information to the map accurately. Please do so with care, and, when in the field, KNOW WHERE YOU ARE AT ALL TIMES. Two sets of water-proofed maps are essential; better still, every person should carry on their person his/her own route maps in case of separation on the river. The CRCA carries several how-to books on the use of maps and GPS.

INSECTS THAT BITE

Insects...those flying, crawling, boring, chewing and biting vexations of the backwoods, heirs to the earth when we finish tampering with it, are without question an integral part of the natural environment. Whether we like it or not, they assume their rightful place alongside us as we trek through the north woods; we are, after all, just part of the cyclical food chain once we step into the realm of nature; we are not at the top of the food chain as we might have thought.

Coming to terms with the negative wilderness elements does not necessarily mean succumbing to the onslaught of biting insects, for example. It does imply the need to prepare ourselves adequately, however, or suffer the consequences. On any wilderness excursion there are always going to be tradeoffs, be they pros or cons to equipment or canoe choices, or even the time of season you decide upon for your trip. Oftentimes the optimum features of a canoe trip, like high water levels for instance, can also connote dealing with one or more negative components...such as cold weather perhaps...or biting insects.

MONTHLY BUG CALENDAR

MAY: Early spring runs on the river do offer the paddler the highest water levels and dramatic, voluminous rapids (although dangerous due to the cold water factor). One can, however, sometimes beat the black fly season by hitting the Atikaki rivers shortly after break-up in May. It is best to check with a local lodge or Natural Resources office first.

Black fly larvae hatch in spring freshets and generally anywhere water is in its mobile state, intensifying by late May and well into June, and July in northern Manitoba.

JUNE: Early to mid-June is peak black fly season. Heavy rain at this time will extend the breeding season, prolonging the scourge of black flies well into July.

Hot, dry weather, often typical for June, will bring a quick demise to the black fly population, usually by the end of the month. First generation mosquitoes, slow and hefty, make an appearance in early June and intensify as the month progresses.

JULY: Mosquitoes peak in early July and fade as the month progresses and the breeding ponds dry up. Horse, deer and sand flies (midges, or no-see-ums) are most bothersome throughout this month.

There is also a species of biting "house" fly that plagues the northland at this time.

AUGUST: Considered the bug-free month, its popularity with canoeists can also translate into running into more people, although July is still the heaviest-travelled month because of water levels. Remnant horse, deer and biting house flies continue to make their appearances. Paddlers can enjoy sleeping outside their tents at this time.

SEPTEMBER: The few parties descending rivers at this time may experience a resurgence of black flies for a short period, mid to late September, as rainfall (and snow flurries towards the Bay) raise water levels.

OTHER BUGS THAT BITE

Yellowjackets: A social wasp of the family Vespidae that can inflict a nasty bite or sting. The nest is usually constructed of "wasp paper", a thick pulp of wood fibre and saliva, either underground, in decaying stumps, or in hanging nests. Wasps feed on carbohydrates (nectar, aphid honeydew or the jam you accidentally dropped on the ground). Nest larvae are fed dead insects. Paddlers walking portages, pitching camp or scrounging for firewood often fall victim to yellowjacket attacks. They are easily provoked if you come within a metre or two of the nest and you'll likely feel the assault before you see or hear them. Move away quickly from the

nest area and have a friend brush off the wasps with a hat or shirt. (this is when you find out who your real friends are!)

White-faced hornets: A rather sizeable wasp that constructs large suspended paper nests and, like the yellowjacket, may become very protective of its territory during the late summer. I have seen these beasts attack, unprovoked, even when their nest was almost 25 metres from the portage. They are attracted to anything sweet and become very bothersome at the campsite, buzzing around your food as you try to prepare a meal. In this situation they'll only bite if stepped on or caught in clothing.

Bees: Social honey or bumblebees are generally non-aggressive, found at lumber camps or other grassy clearings collecting flower nectar. Unless stepped on or caught up in your clothing, bees pose no threat. If you are exploring open fields, nylon jackets and pants are recommended.

PROTECTION

Bee and Hornet Bites: The sting or bite of a bee or wasp can set off allergic reactions, and in some cases can even be fatal. If anyone in your group is subject to allergic trauma then you should carry an antivenom kit in your first aid kit, and more than one person should know how to use it. For mild reaction to stings or bites, an antihistamine will suffice. On the spot relief from the pain of the sting can be given by making a quick salve of spit and peat-earth in your palm and applying it to the bite...or use a commercial ammonia-based "sting-stop" applicator.

Protection from Biting Bugs: Sometimes the protection is more unbearable than the problem. Several brands of insect repellent have been removed from store shelves because of the possibility of birth defects occurring — even the acclaimed DEET is suspected of a variety of nasty things. After all, any body lotion that is poisonous if ingested, harmful to the eyes and can melt plastic, can't be that good plastered over your skin. There are alternatives.

For example...a reliable and safe protection is keeping covered, and maintaining an appropriate diet. Avoid fashionable tightness, blue jeans, and dark clothing. Pants can be tucked into socks, and a lightweight, hooded shell-type jacket with elasticized cuffs and waist draw-string will keep out black flies that like to crawl

Insects —vexations of the backwoods — part of the northern experience

up into your clothing looking for soft, blood-filled flesh. Douse your bandanna with bug "juice" and wrap it around your neck, a most vulnerable target for black flies. Repellent-embalmed bug jackets and head nets are becoming more popular during peak black fly season. Dress appropriately for the weather and minimize sweating.

You are what you eat may be an old cliché but when it's you that becomes the pursued fare during bug season, experience (and suffering) is the mother of resourcefulness – you'll soon discover just how important diet is in protecting yourself from the biting insects. The flavour and odour of your body sweat is governed by food choices, and some aromas either attract or repel biting insects to some degree.

Vitamin B1 (thiamin), taken three times daily (100 mg) creates a smell that bugs don't like (drinking alcohol may counteract the effect of B1). Both garlic and vitamin C have excellent properties as antihistamines, but while relieving the effects of bug bites, really do little else to prevent the actual insect attacks. Garlic supplements dissolve in the lower intestine and do not create a skin odour, whereas eating raw garlic that digests in the stomach will. Garlic contains potassium and like bananas or other high-potassium foods, may actually attract bugs. A high consumption of citrus fruits at this time and abstinence from alcohol is wise counsel. In extreme situations a firm grip and strong embrace of reality ward off the frenzied paranoias of psychological retreat – the only other relief is to stay home or visit a theme park.

BUG CHARACTERISTICS

Black Fly Season: late May to early July and late September.

Diurnal villains shaped like minute bison with rapier jaws that like temperatures of 15°C (60°F) and warmer. They are most persistent on portages, campsites and while paddling close to shore (within 10 m). They won't bite in enclosed areas, such as your tent or under a kitchen fly strung low over a smokey fire. Avoid getting over-bitten as it may lead to infection and illness. Black flies numb the afflicted area and inject an anti-coagulant so you don't realize you're being bitten most of the time. They are attracted to wrists, neck, ears and ankles – wherever blood flows

close to the skin. Keep these areas covered and protected. Blackflies may persist well into the summer months along the Hayes River, and rivers through the tundra lowlands.

Mosquito Season: early June to late July.

A sucking Culicidae with a needle-like stylet used to puncture your tender skin, sent from the moist depths of the black wilderness to bite the undersides of your arms as you portage the canoe. Mosquitoes are most prevalent during the evenings and early mornings, and in heavily shaded or cooler areas along portages having a deciduous canopy. Usually try to bite through clothing on contact rather than crawl through it looking for bare skin. Mosquitoes continue their assault even in enclosed areas.

No see-ums (sand flies, midges) Season: late July to early August.

If your tent is not equipped with no-see-um screening, then these critters will molest you throughout the night. Silent and almost invisible, they leave mosquito-size welts, not to mention a miserable night to forget. Sand flies prefer, what else...sandy environments but also may be present at rocky campsites. Late afternoon and evening is feeding time, and throughout warm nights or just prior to storms or heavy rains.

Deer Fly Season: mid-June to early September.

They love the heat of the day and the crown of your head...or the soft flesh between your fingers and toes. More a nuisance than anything, they try and psych you into displaying total lack of personality control in front of your friends. Wear a hat and shoes to protect your sanity.

Horse Fly Season: mid-June to early September.

How many times have you clobbered a horse fly perched on a body part poised to bite, felt the slight give of carapace in an audible crunch, only to watch it fall to the

bottom of the canoe, buzz in a bewildered legup position, roll over and fly away? A simple slap no longer works...so you develop the slap and palm-grind, administering enough torque until the attacker resembles an exsanguinated raisin. Horse flies are powerful insects that enjoy hot weather and bare skin – usually choosing locations on your body to bite where you can't reach.

If you aim a couple of inches behind a horse fly chances are you'll clobber it. These type of pests actually take off in a backward arc, so set your sights accordingly.

Dene and Cree children often eat the horse fly (known as a "bull dog"). If you pull out the wings and squeeze the meaty thorax gently, a gel-sac pops out filled with delicious nectar which can be scooped up in the tongue.

Bug jackets are invaluable for the early season expeditions

Caribou encounter along an esker, Caribou River

NATURE OBSERVATION

WILDERNESS PHOTOGRAPHY

Our appreciation and enjoyment of the outdoors mature through experience; the fundamental perception of how nature functions allows us to enter into a confrontational acquaintance with the natural world itself, be it spiritual or visual. Those who travel the river solely for the adrenalin charge of whitewater often deprive themselves of other, certainly less physically stimulating experiences that would otherwise enrich a holistic view of the river environs.

Nature observation is more popular today than it has ever been, indicated by current economic contribution; there exists a greater number of camera-toting, binocular-wielding outdoorspeople who disdain viewing wildlife through the sights of a gun. More canoeists are likely to carry cameras than even fishing rods (as an outfitter, guide and venture-tourist consultant I have made personal calculations to this effect, noting that only one in five canoeists were avid anglers, but four out of five carried camera equipment).

Many canoeists, although not crack photographers, are enthusiastic about nature observation all the same and confrontation with wildlife, for them, is often sudden, unexpected, unpredicted but gloriously exciting. Snapshots from disposable cameras concentrate on catching the moment in a chronology of trip events, to be proudly displayed in the coffee table album back home.

For others, nature study goes beyond all insatiable passions – a small fortune is spent on the most sophisticated photo-gadgetry (not to mention processing), and aspirations focus on getting that "shot of a lifetime."

As we urban creatures evolve, or distance ourselves from nature, we lose that primitive ability to gel with the environment, or to understand its peculiarities, nuances or patterns. We then begin to presume that wildlife within the political boundaries of a park will be lined up along the shore waiting serenely for their pictures to be taken at our convenience.

Our disappointment that the forest is devoid of all forms of life pre-empts the notion that we are perhaps not familiar with the way things work.

Being knowledgeable about wildlife

Jöri zooms in. Blending with the environment is key to close-up photography

traits and habitat is essential for successful outdoor photography and confrontation. Methods of approach, wind direction, seasonal variations, even the style in which a canoe is handled, are photo-experience variables and considerations.

Animals and birds are creatures of habit; some are nocturnal, some enjoy the pine forests to the fenlands, some prefer the early hours of the morning to feed along the shore while others move about in the dark void of the forest at night. The exhilaration of nature observation requires perseverance, patience, and an understanding of place and time. Canoeists who fail to extricate themselves from their tents at dawn, for instance, are certain to miss the magic of morning sun and mist, or watch the moose grazing in the shallows only 100 metres from the campsite.

Gunnel-banging or loud verbal intercourse between canoes gliding downriver is likely to send all shore denizens scurrying into the security of the forest beyond our perspective. The bright reflection of sun off a paddle blade is enough to catch the attention of the big bull moose you've been trying so desperately to approach. The methodology in which you apply yourself in the wilderness then, particularly in observing wildlife, enhances confrontation by your ability to remain unobtrusive. Successful photographers enjoy the very same stalking techniques once used by native hunters during the "still hunt."

The following are some helpful suggestions:

1. Carry your camera, film, binoculars in a waterproof case.
2. Carry a spare battery and plenty of film (most northern community stores have only a limited supply of film-types and rarely the brand of camera battery for SLR units).
3. A compact tripod is a must for shooting in low-light conditions, especially if you load with low-speed film.
4. A polarizing filter will cut out the unwanted glare on the water during bright, sunny days (at the expense of a couple of f-stops when filtering).
5. We have indicated on the river maps where prime moose-viewing opportunities exist. Woodland caribou will remain elusive while barren-ground caribou are easily photographed north and west of Nejanilini Lake.
7. Bears may present a problem along the Hudson Bay coast. See bibliography for suggested reading material. Practice clean campsite habits and suspend your food pack where possible if you suspect a problem.
8. DO NOT harass wildlife, disturb nests or pick sensitive plants just for the sake of improving a camera shot.
9. Keep a journal, or mark on your map where each photo was taken so that you have an accurate record of your trip.

ARTIFACTS & SPIRITUAL PLACES

Manitoba is rich in cultural history; this is clearly evident by the high concentration of native pictographs (rock paintings), petroforms (placement of stones/rocks to create outlines of specific shapes), ancient campsites (fire and shelter stone rings), dolmen stones (large boulders supported by small stones, creating a compartment for religious offerings), waymarkers and grave sites.

Within these pages you will notice many references to such places; however, only the sites which have already been well documented and previously scribed onto existing maps (Berard, Canada Parks, Ministries of Natural Resources, Manitoba and Ontario), will indicate correct geographic location as set by our own charts. Through our own research, several new sites have been located to which only approximate placement and/or visual reference is given to the reader.

The Ojibway, Cree and Dene people all continue to use some of these sites for ritual; certainly to a lesser degree today since the need for distant travel has diminished over the last century. Nonetheless, it must be understood by the adventure tourist that the protection of such sites is paramount, not just out of respect for aboriginal peoples, but also for the purpose of scientific study that may yield insight into the lives of early cultures that is not possible by any other means.

These features are sacred places where spirits, or incorporeal beings, communicated with the people, specifically members of the Midewewin, as in the case of the Ojibway culture – medicine men and women who were dedicated to the healing of the upright life; or shamans who may represent other cultures (Cree and Dene). The wilful destruction or altering of such places of worship is no different than defacing a church or synagogue.

In order to preserve and protect these sites, the Manitoba government passed the Heritage Resources Act in 1986. Under terms of this law, it is illegal to collect, move or alter objects of archaeological or heritage significance without obtaining a permit, and a fine may be levied against those who refuse to comply. In addition, Section 46 of the Act specifies that any person finding an object or feature is required to report that finding to the Minister of Culture, Heritage and Citizenship. By so doing, it will be possible to have such sites preserved and protected for future generations.

If you should find an offering left at a religious site, such as tobacco, cloth or medicine bundle, please do not disturb it. In an act of reverence you may leave some tobacco. Similarly, should you happen to come upon an individual or group visiting a site, please respect their right to do so in privacy and withdraw graciously.

Spirit places and artifacts are very susceptible to destruction from natural agents, such as animals and weather; but there are also people who may inadvertently move stones, for example, to build firepits or to anchor tents. If you notice stones placed in specific formation or as cairns, DO NOT MOVE THEM! Some pictographs have also been defaced. It should be a warning to travellers who come upon these sacred sites that, as in the case of the Tramping Lake rock paintings located on the Grass River, that the two white men who painted graffiti amongst the ancient drawings, died untimely and violent deaths soon after.

Stephen Hurlbut holds the remains of John Gray's grave marker carved by S. A Keighley in 1932. Refer to the book, Trader, Tripper, Trapper – The Life of a Bay Man, *pg. 148*

HOW TO USE THIS BOOK

Things You Should Know

*"To stick your hands into the river is to feel the cords
that bind the earth together in one piece."*

Barry Lopez

Hap Wilson

RATING RIVER DIFFICULTY AND SKILL LEVEL

Canoe Route Classifications – International River Grading System (IRGS) Route classifications or "grades" are indicated for each surveyed river. The difficulty of a river (or route) is determined by risk factor and overall stamina required to complete the trip safely. Variables such as weather, wind and water levels are unpredictable and may be considered as individual environmental considerations when choosing a route: for example, the distance you will be travelling against a head wind, or unusually high water levels that may suddenly change the classification of a route section.

Specific rating factors include: the number and difficulty of technical rapids, gradient or elevation drop per kilometre, length and difficulty of portages, remoteness and feasibility of rescue, average water temperature through canoeing season, unusual hazards (tidal currents, bears, fires, etc.) and degree of regular maintenance (specifically portage trails).

Although the I.R.G.S. was developed primarily for closed boats, and there exist minor variations correlated to geographic distinctions, the grading assessment for Manitoba rivers complies with what is considered accurate for Canadian rivers, and using open, unmodified canoes (stock, recreational).

Grading considers three elements: Overall sum of contributing factors to designate a route rating; a detailed rapid classification analysis; and an examination of characteristic hydrology for both low and high waterflow conditions. From the above information, the canoeist is able to determine what river matches their particular skill and energy level.

KNOW YOUR SKILL LEVEL

Few canoeists like to admit that they are, in fact, novice paddlers, and quite often will attempt running a particular rapids, or route, beyond their capabilities. Inexperience coupled with peer pressure are nasty canoe partners.

The number of derelict canoes scattered along the rocks attest to this grim fact. If you do not have the skills then you do not whitewater paddle. You either sign up for a clinic or join a guided expedition where you will learn the compulsory strokes, after which you can then assess your personal level of skill and apply it to a route of comparative grading.

Being able to read whitewater is an acquired skill. It takes years to develop. Relying on what you can pick up from how-to books and videos, or outfitting yourself with the latest outdoor gadgetry won't bail you out of a bad play on a rapid. This is dangerous fun – a lot riskier and less fun if you don't know what you're doing...and canoeists have met untimely deaths and serious accidents because they overestimated their skill and under estimated the power of the river.

The following are a few helpful tips:
- put the strongest paddler in the group with the weakest paddler
- travel in groups of at least two canoes (three is best)
- on difficult whitewater runs the more proficient paddler should be in the bow
- work cooperatively with your partner (screw-ups are usually the fault of both paddlers)
- even good paddlers are known to make poor judgement calls (use your own discretion and don't bend to peer pressure)
- know your limitations and make them known to others
- fatigue is the number one cause of river accidents (stop early even if only one paddler shows signs of stress or diminished strength)

SKILL CLASSIFICATIONS

The following skill level categories are predicated upon the paddler's ability to safely handle a stock recreational open canoe. Each classification indicates: Necessary skills required; route characteristics matched with level of skill; and type of difficulty or hazard one may encounter.

Novice or Beginner:

Skills Required – Canoeists have little or no experience or knowledge of whitewater techniques but do have primary flatwater skills. Capable but not proficient at navigating easy Class I rapids or swifts only, while ALL technical rapids are avoided. May attempt next grade if accompanied by higher grade paddler.

Route Characteristics – Predominantly flat water with some river/creek links that may have swifts or very minor rapids with the option to portage. Portages not excessively difficult; water temperatures are above 16°C (60°F) June through August, and evacuation accomplished within hours.

Hazards – Highwind on lakes and cold weather/water during buffer season trips. Sudden rise in water levels.

Experienced Novice:

Skills Required – Canoeists have basic whitewater skills and are proficient at safely navigating Class I and Class Itech. rapids. Class II rapids and higher are portaged. Lining skills are mediocre. May attempt next grade if accompanied by higher grade paddler.

Route Characteristics – River gradient is generally consistent and gradual with sporadic drops exceeding 5'/km. Predominantly Class I rapids interspersed with more technical, portageable rapids. Portages generally easy, but with a few classic steep climbs, bogs, or long hauls (over one kilometre). Water temperatures above 16°C (60°F) June through August, and evacuation accomplished in 12-24 hours.

Hazards – Same as novice with the addition of potential for capsize in easy grade rapids above dangerous chutes, falls or rapids.

Intermediate:

Skills Required – Canoeists are proficient whitewater paddlers able to safely line or navigate up to Class IItech. rapids without difficulty. Class III rapids are carefully scrutinized and run only with safety and rescue precautions in place and/or if accompanied by an advanced paddler. Eddy-turns and cross-ferries fully understood and implemented. Canoe extrication knowledge mandatory.

Route Characteristics – River gradient is often steep-pitched with at least 50% CII rapids or greater. Some longer CI and CII rapids may not have portages but lining is possible during low water conditions. Water temperatures may be lower than 16°C (60°F) during peak summer season. Portages steep or long (2 km +) and may be partially obstructed or overgrown. Environmental conditions are generally moderate, and evacuation may take longer than 24 hours.

Hazards – Cold weather/water risk during buffer season trips and/or during peak summer at higher latitudes (Seal, Caribou Rivers). Greater risk of capsize in larger rapids. Temptation to run the more difficult rapids greater.

Advanced or Expert:

Skills Required – Canoeists have extensive whitewater experience and high level skills. Ability to safely navigate CIII rapids or greater (with specialized equipment). Paddling skills include all technical rescue and extri-

cont'd on pg. 28

RAPID CLASSIFICATION CHART

The classification of rapids conforms with the International River Grading System (I.R.G.S.) which includes a total of six classifications. Since Class or Grade III rapids are considered the maximum safe rating for open, stock recreational canoes, unmodified for whitewater, only the first three grades are listed. Each class is defined and given an additional "technical" rating for more accuracy. This chart will enable you to assess your own skills and experience and apply them to the routes as described in the book.

CI

CI tech.

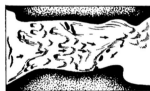

CI: Definite deep water, clear channel with well-defined downstream "V", small regular waves to 1/3 metre. Beginner's level.

**Easy –
Low Risk**

CI tech: As above with greater volume or some minor technical maneouvers requiring basic skills. Advanced Beginner's level.

CII

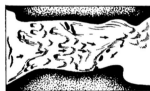

CII tech.

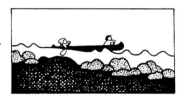

CII: Definite main channel with optional secondary channels visible in high water. Rock gardens, ledges present with standing waves to 2/3 metre. Technical moves such as eddy-turns and ferrying are required. Intermediate level paddler.

**Moderately Difficult –
Moderate Risk**

CIItech: As above with greater volume and larger waves, rock gardens with indefinite main channel; may be clogged with sweepers, snags, log jams, or larger boulders. Low profile canoes may swamp. Experienced intermediate level paddler.

CIII

CIII tech. or CIV

CIII: Maximum for open canoes — spray deck optional for rockered whitewater canoes but recommended for low-profile designs. Definite main channel with high volume, often narrow/steep-pitched "V" ending in a hydraulic/souse. Less reaction time. Boulder gardens, high ledges present with waves to one metre or more. Scouting and rescue spotters mandatory. Advanced level only.

**Difficult –
High Risk**

CIIItech or CIV: As above with greater volume, questionable main channels often split; tight passages and steep drops with serious aerated holes present. Specialized whitewater equipment/canoes required. Playboats with flotation or decked canoes only. Scouting and safety teams required. Expert level only.

cation procedures. High level of stamina/ endurance under duress.

Route Characteristics – River gradient has long, steep-pitched drops with a high proportion of technical rapids. Long rapids may not be portageable or lineable. Water temperatures may be lower than 16°C (60°F) during peak canoeing season. Portages may be difficult or non-existent. Environmental conditions may be extreme (wind, ice, snow, etc.). Evacuation without E.L.T. may take several days.

Hazards – Cold weather/water risk is greater; risk of capsize may be extreme. Wet or dry suits, added flotation, spray decks mandatory.

WATER LEVELS AND HYDROLOGY PATTERNS

The capricious nature of the river makes it next to impossible to indicate a perfectly accurate assessment of any river.

The only thing we can do as researchers and river cartographers is to make the variables and incongruencies known to the paddler – forewarned is forearmed. The ability to adjust to environmental changes, including fluctuating water levels, is inherent to the overall skill of the paddler in making responsible and safe judgement calls.

The information gathered in these pages regarding water levels is based upon average water level conditions that prevail through late June to early September when channels are well-defined. This time period is considered to be the normal canoeing season. Rapids are assessed in relation to the obvious, visible, high-water mark, seen as a darkened line on partly submerged rocks or shoreline striations. Highest water levels generally occur in late April to mid-May. Ice "scars" can be seen on shore trees two to three metres above summer levels.

In the far north, in areas of permafrost, rivers drain quickly after the spring run-off. The detailed descriptions in this book were charted from average June to August flow rates.

CONDITIONS MAY VARY AND ALTER THE RAPIDS DIAGRAMS AS SHOWN. Please take this into consideration.

LOW WATER CONDITIONS

Water levels lower than those described in this book may necessitate more lining, wading, or portaging. Rock gardens may become rockier, actually constricting main channels; ledges become pronounced as actual drop-offs.

Obstacles or obstructions generally become more visible and main channels more defined while secondary channels may totally disappear. It also maximizes the potential for getting "hung-up" if you don't employ good technique.

Because water volume is lower, you have more "adjustment" time while maneuvering but also the increased risk of broaching surface or "pillow" rocks.

Ferries and eddy turns have to be executed with more diligence. Low water levels can also permit more playtime along the rapids normally too difficult to run during high-water flow. This is usually accomplished by a combination of lining, lifting over ledges and running where suitable.

Those who possess good whitewater skills and creative technique also have the opportunity to shorten or eliminate some portages.

HIGH WATER CONDITIONS

Extreme high water level conditions are not only very dangerous, but render the detailed rapid descriptions in this book valueless, except possibly noting spring-level portage landings above dangerous water. Most rapids become unrecognizable, voluminous, often with flooded portage landings and dangerous because of high velocity current. Ice can be present on the lower reaches of some northern rivers up to early June.

Polar bear trips planned during ice run-off may end in polar bear "dips" so canoeists are recommended to don wet/dry suits and run with extra flotation, pack-tethers and spray skirts.

Advantages to high-water levels are smoother ledges, submerged rock gardens, exciting wave action and straighter runs. Concentration is focused less on spontaneous technical moves and more on keeping water out of the canoe. Inherent dangers are as follows:

1. Cold water factor. Water temperatures below 10°C (50°F) actually bump up the individual classification of technical rapids due to risk factor and elapsed rescue time.
2. Capsizing in rapids above dangerous chutes or falls poses extreme risks because of water velocity.
3. Larger volume and greater flow present the risk of "submarining" and less time to maneouver. Washing out at the top of a long rapids translates into a long, cold swim to the bottom.
4. Increased difficulty of rescue and canoe extrication.

HYDROLOGY

For some whitewaterists it is important to know water flow in terms of monthly and annual mean discharge.

Discharge is calculated in cubic metres per second or millions of gallons per day. Average mean figures do not tell a great deal unless compared with the outflow of another river system you may be familiar with. Monthly mean readings will indicate, however, a more useful determination of seasonal highs and lows, periods of dangerous ice-flows and so on.

Randy Todd of the Water Survey of Canada in Thompson compiled the average flow rates of rivers as shown for each described route in the book. The canoeist should be aware that they may experience a "high" or "low" flow rate different than the average. For more information and current data you may contact:

Water Survey of Canada
150-123 Main Street
Winnipeg, MB R3C 4W2
204-984-0240
or
Water Survey of Canada
5204-50th Ave. Suite 301
Yellowknife, NWT
X1A 1E2
(For the lower Thlewiaza north
of Nueltin Lake.)

For over 90 years the Water Survey of Canada has been a national agency responsible for the collection, interpretation and dissemination of standardized water resource data and information in Canada. It plays an important role in the national water survey program to ensure beneficial and wise use of water in this country.

"For 15 years I have been monitoring the rivers in Northern Manitoba and have witnessed the extremes of flows on all the major rivers. The significance of our data was shown in the spring of 1997 during the flood of the century in southern Manitoba.

"Having canoed many of the northern rivers you realize that this is a resource for all to use and respect. I have listened to wolves serenade me at night while the northern lights danced in the sky, but I have also experienced the garbage and litter left behind from other people. Inscribed on the wall of our Hayes River cabin I read, 'For years the river carried men of many different nations. Preserve her now with due respect for future generations,' a wise epitaph to be considered while enjoying the beauty of Manitoba rivers."

Randy Todd, Thompson
Water Survey of Canada

NOTE: Determining water flow and rainfall prior to an expedition is essential in assessing conditions of the river when you get to it. By comparing up-to-date readouts for water flow with the averages listed you should be able to determine whether you will be confronted with high or low level conditions. Heavy rainfall of 50 mm (2") or more over a period of a few days will affect water levels dramatically.

ADDITIONAL SERVICES

For a current listing of tourist outfitters and service contact:

Travel Manitoba
155 Carlton St.
Winnipeg, MB
R3C 3H8
1-800-665-0040

For information concerning provincial parks and fishing regulations, tide charts and ferry schedules you can contact:

Manitoba Conservation
Box 22, Winnipeg, MB
R3J 3W3
1-800-214-6497

USING THE MAPS

Map Scales: Each route begins with a bird's-eye location map that shows access and egress points, and the number of route maps (shown as red boxes). River maps are drawn from the 1:250,000 topographical scale in order to save space within the book. Detail maps of rapids or sections of river that may require more definition are drawn from the larger scale 1:50,000 topographical maps; *NOTE:* actual field drawings of

rapids are scaled individually by portage length, or by average site length calculated in metres. All maps are aligned north/south unless otherwise indicated.

Canoeists should transfer pertinent information from the guidebook to the 1:50,000 topographical maps which are listed at the beginning of each route description.

Keep the book handy for quick reference and learn to use the Legend for speedy interpretation of field info.

DETAILED RAPID MAPS

The seasoned whitewater paddler may not require this much information but I know for a fact that most guides have carried copies of my book with them even if not openly admitted. The purpose of such detail is to:
1. Grade the difficulty of the rapid
2. Describe general conditions, hazards, etc.
3. Illustrate primary and/or secondary running channels
4. Detail portage locations around difficult runs
5. Indicate the length of run (to determine the amount of water you can safely ship

before losing control of the craft by running or avoiding larger-volume waves).

Rapid cartography is NOT intended to make the running of whitewater easier for the inexperienced paddler or neophyte. It is very important to note that NAVIGABLE CHANNELS MAY VARY WITH WATER LEVEL and canoeists should use their own discretion based on the key factors affecting the safe navigation of any fast-water situation. Rapids that round bends may be impeded by sweepers or strainers (fallen trees and log jams). Each spring freshet scours the shores and washes timber downriver, frequently to become lodged in the most inappropriate places. Rapid diagrams are for reference only and gauged at optimum running conditions with all safety procedures in place. Although many rapids "flood-out" during high water, making primary channels barely discernible, the diagram will still indicate areas to avoid or rocks that may be just beneath the surface of the water, outside the low-water running channel but submerged.

Planning tomorrow's schedule

SCALE USED FOR ROUTE MAPS – 1:250,000

HELPFUL NOTES ON USING THE LEGEND

GENERAL MAP DETAIL

Portage in Metres — All portages have been accurately assessed for length and location. Where applicable, both high and low water portage access points are indicated on detailed rapid maps.

Rapids or Swifts, Class I-II Only — Navigable fast water under optimum conditions; however, water levels may alter classification which may present certain hazards. Novices should approach with care and scout.

Technical Rapids, Class II Tech. – CIV — Fast water that requires careful scouting or portaging. Mandatory portaging for novices.

Falls/Dangerous Chutes – DO NOT RUN! Portage required.

Rapid or Rapid/Fall in Sequence — Some rivers have numbered runnable rapids for easy clarification; or, numbered rapids and falls that may or may not be runnable. This is clarified on the General Information page for each river.

Kilometres to End of Route — These are mileage reference points that make daily planning easier.

Pictograph site — Native rock paintings (general location). Refer to section on "Artifacts and Spiritual Places."

Moose Viewing Opportunity — Higher potential for observing moose in their natural feeding environment.

Viewpoint — Vistas that afford a panoramic view of surrounding environs but do not generally have an established trail to the summit. In most cases, bedrock predominates in the Shield ecozone, whereas viewpoints in the boreal/tundra fringe consist of glacial drumlin or esker formations.

Air Access/Egress — These are optional start and end points accessible by floatplane or land-based charter.

Remote Phone — Located at wilderness-based tourist lodges, these radio-phones are for emergency use only.

Road – Only roads pertaining to access/egress points are shown for easy reference.

Campsites – Sites were assessed for their ability to accommodate a specific number of 2-person, self-standing tents.

RAPID DETAIL

Deepwater "V" – This is generally the initial point of entry into a runnable rapid.

Standing Waves/Haystacks — Usually deepwater waves following the "V" which can be run with care while applying the proper "braces," employing the use of a spray deck "for waves in excess of one metre," or to be avoided by maneuvering left or right as the situation demands. In cases such as the Seal River, many rapids are classed higher where centre flow creates large standing waves. Easier runs are then negotiated to either side of the main flow.

Boils/Aerated Water — Deepwater turbulence following heavy waves or below falls and chutes, particularly noticeable where the geology rises abruptly from the shores, and during peak flow periods. Boils move and pulse in circular patterns and can overturn canoes if paddlers are not wary of conditions while aerated water (white/foamy) has little buoyancy where balance and maneuverability could be compromised.

Running Channel — These indicate maneuvers under optimum conditions only. Each rapid should be assessed individually by each paddler.

Ferries — Maneuvers required by experienced whitewater paddlers, most often applied where rapids are long and unscoutable (Seal & Hayes), or, where applicable as indicated on the detailed rapid maps.

Eddy — Static pools formed behind obstacles and along shores, used as safe havens or escape from the main river flow. Eddy turns in and out of eddies are mandatory skills required for intermediate classed rivers and rapids.

Ledges — These are to be avoided. Large ledges during heavy flow may create "souse holes" or "keepers," dangerous aerated water where attempts at rescue may be difficult (Pigeon, Seal & Hayes). On smaller rivers, an on-shore safety "spotter" may be required.

Dangerous Current — STAY OUT! Usually indicates extreme current at the head of dangerous rapids, falls, or chutes. Wider berth should be given during periods of heavy or peak flow.

Rapid Classification — All rapids are classified according to difficulty under the International River Grading System (refer to section on "reading rapids.")

General Map Detail:

Portage in meters	℗175
Rapids or Swifts, Class 1~11 only	
Technical Rapids, Class 11 tech. ~ CIV	
Falls/Dangerous Chutes	
Rapid or Rapid/Fall in sequence	(18) or ◯18
Kilometers to end of route	(30)—
Pictograph site	
Moose viewing opportunity	
Viewpoint, Eagle nest	Ⓥ ⒺⓃ
Air access/egress	
Remote phone	
Roads	—(6)—or —(6)—
Campsites: **Large** 6 or more tents	▲
Medium 3 to 5 tents	▲
Small 1 to 2 tents	△

Rapid Detail:

Deepwater 'V'	
Standing waves/haystacks	
Boils/aerated water	
Running channel	flow→ ... or → ↗ →
Ferry: **Downstream**	
Upstream	
Eddy	ⓔ
Ledge	
Dangerous current	ⓘ
Rapid classification	CI, CIV

WILDERNESS RIVERS OF MANITOBA
Regional Divisions

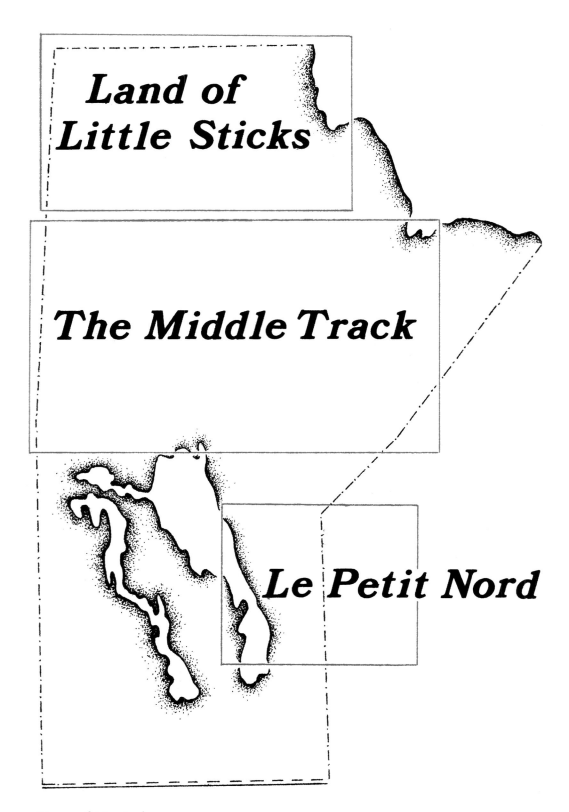

Land of Little Sticks

The Middle Track

Le Petit Nord

SECTION IV

THE RIVERS

*"It is pleasant to have been to a place the way
a river went."*

Henry David Thoreau

Tranquil scene along the Leyond

Le Petit Nord
The Rivers of Atikaki

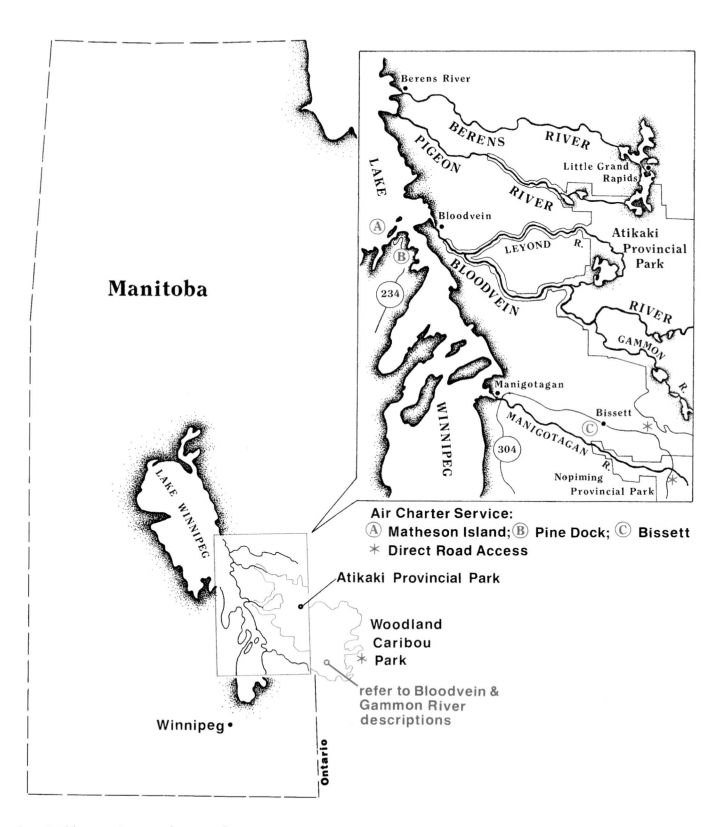

Berens River

BERENS RIVER

PIGEON

RIVER

Little Grand Rapids

LAKE

Bloodvein

Ⓐ

Ⓑ

234

LEYOND R.

Atikaki Provincial Park

BLOODVEIN

RIVER

GAMMON

R.

Manigotagan

Bissett

WINNIPEG

Ⓒ

MANIGOTAGAN R.

304

Nopiming Provincial Park

Manitoba

LAKE WINNIPEG

Winnipeg•

Ontario

Air Charter Service:
Ⓐ **Matheson Island;** Ⓑ **Pine Dock;** Ⓒ **Bissett**
✳ **Direct Road Access**

Atikaki Provincial Park

Woodland Caribou Park ✳

refer to Bloodvein & Gammon River descriptions

LE PETIT NORD
The Rivers of Atikaki

Atikaki is Saulteaux Ojibway meaning "country of the caribou," There is evidence of aboriginal settlement here that dates back several thousand years; the number of archaeological sites and rock paintings attest to the frequent use of the rivers for travel, trade, hunting, fishing, the gathering of wild rice in the fall, and for spiritual purposes.

During the fur trade, specifically in the late 1700's to early 1800's, there was intensive competition for furs by independent traders of the North West Company who were based in Montreal, and traders for the Hudson's Bay Company who operated out of Fort Albany and later York Factory on Hudson Bay. The trading area north and west of Lake Superior to Lake Winnipeg became known as "Le Petit Nord," an area that fringed on the southern extremity of Rupert's Land – a vast area which the HBC held by royal charter from 1670 to 1869. The main trade route from east to west, along the voyageur highway, followed the Winnipeg River to the south but some traders used the Berens and Bloodvein routes as an alternative passage connecting Lake Winnipeg to Hudson Bay. Suggested reading about the history of Le Petit Nord is Victor Lytwyn's book, *The Fur Trade of the Little North.*

In 1985 the government of Manitoba designated a 4,000 sq. km. area east of Lake Winnipeg which included the Pigeon and Bloodvein watersheds resulting in the formation of the province's first wilderness class park. Two years later, the Bloodvein received honour as a Canadian Heritage River, significant in terms of human, natural heritage and recreational values for wilderness tourism.

Atikaki is perched atop some of the world's oldest rock, formed 3 billion years ago; time-worn and molded by several glaciers, this part of the great Precambrian Shield was then flooded by glacial Lake Agassiz 9,000 years ago, whose meltwater nourished a lush boreal forest carpeted beneath with a thick matt of moss, decorated by Indian Paint-brush, Lady's Slipper and numerous other wildflowers.

At this time there are no fees and few regulations governing the use of the park; nonetheless, canoeists should abide by the "no trace camping" code of ethics. The rivers are extremely pristine and refreshing with minimal impact by man; campsites are nothing short of spectacular, rapids are multi-graded, capricious and exciting, and portages are generally short. Most difficult rapids and chutes can be bypassed.

Novice paddlers are encouraged to travel with experienced guides or join a scheduled expedition with a reputable tour company. There are seven distinctly different rivers featured in this section; some routes can be paddled upstream, some join adjacent rivers, or canoeists can stay with a chosen river from headwater lake to Lake Winnipeg. Maps illustrating both Atikaki and Woodland Caribou parks are available from Natural Resources District Offices, or the CRCA.

Please read all river descriptions over thoroughly before selecting a route and make sure that it suits your requirements and skill level.

WOODLAND CARIBOU PARK ONTARIO

Since Ontario shares specific headwaters of rivers flowing through Manitoba, it was only natural to include the upper reaches of both the Bloodvein and Gammon Rivers. For those wanting extended canoe trips, you may consider travelling through Woodland Caribou Park in Ontario.

The Ontario government first set aside this border region adjoining Manitoba in 1948. It was then known as the Caribou Game Preserve and later became a full-fledged member of the provincial park system in 1983; encompassing nearly half a million hectares (1.2 million acres), it is the fifth largest provincial park in the province.

Of provincial and national distinction are the numerous rock art sites, one of the largest resident woodland caribou herds south of the Hudson Bay lowlands, excellent fisheries and pristine wilderness. This "prairie boreal" landscape is quite similar to that of Manitoba's Atikaki Park; the provincial boundary only represents a difference in management ethics. The canoeist should think of Atikaki and Woodland Caribou parks as one contiguous multi-river ecosystem that has evolved through thousands of years, or rivers without boundaries.

Le Petit Nord, without dispute, offers the paddler the finest adventures in a truly remarkable Canadian wilderness landscape. The only worry will be whether or not you've brought along enough film for your camera.

Morning mist on the Pigeon

MANIGOTAGAN RIVER OVERVIEW

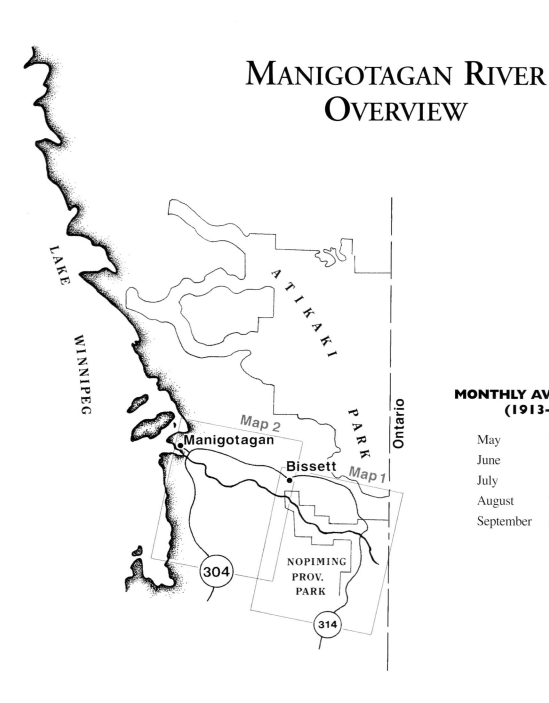

MONTHLY AVERAGE FLOW (1913-1992)

May	24.2	m³/sec.
June	18.8	m³/sec.
July	12.4	m³/sec.
August	7.89	m³/sec.
September	6.54	m³/sec.

MANIGOTAGAN RIVER

GENERAL INFORMATION

Classification: Experienced Novice
(portaging all technical rapids)
Intermediate
(CII tech. to CIII rapids negotiated)
Distance: 100 km. (Long Lake to Manigotagan village)
Elevation Drop: 79m. (260') or .8m/km. (2.6'/km.)
Time: 4-7 days
Number of Campsites: 28 (approx. 3 every 10/km.)
Number of Rapids & Falls: 32 (numbered in sequence)
Number of Runnable Rapids: 22 (85% CI to CII)
Portages: Experienced Novice – 24 (3,205m.)
Creative Intermediate – 15 (1,670m.)
Season: Late May through early October (canoeists should avoid travelling during hunting season).
Maps Required: 52 L/14 52 L/13 52 M/4 62 P/1
Access: *6-7 day trips* – Hwy #304 (gravel base) to public access at Long Lake (mileage 100). Shuttles can be arranged in advance at Windsock Lodge, 204-254-0901. Campsites are located 11/2 hrs. paddle down Long Lake.
4-5 day trips – Take Quesnel Lake Rd., 18 km. south from Bissett to Caribou Landing (mileage 70). Shuttles may be arranged locally or in Bissett. Camping is possible at the landing or 1/2 km. downriver at the chutes.
Egress: Hwy. #304 bridge at Wood Falls near the village of Manigotagan. Campsites are available at the Wayside Park, 450m. from the portage landing at the upstream side of the bridge, cross highway to park entrance. The village of Manigotagan is a 1/2 hr. walk or paddle from the campsite. Campsites should not be left unattended and arrangements should be made to leave your vehicle in a secure place.
Features: The Manigotagan is a short, easily accessed and very pretty river corridor with the upper section lying within the Nopoming Provincial Park. It drains a relatively small area and typifies the Boreal Shield Ecozone by its rolling Precambrian landscape and thin layers of silt and clay-rich sand, deposited during post-glacial submergence by Lake Agassiz. The corridor traces a course through billion-year-old granitic bedrock, noted distinctly by the irregular river pattern and numerous white-water stretches through steep, rock-sloped shores. Bedrock barrens are common where coniferous forests dominate and frequent natural fires have changed the forest cover in recent years, but remain as a crucial force in maintaining ecological diversity and habitat renewal. The climate of the corridor is "prairie-boreal," with a hot, dry, prairie-like influence that actually encourages frequent wild fires. The forest cover, conspicuous of past fires, supports a mosaic of jackpine on the drier sites, with black spruce and larch (tamarack) emerging from shoreside wetlands.

Fauna is characteristic of "warm-boreal" species which include: Woodland caribou, Great Gray owl, Timber wolf, Fisher, Lynx, Black bear, Snowshoe hare, beaver, Least chipmunk, Common loon, Palm warbler, Red-sided garter snake and Evening grosbeak. Prairie-parkland elements contribute to the occurrence of Prickly-pear cactus, Bur oak, Franklin's ground-squirrel and wood ticks.

The archaeology of the river attests to thousands of years of use by Paleo Indian, Shield Archaic and Woodland cultures, clustered chiefly around the Quesnel, Manigotagan and Long Lake area. Being close to the plains, hunters could wait at the forest fringe for bison, while the upper resources of the river supplied fish, waterfowl, wild rice and bark for canoes.

The Manigotagan was spared heavy use by fur traders but remained as an important route for the resident Ojibway and Metis from the Manigotagan and Hollow Water communities where trapping and wild rice harvesting continues to be an important part of the Anishnabai culture.

During the 1900's mineral exploration resulted in the staking of several mine sites, particularly gold at Bissett. The historic "Jackpine Trail," still used as a snowmachine route, connects Pine Falls with the town of Bissett. Although there is a fair bit of activity north of the river, the Manigotagan enjoys a pristine, semi-wilderness character with the few cottages and lodges restricted to Quesnel and Long Lakes only.

WHITEWATER CHARACTERISTICS AND GENERAL HAZARDS

Route maps indicate both runnable rapids, and serious chutes and falls, in numbered sequence for easy reference (1 to 32). Many of the rapids do become quite rocky as the flow diminishes which may necessitate additional portaging, lining or greater skills to avoid broaching on "pillow" rocks.

Higher water levels may present greater risk at chutes and falls where portage access lay close to pitch-offs. This is generally not a serious concern on the Manigotagan. The river enjoys a good flow throughout the paddling season.

Wood ticks can be somewhat of a nuisance and easily picked up along some of the portages. Just make sure that you brush off your outerwear after each carry and wear a hat to keep the pests out of your hair. Tick bites can spread diseases such as babesiosis, Lyme disease or Rocky Mountain spotted fever. To remove ticks it is best NOT to use home remedies such as kerosene, or the end of a cigarette; instead, use tweezers to grasp the head firmly close to the skin and remove by pulling backwards. Do not leave tick parts in the skin! Although undesirable, ticks should not be a deterrent from enjoying the beauty of the Manigotagan.

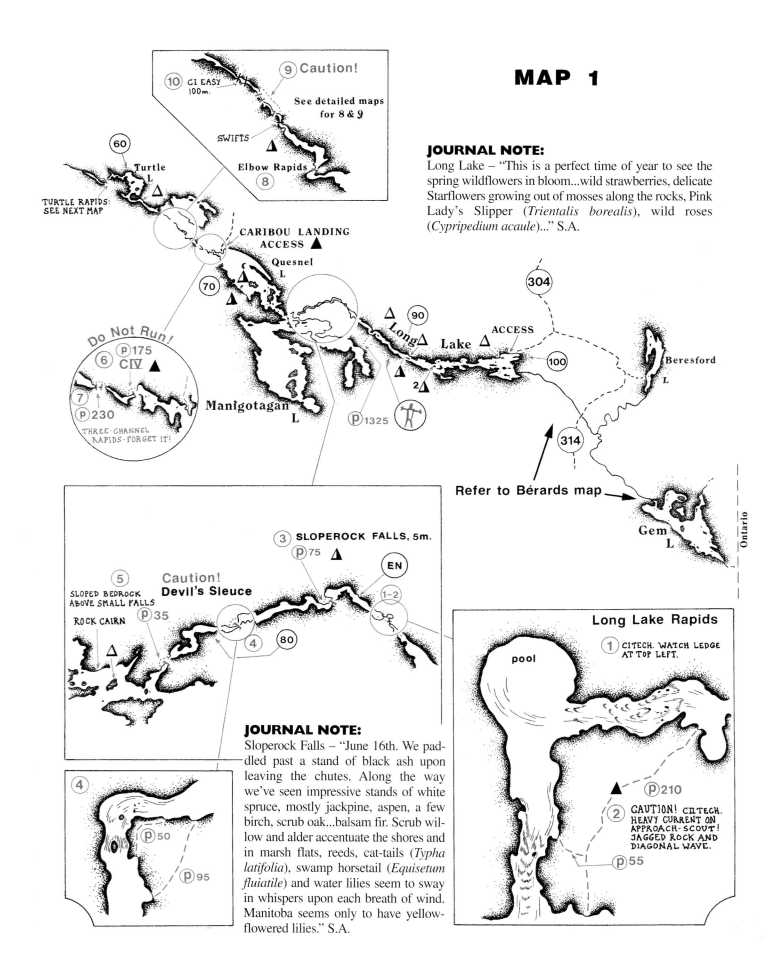

MAP 1

JOURNAL NOTE:
Long Lake – "This is a perfect time of year to see the spring wildflowers in bloom...wild strawberries, delicate Starflowers growing out of mosses along the rocks, Pink Lady's Slipper (*Trientalis borealis*), wild roses (*Cypripedium acaule*)..." S.A.

⑨ Caution!

See detailed maps for 8 & 9

⑩ CI EASY 100m.

SWIFTS

Elbow Rapids

⑧

60

Turtle L

TURTLE RAPIDS: SEE NEXT MAP

CARIBOU LANDING ACCESS ▲

Quesnel L

70

Do Not Run!

⑥ Ⓟ175 CIV ▲

⑦ Ⓟ230

THREE-CHANNEL RAPIDS-FORGET IT!

Manigotagan L

Long ▲ Lake ▲

90

2▲

ACCESS

304

100

Beresford L

314

Refer to Bérards map

Gem L

Ontario

Ⓟ1325

③ **SLOPEROCK FALLS, 5m.**
Ⓟ75 ▲

⑤ Caution!
Devil's Sleuce

SLOPED BEDROCK ABOVE SMALL FALLS

ROCK CAIRN Ⓟ35

④ 80

EN

1-2

Long Lake Rapids

① CITECH. WATCH LEDGE AT TOP LEFT.

pool

▲ Ⓟ210

② CAUTION! CITECH. HEAVY CURRENT ON APPROACH-SCOUT! JAGGED ROCK AND DIAGONAL WAVE.

Ⓟ55

④ Ⓟ50
Ⓟ95

JOURNAL NOTE:
Sloperock Falls – "June 16th. We paddled past a stand of black ash upon leaving the chutes. Along the way we've seen impressive stands of white spruce, mostly jackpine, aspen, a few birch, scrub oak...balsam fir. Scrub willow and alder accentuate the shores and in marsh flats, reeds, cat-tails (*Typha latifolia*), swamp horsetail (*Equisetum fluiatile*) and water lilies seem to sway in whispers upon each breath of wind. Manitoba seems only to have yellow-flowered lilies." S.A.

JOURNAL NOTE

"It is always such a thrill to come across a spiritual or archaeological site. This one on the Manigotagan was particularly interesting as it contained an impressive rock art display, two primitive campsites and a dolmen type petroform as shown in the diagram. The triangle configuration of the petroform pointed to the pictographs and each of the respective campsites. A speculative interpretation may suggest that the petroform 'joins' the corporeal subjects with the incorporeal or 'spirit' world as depicted by the rock paintings. A suggestion of 'harmony' through a sort of pyramid power. A shaman holding a memegishiwok, the rabbit-eared Nanabush and many more symbols demanded we leave an offering of tobacco." S.A.

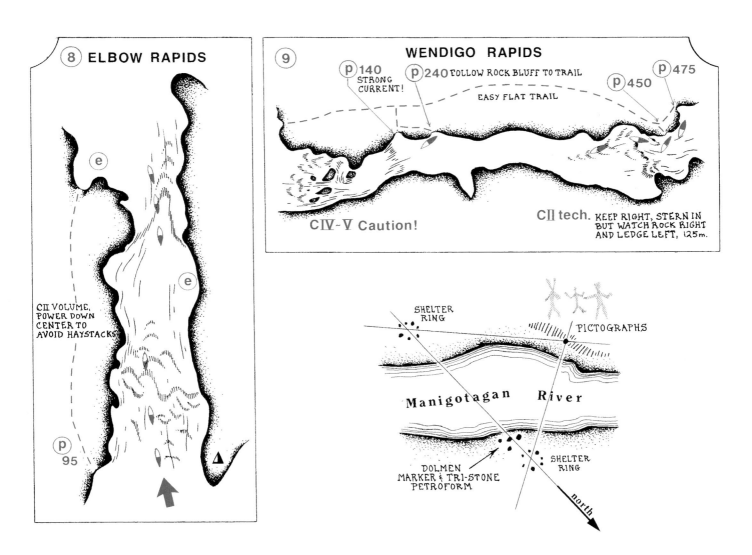

JOURNAL NOTE:

Sand River Falls – "We paddled a short piece past the falls which really was no more than a Class II rapid, after having enjoyed a rest day camped high on the rocks; pulling ashore on the south side to photograph the old 'alligator.'

"Alligators are relics from the timbering days, used primarily to draw log booms down lakes. Powered by steam and paddlewheel on the lakes, they needed their powerful winches to haul its bulk over the portages. This particular alligator was modified to process ore and was heading upriver to the Long Lake mines in 1921, fell upon hard going until the cook walked out and took the rest of the crew with him. It is purported that the vessel was so heavy that it pulled the trees out by the roots to which the winch had been anchored." H.W.

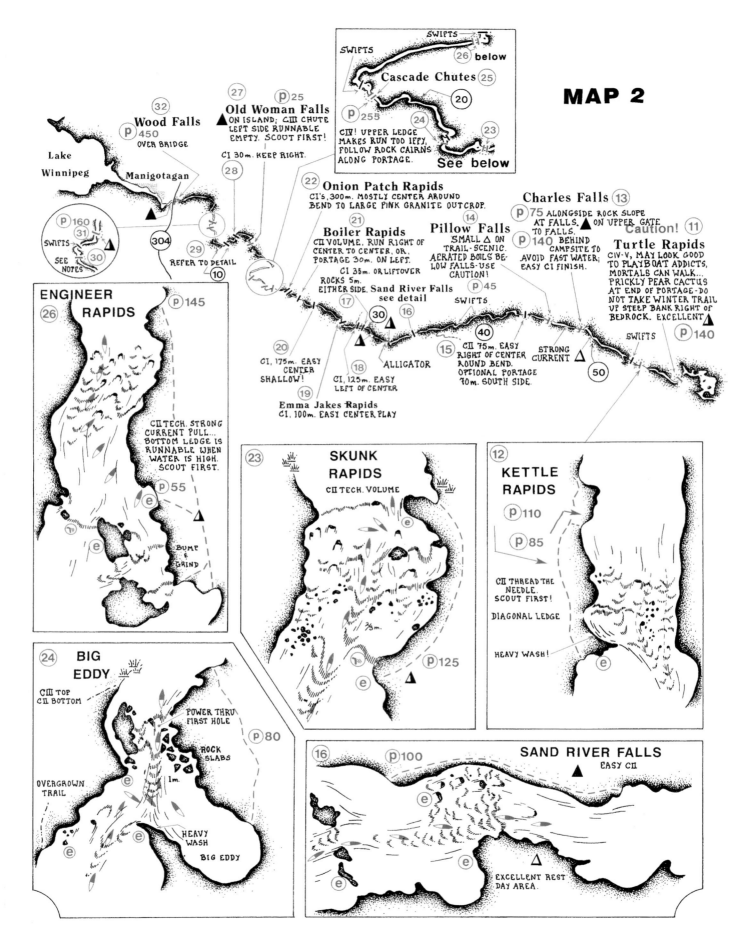

JOURNAL NOTE

"Tonight we're camped at Turtle Rapids, a most exquisite spot where the river tumbles over granite ledges in no particular hurry. I explored the trail leading to the end of the falls and elected to sit and watch the evening unfold to a chorus of spring peepers, almost sitting on a prickly pear cactus! Something of an anomaly in such northern Shield country, but really quite remarkable just to see how it has taken root in all the tiny crevices of the overlaying rock. I think that I will keep my shoes on." S.A.

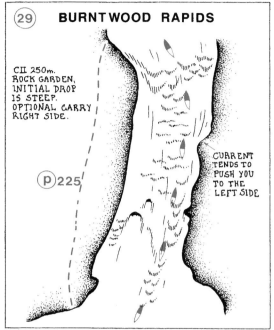

Post Office at Bissett

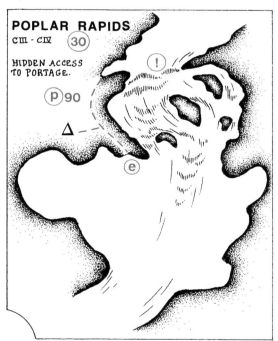

Falls along the Manigotagan

JOURNAL NOTE

"It's comforting to know that the river survived the east-central Manitoba gold rush of 1910. What with all the activity upriver back then, and even today to a lesser degree, one would think the spirit of the wilderness would be subdued, but it's not. The odd cougar wanders riverside and you're sure to see a moose wading through the water lilies somewhere along the course. Listen carefully...you might even hear manigodagan, old 'bad throat,' the bull moose with the feeble voice that gave the river its name." S.A.

BLOODVEIN RIVER
OVERVIEW

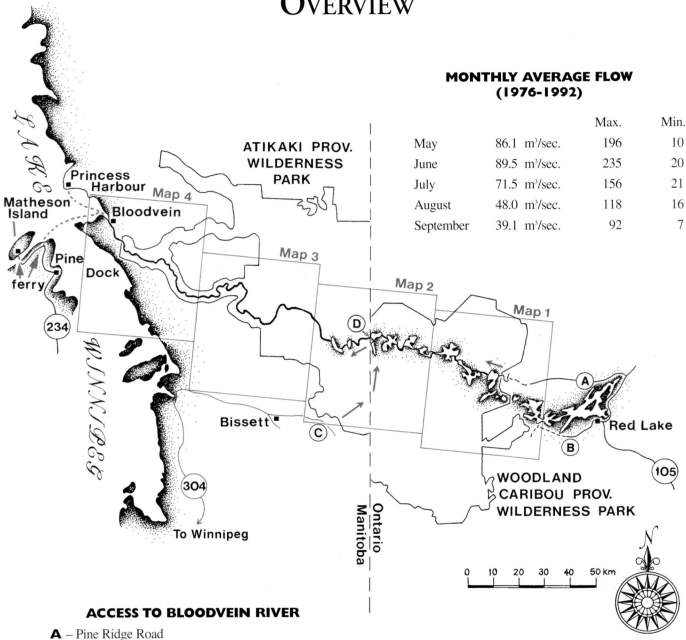

MONTHLY AVERAGE FLOW
(1976-1992)

			Max.	Min.
May	86.1	m³/sec.	196	10
June	89.5	m³/sec.	235	20
July	71.5	m³/sec.	156	21
August	48.0	m³/sec.	118	16
September	39.1	m³/sec.	92	7

ACCESS TO BLOODVEIN RIVER

A – Pine Ridge Road

B – Suffel Lake Road

C – Wallace Lake (see Gammon River Route)

D – Artery Lake (Fly-in from Matheson or Pine Dock)

BLOODVEIN RIVER

GENERAL INFORMATION

Classification: Experienced Novice
(portaging all technical rapids)
Intermediate
(CII tech. to CIII rapids negotiated)
Distance: From Red Lake, Ontario: 340 km.
From Knox Lake/headwaters: 300 km.
From Artery Lake/Ont. Manitoba border: 225 km.
*all to Bloodvein village on Lake Winnipeg
Elevation Drop: Red Lake to Lake Winnipeg –
137m. (450') (.4m./km.)/(1.3'/km.)
Artery Lake to Lake Winnipeg –
104m. (341') (.46m./km.)/(1.5'/km.)
Time: From Red Lake – 18-21 days
From Artery Lake – 12-14 days
Number of Campsites: Red Lake (Pipestone Bay) to Artery
Lake: 34 115 km. or 1 campsite every 3 km.
Artery Lake to Bloodvein: 71 225 km. or 1 campsite every 3 km.
Number of Runnable Rapids: 85 (70% CI to CII) Numbered in
sequence.
Portages: Red Lake to Artery
Experienced Novice – 15 (8,160m.)
Creative Intermediate – 16 (7,660m.)
Artery to Lake Winnipeg
Experienced Novice – 48 (5,378m.)
Creative Intermediate – 27 (2,440m.)
Total: Experienced Novice – 63 (13,538m.)
Creative Intermediate – 43 (10,100m.)
Season: Late May through early October (canoeists should avoid
travelling during hunting season).
Maps Required: 52 M/1 52 M/2 52 M/5 52 M/6 52 M/7 52
M/12 62 P/8 62 P/9 62 P/10 62 P/15
Access: By vehicle: Red Lake/Woodland Caribou Provincial Park;
Suffel Lake Rd. west of Red Lake village to Black Bear Lodge
(400m. portage from gate to lake). Atikaki via Wallace Lake (Hwy
#304), refer to Gammon River General Information.
By air: Floatplane service available from Bissett, Matheson Island
or Pine Dock.
Egress: There is a free, daily ferry service (except weekends and
holidays), back to Hwy #234 at Matheson Island from Bloodvein
village. Ferry does not operate during severe wind conditions.
Features: Miskowisibi, the "Bloodvein," best represents the
drama of place both geologically and spiritually. The exceptional
natural beauty of the Precambrian Shield is marked by abrupt grey
granite outcroppings often brilliantly decorated with patches of
orange lichen and lush green mosses. The concentration and variety of native rock paintings constitutes a most celebrated prehistoric art gallery of international scope and importance.

This roadless treasure was protected within the confines of
Manitoba's first wilderness park in 1985. "Atikaki," pronounced a-
tick-a-kee, is Saulteaux (pronounced so-toe) Ojibway meaning
"country of the caribou," and is presently home turf for the 350
Woodland caribou who thrive on the boreal lichen, "old man's
beard," and reindeer moss which grows abundantly in the mature
jackpine stands and boreal flats of the park interior.

The Bloodvein River, which originates in the uplands of
Ontario's Woodland Caribou Provincial Park (designated in 1983),
can be enjoyed by virtually all levels of paddlers with various
skills. Novices, though, should be aware of the inherent risks present at several of the larger and capricious rapids and falls.

WHITEWATER CHARACTERISTICS AND GENERAL HAZARDS

The Bloodvein is a typical "pool & riffle" type river where most
of the current is restricted to the actual outflow of the individual
rapid or fall only. This characteristic makes the river appealing for
both up and downstream travel, and probably the establishing factor why the corridor was heavily used by native peoples over the
last several thousand years.

Compared with the Manigotagan, the Bloodvein has a much
higher flow rate which produces a greater number of technical or
volume rapids greater than Class IItech., and this would appeal to
the more experienced canoeist. Many of the short, steeply-pitched
runs often create various sized "keepers" or souse-holes which
could present a problem if the paddler is not familiar with rescue
techniques.

Only the runnable rapids (all grades) are numbered in
sequence on the Bloodvein maps, and paddlers should study well
the detailed rapids as illustrated on the inset diagrams. The temptation to challenge the more serious ledge-type rapids does exist
and the danger in doing so may be life-threatening and foolhardy.
Diminishing flow by August does make accessing portage landings easier and safer; however, ledges and rock-gardens become
more pronounced making ferries and eddy-turns more difficult.
Canoeists should scout each run carefully before attempting to
run. Rapid detail illustrates a moderately "high" flow as typical for
early summer.

During the past few seasons, the Bloodvein has experienced
a much diminished seasonal flow. Some paddlers will actually
prefer this as many non-runnable rapids can now be negotiated
safely, and more lining reduces the number of portages required.
Paddlers must be aware of the rather dramatic changes that occur
on some rapids: class I's may disappear or become ledges; class
II's may become class I's, class III drops may not be navigable at
all. This alters the detailed rapid maps which have been drawn to
scale for higher water levels. CHECK EACH RUN CAREFUL-
LY!

MAP 1

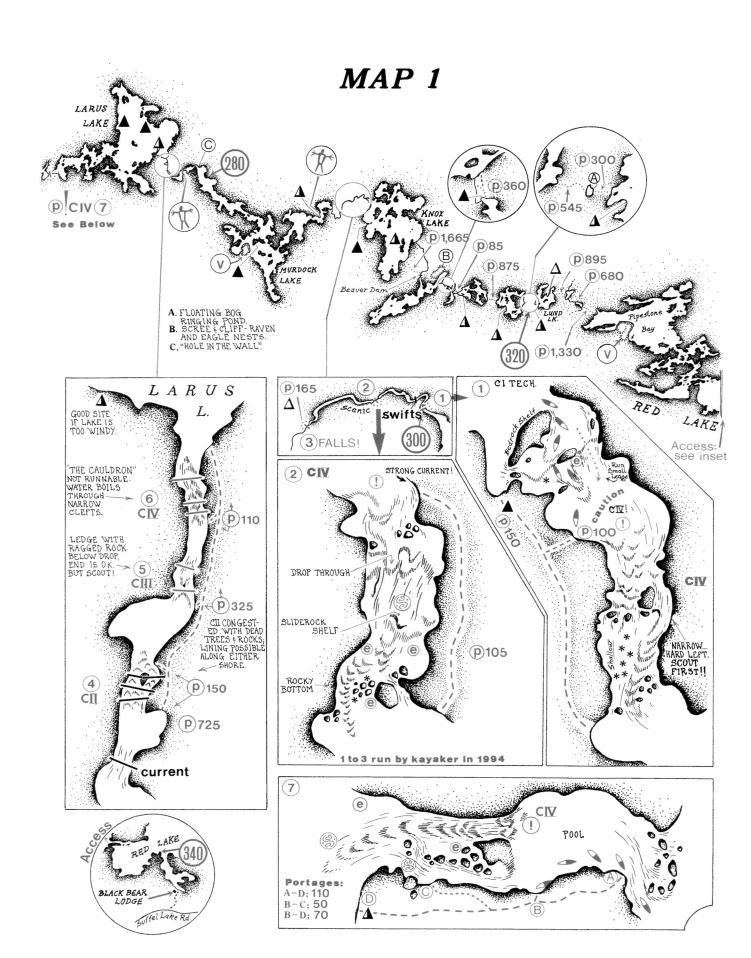

LARUS LAKE

C
(280)

(p)! CIV (7)
See Below

V

MURDOCK LAKE

A. FLOATING BOG RINGING POND.
B. SCREE & CLIFF - RAVEN AND EAGLE NESTS.
C. "HOLE IN THE WALL".

Knox Lake

(p)1,665

Beaver Dam

B

(p)85

(p)875

(p)895

(p)680

(p)360

(p)300
A
(p)545

Lund LK.

(320)

(p)1,330

V

Pipestone Bay

RED LAKE

Access: see inset

LARUS L.

GOOD SITE IF LAKE IS TOO WINDY.

"THE CAULDRON" NOT RUNNABLE. WATER BOILS THROUGH NARROW CLEFTS.
(6) CIV.

LEDGE WITH RAGGED ROCK BELOW DROP, END IS O.K. BUT SCOUT!
(5) CIII.

(p)110

(p)325

CII CONGEST-ED WITH DEAD TREES & ROCKS; LINING POSSIBLE ALONG EITHER SHORE.

(4) CII

(p)150

(p)725

current

(p)165

(2)

Scenic

swifts

(3) FALLS!

(300)

(2) CIV
STRONG CURRENT!

DROP THROUGH

SLIDEROCK SHELF

ROCKY BOTTOM

e

e

e

(p)105

1 to 3 run by kayaker in 1994

(1) CI TECH.

Bedrock Shelf

Run Small Ledge

e

*

caution
CIV!

(p)150

(p)100

CIV

Shallow

NARROW... HARD LEFT. SCOUT FIRST!!

Access

RED LAKE
(340)

BLACK BEAR LODGE

Suffel Lake Rd.

(7)

e

CIV
!
POOL

e

A

D

C

B

Portages:
A–D; 110
B–C; 50
B–D; 70

THE BLOODVEIN RIVER/ JOURNAL NOTES SUMMER '95

We were detained in Red Lake by the Ministry of Natural Resources since our prescribed route lay in the smoke drift of a wild fire that wasn't quite under control. I was paddling with a friend from London, and we met up with a couple of Swiss lads who worked at Enid and Hugh Carlson's Viking Outpost lodge for the summer. They would join us for the trip down the Bloodvein. I was anxious to get going, fires or no fires, thinking that it couldn't be half as bad as the fires on the Seal River the year previous.

The three day delay did give me time to peruse the large volume of archaeological data given to me by park staff, which then allowed us to chart out the best route through Woodland Caribou Park in order to explore all of the upper Bloodvein rock art sites. It was like joining the dots and I half expected the finished etching to resemble some magical symbol of ancient Ojibway folklore, but Mishapeshu didn't jump off the topographic map and into the canoe.

I've always been fascinated by our Canadian native culture having first been introduced to the Stony Lake petroglyphs

Summer storm near Artery Lake

in Ontario when I was only six years old. My father was producing survival movies for the Department of Lands and Forests in the mid 1950's, and old Charlie, an Ojibway elder who worked on the movie set, took us along an old, overgrown trail that led to a "religious site" that was located not far from my childhood cottage in the Kawartha Lakes district.

Almost 40 years later, here I was about to experience another journey back in ancient cultural time when rock art depicted soul journeys by medicine people – the Mides and the Jeesekeewinini. The prehistory of human occupation along the Bloodvein dates back 9,000 years when Paleo Indian people followed the retreating glaciers and glacial Lake Agassiz. The Archaic peoples, who evolved some 3,000 years ago, were the first to trade native copper and were probably responsible for the first known rock paintings. They were followed by the Laurel people (200 BC) who introduced the use of pottery, succeeded by the Blackduck and Selkirk peoples around 1,000 AD, who were most commonly associated with the creation of rock art.

Archaeological surveys along the river have literally "unearthed" burial mounds, middens, whole village sites, bones, chipped stone and pottery, native-worked copper and, of course, the largest conglomeration of pictograph sites in Canada. Later, during the fierce struggle

Chap Falls waterplay

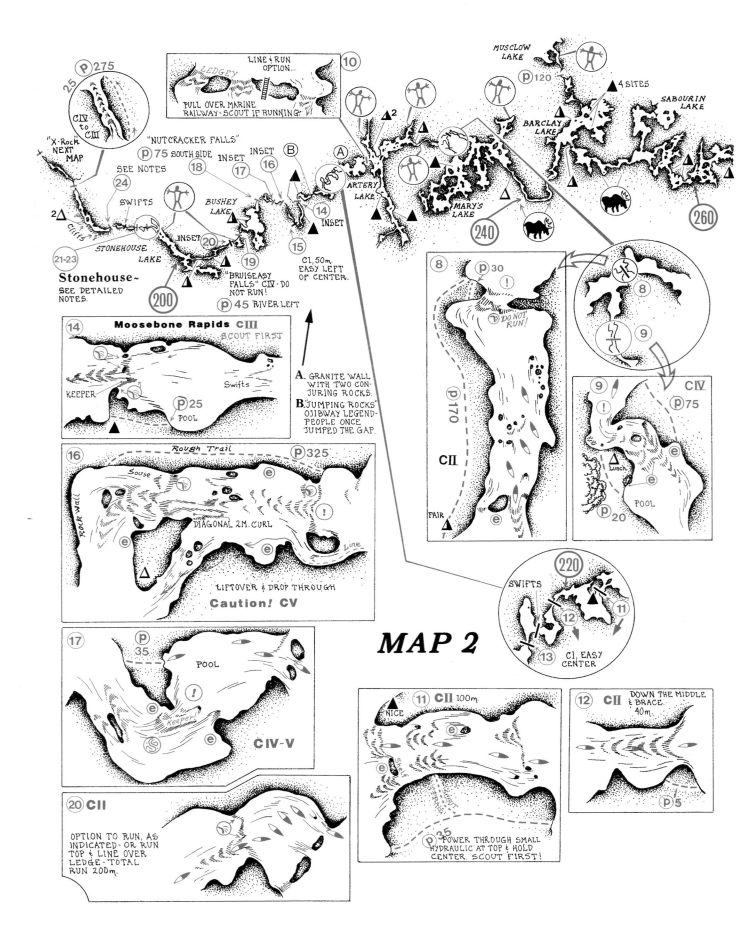

for fur-power, both the Hudson's Bay Company and the Northwest Company used the Bloodvein as a secondary waterway between the Albany and English river systems connecting Hudson Bay with the frontier beyond Lake Winnipeg.

The name "Bloodvein" has many origins. Some portend that the river flowed with the blood of the Sioux after having lost a battle with the united Ojibway and Cree. This story is backed posthumously by one Brother Leach, O.M.I., who resided at Berens River village for 50 years.

Geologists will lay a rock-solid claim that its name was derived from the intrusive "veins" of trapped red rock in the Precambrian gneiss and granite, whereas spiritualists, leaning towards anishnabeg cosmological theory, contend that it was the blood of the memegwishiwok, stone fairies that reside in the cliffs, whose life essence was used by ancient shamans to produce the myriad picto-images; but, according to Kaminotahkosit or "good voice" — chief of the Bloodvein Ojibway, the river may actually have received its English cognomen as a tribute to Treaty or "Indian Day," whereby the anishnabeg were recompensed for their land by the Canadian government to the tune of $5.00 per head, doled out with all the pomp and ceremony by the red-coated Royal Canadian Mounted constabulary.

RED LAKE TO ARTERY LAKE:

Regardless of how creative you are, riverwise, you won't be able to whittle down the more than 8 kilometres of portaging by any more than a few hundred paces; and that's because there are more unconnected lakes and unrunnable chutes along this initial stretch of the route.

And the portages might have been considerably easier had the area from Pipestone Bay to the headwaters of the Bloodvein at Knox Lake not been razed by several fires over the last two decades, leaving a bone yard of dead jackpine and pungy-snags over the trails.

One has to acknowledge fire as an ecological requirement and just revel in the biological process of natural regeneration. It was worth the extra toil, but then I have no distaste for a hard carry. The magic is still there, it's just different. Lichen-encrusted bedrock and the lush growth of fire-spawned jackpine seedlings created a resplendent mosaic of habitat types where lowland valleys survived the fires.

Bunchberry, blueberry, fireweed, Labrador tea, pitcher plant, floating bog, vultures, bald eagles, mosquitoes and deer flies – part of an ongoing life, death and rebirth cycle. It was worth the extra effort, nonetheless, especially to see the pictograph sites located at either extremity of Murdock Lake.

The headwaters of many rivers often subscribe to little traffic by humankind and that sense of aloneness always seems to elevate that sometimes inane feeling that you were the only person ever to dip their paddle here. Certainly, that elation of discovery through exploration and hard work is compensation enough to offset the sufferings endured along the portage. I also didn't want to think of the Bloodvein as a river divided by political borders; whether I was in Ontario or Manitoba had little to do with the journey; rather, it was the journey itself from start to finish that dictated the reasons for route selection even though this is, technically, a book about Manitoba rivers only.

The "Canaux-et-Lacs" drainage pattern of Woodland Caribou Park is the result of the fractures and faults concocted by 2.5-billion-year-old geological processes, and more recent scouring by glacial ice. All this has left a scant layer of nutrient-poor soil and a limited vegetative diversity. If I were to adequately describe this portion of the Bloodvein, I would have to express it in terms of which natural force had the most profound impact...fire, glacially-gouged and polished bedrock knolls, or just time itself? There was that sense of place predicated by that very earth time-clock that has etched the life story of Mother Earth in well-worn Precambrian wrinkles and melt-water channels. We were travelling through time in an ancient land that demanded the deepest respect for such a revered elder, the earth itself worn to the carapace by the ravages of nature.

ARTERY LAKE TO LAKE WINNIPEG

We picked up the rest of our party at Barclay who had been cont'd on pg. 54

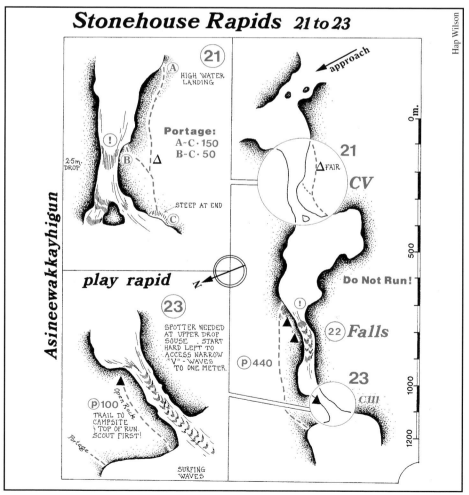

Stonehouse Rapids 21-23

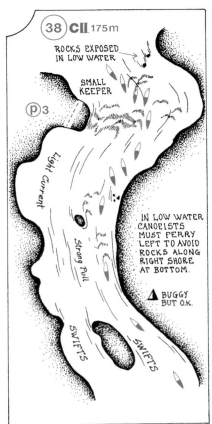

38 **CII** 175m

ROCKS EXPOSED IN LOW WATER

SMALL KEEPER

p 3

Light Current

Strong Pull

IN LOW WATER CANOEISTS MUST FERRY LEFT TO AVOID ROCKS ALONG RIGHT SHORE AT BOTTOM.

△ BUGGY BUT O.K.

SWIFTS

SWIFTS

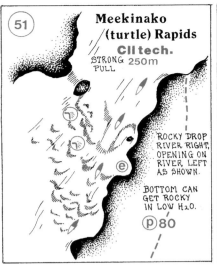

51

Meekinako (turtle) Rapids
CII tech.
STRONG PULL 250m

ROCKY DROP RIVER RIGHT, OPENING ON RIVER LEFT AS SHOWN.

BOTTOM CAN GET ROCKY IN LOW H2O.

e

p 80

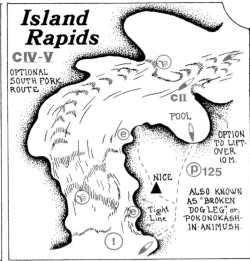

Island Rapids
CIV-V

OPTIONAL SOUTH FORK ROUTE

CII

POOL

e

OPTION TO LIFT-OVER 10 M.

p 125

NICE ▲

e

Tight Line

!

ALSO KNOWN AS "BROKEN DOG LEG" or, POKONOKASH-IN-ANIMUSH.

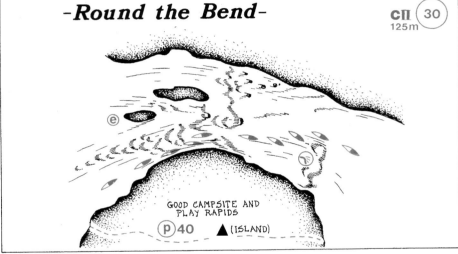

-Round the Bend-

CII 30
125m

e

GOOD CAMPSITE AND PLAY RAPIDS

p 40   ▲ (ISLAND)

36B **Do Not Run**

(Approach carefully)

STRONG CURRENT!!

!   !

SUMMER TAKE OUT (ISLAND)

p 15

2M. DROP WITH NICE KEEPER.

e

SPRING TRAIL

p 40

N ⊕

North Channel

SOUTH CHANNEL

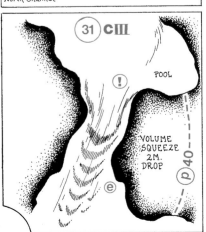

31 **CIII**

!

POOL

VOLUME SQUEEZE 2M. DROP

e

p 40

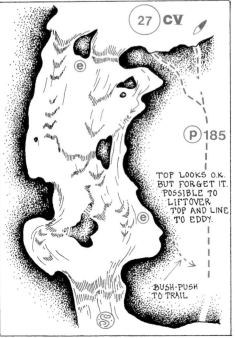

27 **CV**

e

P 185

Line

e

TOP LOOKS O.K. BUT FORGET IT. POSSIBLE TO LIFTOVER TOP AND LINE TO EDDY.

S

BUSH-PUSH TO TRAIL

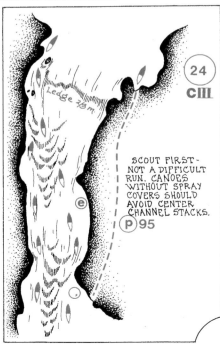

24 **CIII**

Ledge 78m

e

SCOUT FIRST-NOT A DIFFICULT RUN. CANOES WITHOUT SPRAY COVERS SHOULD AVOID CENTER CHANNEL STACKS.

p 95

!

Goose Rapids~Nekesepe 29

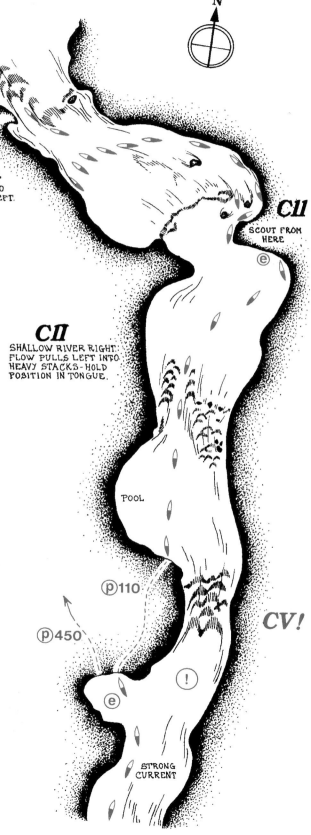

CII tech
"THE FISH HOOK"
LIFTOVER RIGHT SIDE
OR RUN LEFT TONGUE
AND BRACE! DON'T GET
HOOKED! POSSIBLE TO
SCOUT FROM RIVER LEFT.
SPOTTER REQUIRED.

CII
SCOUT FROM
HERE

CII
SHALLOW RIVER RIGHT:
FLOW PULLS LEFT INTO
HEAVY STACKS - HOLD
POSITION IN TONGUE.

POOL

ⓟ110

ⓟ450

CV!

ⓔ

❗

STRONG
CURRENT

NEKESEPE RAPIDS

Nekesepe in Ojibway does not mean "goose" (wawe) and I had some problem in the interpretation, knowing well that there do exist variations in the spelling of particular words; river, for example, can be spelled sibi, sippi, or sepe. If this is the case, then neke-sepe could very well suggest "this side of the river," possibly as a warning that others to follow should portage "this side of the river before the goose neck bend."

This series of four drops, depicted as # 29, can be said to typify the rapids of the Bloodvein River. For novice paddlers the initial CV falls is suggestion enough to warrant a carry over high ground, but for the experienced or intermediate paddler with the curiosity of a stray cat, viewing the CII below the chutes from the end of the 110m. trail, will only taunt the weak minded. You have to ask yourself, "What's around the corner?" This map makes it a little easier...but. Paddlers who enjoy running easier CII's without a lot of work may get a reality shock when they reach the last pitch where it's "run or nothing"; the drop is tight and fast, hemmed in by steep-sided rock embankments which cancel out the option of carrying around or easy lining.

Whatever you decide to do, make the decision at the first portage and be honest about your skill level and abilities. Jawendâgosiwin good luck!

Low Water Note: after the CV portage, the rapids vary considerably from this detail map — the "fish hook" for example becomes an easy CI during low flow.

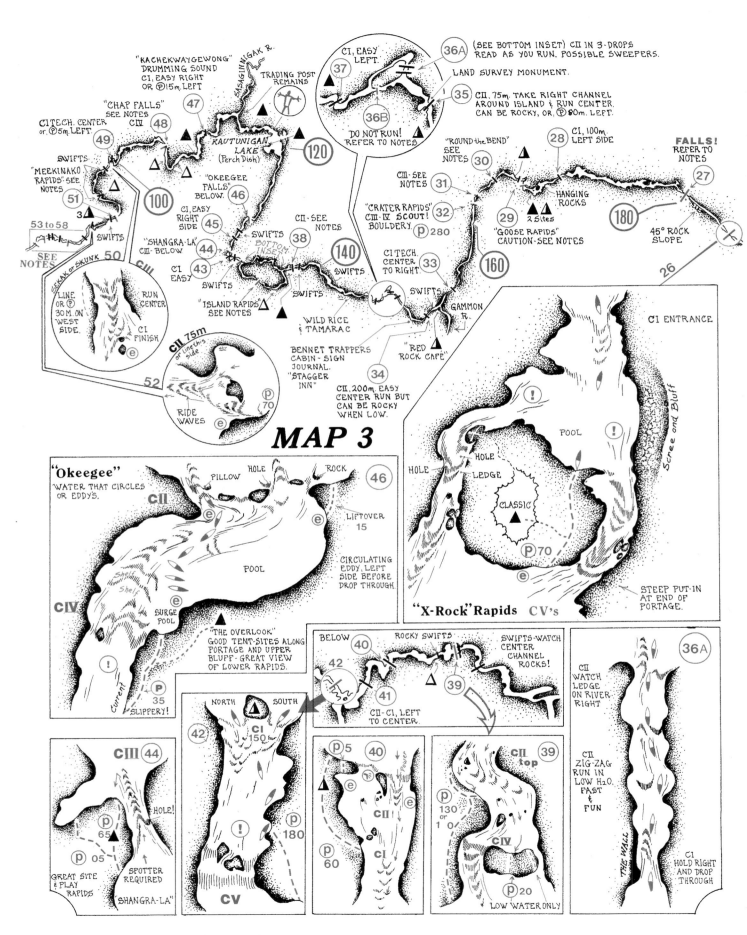

"MAP 3"

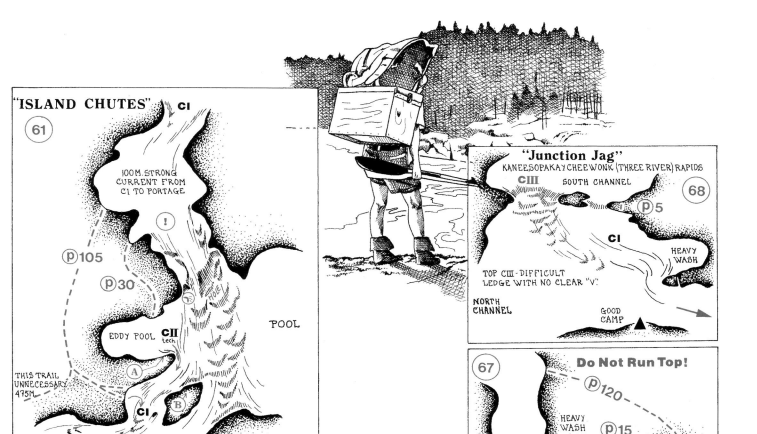
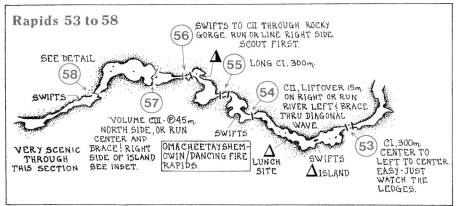
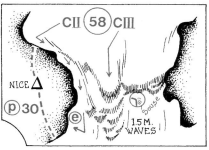
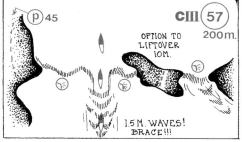
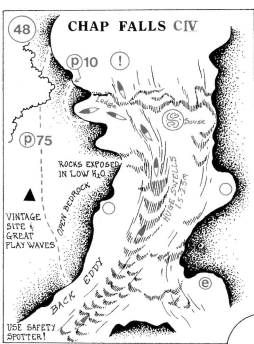

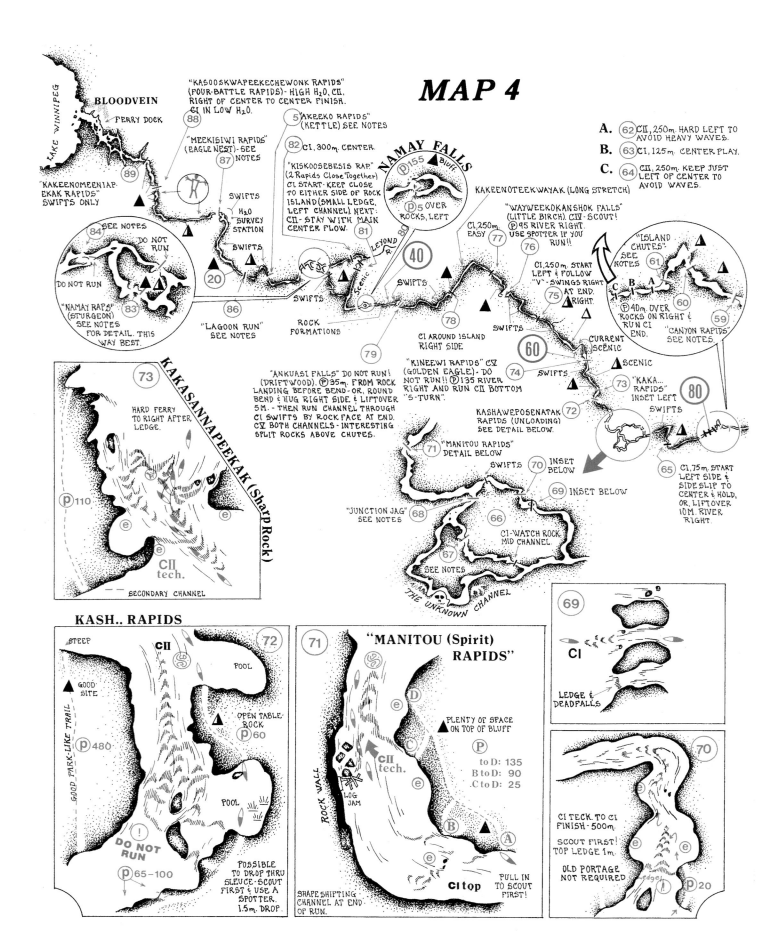

MAP 4

BLOODVEIN

LAKE WINNIPEG

FERRY DOCK

"KASOOSKWAPEEKECHEWONK RAPIDS" (FOUR-BATTLE RAPIDS)- HIGH H_2O, CII, RIGHT OF CENTER TO CENTER FINISH. CI IN LOW H_2O.

(88)

"MEEKISIWI RAPIDS" (EAGLE NEST)- SEE NOTES

(87)

(89)

"KAKEENOMEENIAP-EKAK RAPIDS" SWIFTS ONLY

SWIFTS

(5) "AKEEKO RAPIDS" (KETTLE) SEE NOTES

(82) CI, 300m. CENTER.

"KISKOOSEBESIS RAP." (2 RAPIDS CLOSE TOGETHER) CI START- KEEP CLOSE TO EITHER SIDE OF ROCK ISLAND (SMALL LEDGE, LEFT CHANNEL) NEXT: CII- STAY WITH MAIN CENTER FLOW.

H_2O SURVEY STATION

SWIFTS

(20)

NAMAY FALLS

(P)155 Bluff

(P)5 OVER ROCKS, LEFT

(81)

BEYOND R. 80

(40)

SEE NOTES

(84)

DO NOT RUN

(83)

DO NOT RUN

"NAMAY RAPS" (STURGEON) SEE NOTES FOR DETAIL. THIS WAY BEST.

(86)

"LAGOON RUN" SEE NOTES

Scenic

SWIFTS

ROCK FORMATIONS

(79) CI AROUND ISLAND RIGHT SIDE

KAKEENOTEEKWAYAK (LONG STRETCH)

"WAYWEEKOKANSHOK FALLS" (LITTLE BIRCH). CIV- SCOUT! (P)95 RIVER RIGHT. USE SPOTTER IF YOU RUN!!

(77) CI, 250m. EASY

(76)

CI, 250m. START LEFT & FOLLOW "V" - SWINGS RIGHT AT END. RIGHT.

(75)

SWIFTS

(78)

SWIFTS

A. (62) CII, 250m. HARD LEFT TO AVOID HEAVY WAVES.

B. (63) CI, 125m. CENTER PLAY.

C. (64) CII, 250m. KEEP JUST LEFT OF CENTER TO AVOID WAVES.

"ISLAND CHUTES". SEE NOTES

(61)

C B A

(P)40m. OVER ROCKS ON RIGHT & RUN CI END.

(60)

(59)

"CANYON RAPIDS" SEE NOTES

(60)

CURRENT SCENIC

SCENIC

(74)

SWIFTS

(73) "KAKA... RAPIDS" INSET LEFT

SWIFTS

(80)

"ANKUASI FALLS" DO NOT RUN! (DRIFTWOOD). (P)35m. FROM ROCK LANDING BEFORE BEND- OR, ROUND BEND & HUG RIGHT SIDE & LIFTOVER 5M. - THEN RUN CHANNEL THROUGH CI SWIFTS BY ROCK FACE AT END. CV BOTH CHANNELS - INTERESTING SPLIT ROCKS ABOVE CHUTES.

"KINEEWI RAPIDS" CV (GOLDEN EAGLE)- DO NOT RUN!! (P)135 RIVER RIGHT AND RUN CII BOTTOM "S-TURN".

KASHAWEPOSENATAK RAPIDS (UNLOADING) SEE DETAIL BELOW.

(72)

(65) CII, 75m. START LEFT SIDE & SIDE SLIP TO CENTER & HOLD, OR, LIFTOVER 10M. RIVER RIGHT.

(71) "MANITOU RAPIDS" DETAIL BELOW

(70) INSET BELOW

SWIFTS

(69) INSET BELOW

(68) "JUNCTION JAG" SEE NOTES

(66) CI- WATCH ROCK MID CHANNEL

(67) SEE NOTES

THE UNKNOWN CHANNEL

KAKASANNAPEEKAK (Sharp Rock)

(73)

HARD FERRY TO RIGHT AFTER LEDGE.

(P)110

e

e

CII tech.

SECONDARY CHANNEL

KASH.. RAPIDS

STEEP

CII

(72)

POOL

GOOD SITE

(P)480

GOOD PARK-LIKE TRAIL

OPEN TABLE-ROCK

(P)60

POOL

(!) DO NOT RUN

(P)65-100

POSSIBLE TO DROP THRU SLEUCE- SCOUT FIRST & USE A SPOTTER. 1.5m. DROP.

(71) **"MANITOU (Spirit) RAPIDS"**

D

e

C

CII tech.

B

e

A

ROCK WALL

LOG JAM

CI top

SHAPE SHIFTING CHANNEL AT END OF RUN.

PLENTY OF SPACE ON TOP OF BLUFF

(P)

to D: 135
B to D: 90
C to D: 25

PULL IN TO SCOUT FIRST!

(69)

CI

LEDGE & DEADFALLS

(70)

CI TECK. TO CI FINISH- 500m.

SCOUT FIRST! TOP LEDGE 1m.

OLD PORTAGE NOT REQUIRED

e

e

Ledge

(P)20

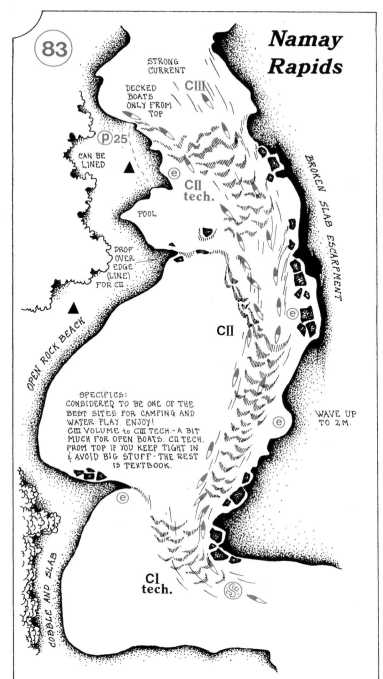

83

Namay Rapids

STRONG CURRENT

CIII

DECKED BOATS ONLY FROM TOP

(p)25

CAN BE LINED

(e)

CII tech.

POOL

DROP OVER EDGE (LINE) FOR CII

BROKEN SLAB ESCARPMENT

OPEN ROCK BEACH

CII

(e)

SPECIFICS:
CONSIDERED TO BE ONE OF THE BEST SITES FOR CAMPING AND WATER PLAY. ENJOY!
CIII VOLUME to CIII TECH.–A BIT MUCH FOR OPEN BOATS. CII TECH. FROM TOP IF YOU KEEP TIGHT IN & AVOID BIG STUFF–THE REST IS TEXTBOOK.

WAVE UP TO 2 M.

(e)

(e)

COBBLE AND SLAB

CI tech.

MEEKISIWI RAPIDS CIItech. 100m.

87

(p)40

LINE

SHELF

HOLE

IN LOW H₂O SHELF IS COMPLETELY EXPOSED. OPTION TO LIFT DOWN "RAMP" & FINISH CL BOTTOM.

SIDE SLIP RIGHT TO AVOID WASH.

(e)

SMALL HOLE

KEEP HARD LEFT JUST TO CLEAR HOLE. THEN POWER LEFT TO AVOID WAVES–FINISH WITH BOTTOM SIDESLIP.

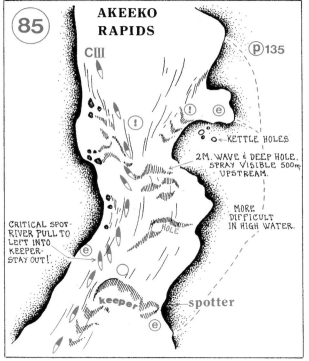

85

AKEEKO RAPIDS

CIII

(p)135

(!)

(!)

(e)

KETTLE HOLES

2 M. WAVE & DEEP HOLE. SPRAY VISIBLE 500m UPSTREAM.

HOLE

MORE DIFFICULT IN HIGH WATER.

CRITICAL SPOT- RIVER PULL TO LEFT INTO KEEPER- STAY OUT!

(e)

keeper

spotter

(e)

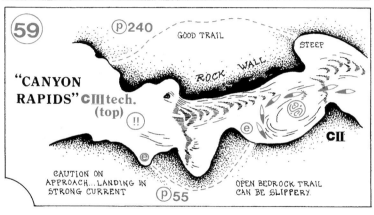

59

(p)240

GOOD TRAIL

STEEP

ROCK WALL

"CANYON RAPIDS" CIII tech. (top)

(!!)

(e)

CII

(e)

CAUTION ON APPROACH...LANDING IN STRONG CURRENT

OPEN BEDROCK TRAIL CAN BE SLIPPERY.

(p)55

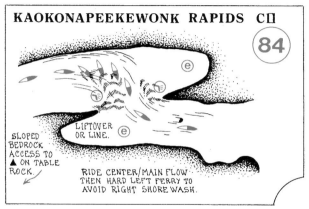

KAOKONAPEEKEWONK RAPIDS CII

84

(e)

(e)

SLOPED BEDROCK ACCESS TO ▲ ON TABLE ROCK.

LIFTOVER OR LINE.

(e)

RIDE CENTER/MAIN FLOW THEN HARD LEFT FERRY TO AVOID RIGHT SHORE WASH.

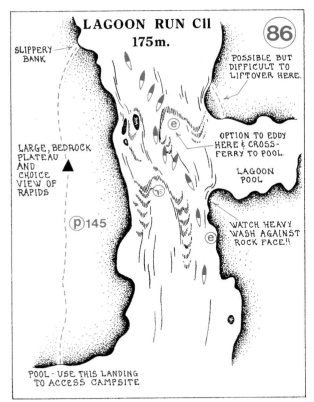

LAGOON RUN C11
175 m.
86

SLIPPERY BANK

POSSIBLE BUT DIFFICULT TO LIFT OVER HERE.

LARGE, BEDROCK PLATEAU AND CHOICE VIEW OF RAPIDS

OPTION TO EDDY HERE & CROSS-FERRY TO POOL.

LAGOON POOL

(e)

(P)145

WATCH HEAVY WASH AGAINST ROCK FACE!!

(e)

POOL - USE THIS LANDING TO ACCESS CAMPSITE

cont'd from pg. 47

flown in from the town of Red Lake, "Norseman capital of the North", and we promptly steered a course to the west toward the Manitoba border.

Within a period of four days we examined 10 different rock art sites. It was not hard to understand why the Bloodvein had been a popular home to a succession of aboriginal people for several thousand years. Traditional lifestyles melded with the environment of the river and adapted simply to the changing seasons; securing food and clothing here, harvesting wild rice there, gathering in small communities in the spring to take advantage of the spawning walleye, collecting summer berries, and eventually moving off in family units for the winter to seek out moose and caribou.

But most amazing, though, is the pictorial history emblazoned on the rock faces of the Bloodvein in a myriad of spirit characters depicted by ancient shaman artists. "Contextual" or cognitive archaeology is used to attempt to interpret the meaning of the figures, still not an exact science, but at least modern methodology transcends analyzing the artifact and reconstructing what was actually going on in the mind of the artist-shaman. Pictographs and their explanation derive from the spiritual and not the scientific.

The paintings were done using a

chalky mineral known as red ochre, "wunnamin" or "miskwassin" to the Ojibway, and mixed with the fish oil from Sturgeon. As a bonding agent it could outlast any commercial house paint by a thousand years, but personally, I believe the agent that sealed the paint to the cliff wall had supernatural connotations. Since ceremony took place here, and as it has been said that the shaman used the blood of the memegwishiwok, or stone people, very powerful spirits who dwelled within the confines of the rock face itself, in which to paint the pictures, may have been the actual force that transfixed the images onto stone forever.

Two of the most impressive sites: one upriver near Larus and the most famous site located just east of Artery, are best viewed under the subtle influences of the early evening sun. Selwyn Dewdney, in his book, *Indian Rock Paintings of the Great Lakes*, says of these two sites:

"Both sites have a northerly exposure. This would normally ensure a heavy growth of lichens because of the lack of sunlight that would speed the drying surface after a wind-driven rain. On both these sites, however, the granite has been so smoothed by glacial action that the algae and fungus spores, whose union makes the plant possible, find little encouragement to lodge on any rock faces that are also protected by overhangs."

About the unique bison painting Dewdney goes on to say, "...the site is perhaps a hundred miles north of the parklands where the bison herds once roamed; but the artist shows a familiarity with the animal that suggests either frequent hunting excursions southward, or his own southern origin."

It was bad luck to pass by these places without ceremony so a little tobacco was handed around to all paddlers who each, in their own act of reverence, said a little prayer and dropped the "assema" or tobacco into the river below the cliff face.

Besides the many venerable and sometimes obscure traces left behind by prehis-

toric hunter-gatherers and shaman artists, the river offered many opportunities for excellent fishing for walleye and even channel catfish which we caught at Chap Falls while spending the day playing in the rapids.

The river corridor seemed to enjoy a more diverse environment than that which lay beyond the shore fringe being that it displayed more of a boreal appearance dominated by an endless morass or fenland. Here, we marvelled at huge broken chunks of granite and gneiss along the water's edge, rapids spilling out into deep pools and excellent places to camp, swim and fish.

The Bloodvein proved itself to be unsurpassed for wildlife viewing although we did not see any of the elusive caribou. The Ontario segment of the river supports over 420 vascular species of plants including the Prairie Spikemoss and the Prairie Gray-stemmed Goldenrod which are a totally new species for this province. The river as a whole entity represents a unique Boreal Upland forest throughout, sharing the same bio-diversity regardless of provincial border. Jackpine, white birch, poplar and black spruce, of course, dominate the landscape, with scattered stands of elm, ash, bur oak and maple. The prairie-boreal influence also supports an uncommon collection of lichens and mosses, prairie crocus and floating marsh marigold.

Animals and birds that are uncommon, rare or endangered elsewhere are common along the river; such as the bald eagle, double-crested cormorant, white pelican, osprey, Great Gray Owl and Woodland Caribou.

From Artery to Lake Winnipeg we found that we could reduce the number of portages considerably by creative river work – lining, lifting over ledges and careful running. There were a couple of tense moments when there was a dumping while playing a larger rapid or two, nothing too serious, although we did have to use a throw-bag to rescue Art from a hole at Moosebone Rapids.

At the village of Bloodvein we caught the *Edgar Wood* ferry that would take us across the 22 kilometres of Lake Winnipeg to our vehicles left at Matheson Island. You had the choice of taking the free ferry when it was running, or hiring a local Ojibway to haul your gear across, but according to David Stephanson, captain of the *Edgar Wood* for 13 years, "It's pretty risky business" to even attempt paddling across. The captain also told us that the boat doesn't run the lake when the winds blow up to 15 knots because the waves can whip up 4-5 metres in no time flat. At 8 knots (on a good day even faster), the ferry can make the crossing in an hour and a half, loaded with 45 people, 13 tons of supplies or two semi-trailers. Captain Stephanson also remarked that the 300-400 canoeists that descend the Bloodvein come from the States and start at either Artery or Wallace Lake. It was July and we saw only two other parties en route upriver heading somewhere else.

In retrospect the saddest part about the Bloodvein was having to leave; it endeared itself to all and the magic remains as it always has, in the sound of the rapids and the music of thrushes on a hot summer's day; the pungent, sweet smell of moss and Labrador tea after the rain has stopped and the night air is still. The paueehnsujk and the memegwishiwok still play tricks and the red ochre paintings come alive in my dreams.   H.W.

GAMMON RIVER OVERVIEW

GAMMON RIVER

GENERAL INFORMATION

Classification: Experienced Novice
(portaging all technical rapids)
Intermediate
(CII tech. to CIII rapids negotiated)

Distance: A – 174 km. (Red Lake access at Suffle Lk. Rd. to Bloodvein Jct.)
B – 106 km. (Wallace Lake access to Bloodvein Jct.)
To Bloodvein village add 150 km.

Elevation Drop: 90m. (295') or .5m/km. (1.6'/km.)
*Red Lake to Bloodvein Jct.

Time: A – 9-11 days B – 6-7 days
(* add 8-9 days to Lake Winnipeg)

Number of Campsites: 55 from Red Lake, or approx. 4 campsites every 10 km.

Number of Rapids & Falls: 38 (not numbered & excluding Haggart River).

Number of Runnable Rapids: 19 (85% CI to CII)

Portages: Experienced Novice – 36 (4,950m.)
Creative Intermediate – 30 (3,885m.)

Season: Late May through early October

Maps Required: 52 M/5 52 M/6 52 M/3 52 L/14 (Wallace Lake Route) From Red Lake add: 52 M/2 52 L/15 52 L/16

Access: Wallace Lake campgrounds via Hwy. #304, or Suffle Lake road east from Red Lake, Ontario, or floatplane from either Matheson Island or Pine Dock to Carroll Lake.

Egress: Bloodvein village on Lake Winnipeg and ferry service to Matheson Island and Hwy. #234.

Features: For those who have already paddled the Bloodvein then you may want to consider the Gammon. This river is small but deceivingly punchy with an ever-changing landscape and it shares much of the same inherent charm as the Bloodvein with the exception that the Gammon has more scenic chutes and falls and fewer rapids. Once you reach the Bloodvein, though, the pace picks up considerably. The Gammon River is an excellent choice for those who enjoy the relaxing peace of lake touring combined with the excitement of a small river.

WHITEWATER CHARACTERISTICS AND GENERAL HAZARDS

The Gammon is a "pool and riffle" type river with a fair amount of flatwater paddling. If the many falls are approached carefully, the Gammon presents itself as a very novice-friendly river. Canoeists should have basic moving-water skills or have someone in their party that has intermediate level capabilities. Because of its size, the Gammon drains fairly quickly during the summer and the rapids may become choked with rocks; this may necessitate additional lining and portaging. Kayakers may consider some of the larger rapids during peak flow periods, making sure a safety spotter is on hand with the required rescue equipment. Portages along the Gammon are, on average, relatively short with the longest carry being only 350m. (from Red Lake). The biggest hazard would be the tendency to shorten portages by running fast water to the brink of some chutes.

MAP 1 Gammon River~access from Woodland Caribou Provincial Park·ONTARIO

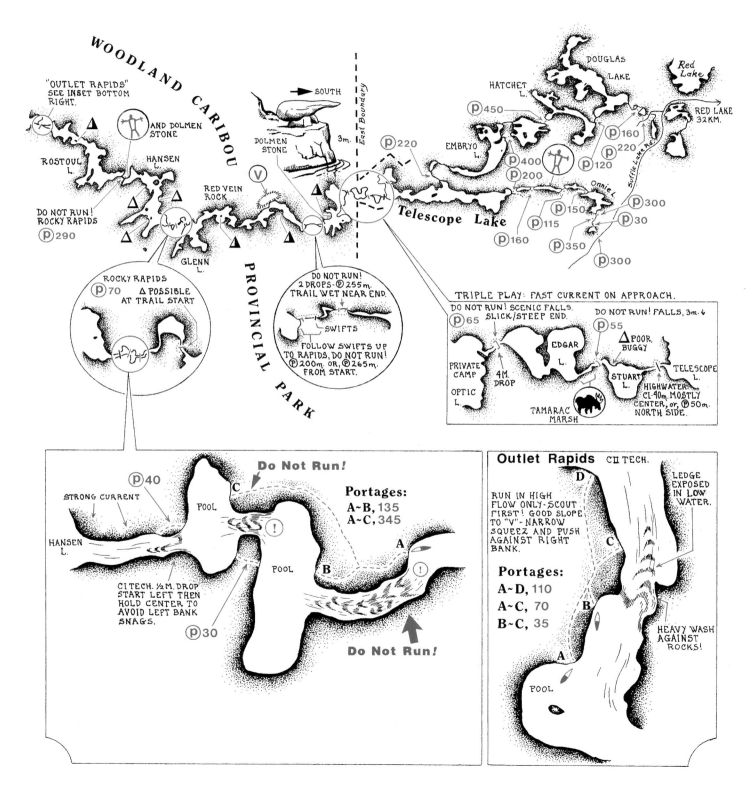

"OUTLET RAPIDS" SEE INSET BOTTOM RIGHT.

AND DOLMEN STONE

ROSTOUL L.

HANSEN L.

RED VEIN ROCK

DOLMEN STONE

3m.

SOUTH

East Boundary

DO NOT RUN! ROCKY RAPIDS
(P)290

GLENN L.

WOODLAND CARIBOU

PROVINCIAL PARK

Telescope Lake

(P)220

DOUGLAS LAKE

HATCHET L.

Red Lake

(P)450

EMBRYO L.

(P)160
(P)220
(P)120

RED LAKE 32 KM.

Soffie Lake Rd.

(P)400
(P)200

Orrie L.

(P)150
(P)115

(P)300
(P)30

(P)160
(P)350

(P)300

ROCKY RAPIDS
(P)70 △ POSSIBLE AT TRAIL START

DO NOT RUN!
2 DROPS-(P)255m.
TRAIL WET NEAR END.

SWIFTS

FOLLOW SWIFTS UP TO RAPIDS, DO NOT RUN!
(P)200m. OR (P)265m. FROM START.

TRIPLE PLAY: FAST CURRENT ON APPROACH.

DO NOT RUN! SCENIC FALLS. SLICK/STEEP END.
(P)65

DO NOT RUN! FALLS, 3m.↓
(P)55

△POOR, BUGGY

PRIVATE CAMP

EDGAR L.

OPTIC L.

4M. DROP

TAMARAC MARSH

STUART L.

TELESCOPE L.

HIGHWATER: CI-40m. MOSTLY CENTER, or, (P)50m. NORTH SIDE.

Do Not Run!

(P)40

STRONG CURRENT

HANSEN L.

CI TECH. ½ M. DROP START LEFT THEN HOLD CENTER TO AVOID LEFT BANK SNAGS.

(P)30

C

POOL

!

POOL

B

A

!

Portages:
A~B, 135
A~C, 345

Do Not Run!

Outlet Rapids CII TECH.

D

LEDGE EXPOSED IN LOW WATER.

RUN IN HIGH FLOW ONLY-SCOUT FIRST! GOOD SLOPE TO "V"-NARROW SQUEEZ AND PUSH AGAINST RIGHT BANK.

C

B

Portages:
A~D, 110
A~C, 70
B~C, 35

A

POOL

HEAVY WASH AGAINST ROCKS!

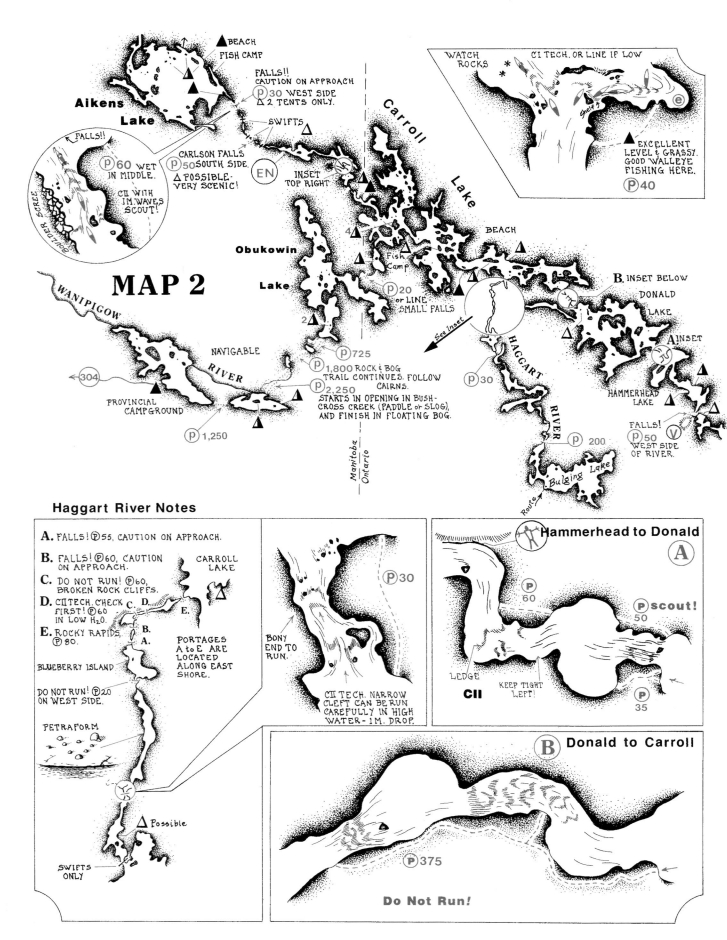

BEACH
FISH CAMP

FALLS!!
CAUTION ON APPROACH
Ⓟ30 WEST SIDE
△ 2 TENTS ONLY.

Aikens Lake

SWIFTS △

Carroll Lake

Ⓟ60 WET
IN MIDDLE.
↖FALLS!!

CII WITH
1M. WAVES
SCOUT!

CARLSON FALLS
Ⓟ50 SOUTH SIDE.
△ POSSIBLE -
VERY SCENIC!

ⒺN

INSET
TOP RIGHT

MAP 2

WATCH
ROCKS

CI TECH. OR LINE IF LOW

Ⓔ

Shelf

EXCELLENT
LEVEL & GRASSY.
GOOD WALLEYE
FISHING HERE.
Ⓟ40

BEACH △

Obukowin Lake

4△
△
Fish
Camp
△

B. INSET BELOW

DONALD LAKE

△ A INSET

WANIPIGOW RIVER

NAVIGABLE RIVER

→304

PROVINCIAL CAMPGROUND △

Ⓟ1,250

△

Ⓟ20
or LINE
SMALL FALLS

2△

Ⓟ725

Ⓟ1,800 ROCK & BOG
TRAIL CONTINUES. FOLLOW
CAIRNS.
Ⓟ2,250 STARTS IN OPENING IN BUSH-
CROSS CREEK (PADDLE or SLOG),
AND FINISH IN FLOATING BOG.

See Inset

HAGGART RIVER

Ⓟ30

△

HAMMERHEAD LAKE

△
△

FALLS!
Ⓟ50 Ⓥ
WEST SIDE
OF RIVER.

Ⓟ200

Bulging Lake

Route →

Manitoba / Ontario

Haggart River Notes

A. FALLS! Ⓟ55, CAUTION ON APPROACH.

B. FALLS! Ⓟ60, CAUTION ON APPROACH.

C. DO NOT RUN! Ⓟ60, BROKEN ROCK CLIFFS.

D. CII TECH. CHECK FIRST! Ⓟ60 IN LOW H₂O.

E. ROCKY RAPIDS, Ⓟ80.

CARROLL LAKE
△

PORTAGES
A to E ARE
LOCATED
ALONG EAST
SHORE.

C. D.
B.
A.

BLUEBERRY ISLAND

DO NOT RUN! Ⓟ20
ON WEST SIDE.

PETRAFORM

△ Possible

SWIFTS
ONLY

Ⓟ30

BONY
END TO
RUN.

CII TECH. NARROW
CLEFT CAN BE RUN
CAREFULLY IN HIGH
WATER - 1M. DROP.

Ⓐ Hammerhead to Donald

Ⓟ60

Ⓟ scout!
50

LEDGE
KEEP TIGHT
LEFT!

CII

Ⓟ35

Ⓑ Donald to Carroll

Ⓟ375

Do Not Run!

THE GAMMON RIVER NOTEBOOK

There are two main watersheds that traverse the whole of Woodland Caribou Park in Ontario before making the decline into Atikaki; the Bloodvein, and the Gammon. The Gammon maintains the greater elevation drop within Ontario (75m.), passing through many precipitous waterfalls and chutes before levelling out past Carroll Lake.

We continued our "rivers without boundaries" journey, once again beginning our trip from Red Lake, hopping over several small lakes to gain access to the Gammon headwaters at Telescope Lake. In 1974 and 1987, wildfires raged through much of the Gammon highlands razing over 600 sq. km. of forest vegetation. Because of the thin podzol soil-type, regeneration is extremely indolent. The boreal forest of Woodland Caribou and Atikaki parks is a fire-dependent ecosystem in which all living things evolve in response to the frequency and intensity of natural wild fires. Regular burning of these upland forests releases nutrients to the soil in an environment where surface cover breakdown is quite slow otherwise.

As we steered westward from Telescope, the scrub second growth of poplar, birch and alder actually helped accentuate the glacially constructed landscape; at least we could easily see into the beyond and pick out the occasional moose, eagle nest atop a dead jackpine, and marvel in the hodge-podge of glacial debris consisting of boulders or erratics strewn across the scene like a giant-sized Chinese checkers game. Slabs of glacial litter bared their white souls to the sun and more than once I had thought someone had pitched several tents upon a slope of dwarf spruce and juniper.

The most notable features about the Gammon were the rock barrens and exposed granite cliffs. There was virtually no soil, though ribbons of moss and lichen formed a patchwork of floral activity in the crevices where scant nutrients collected from rainwash, in turn acting as anchors for other vascular plants such as Lycopodium *obscurum isophyllum* and the viola adunca, serviceberries and juniper.

Of particular interest is the lack of eastern white cedar within Woodland and Atikaki parks, and the absence of silver birch large enough to produce canoe bark. If this is the case through many successions of growth and burn, then the Ojibway of the east Lake Winnipeg region would have had to import their canoes from the Lake Superior anishnabeg where canoe building was possible.

While mapping out the Haggart River we camped on a rocky ledge overlooking Carroll Lake. For two days we marvelled at its lush treed landscape and wondered how it could possibly get any better than this. It wasn't until later that we discovered that the inconspicuous fern which is normally found in open grasslands, known as Prairie Spikemoss (*Selaginella densa*), grew in the rock cracks that framed in our tent.

As with the Bloodvein, once we ventured closer to Lake Winnipeg (within about 200km.), we began seeing white pelicans. Often circling overhead in a procession of four or five birds, flying in lazy half-circles seemingly at the whim of the summer thermals, they resembled the tail of a child's kite dipping and rising in and out of our view and seen at almost any hour of the day.

Bald eagles were as common as ravens, even within the Ontario section where the species is indicated on the Endangered Species List, meaning per-

Lucifer's Boiler

The most notable features on the Gammon were the rock barrens and exposed granite cliffs

haps that kiniw, the war-eagle, is making a comeback. Like wolves to ungulates, eagles have a symbiotic union with resident fish populations where productivity is high.

Forster's Tern, another prairie species, has expanded its range eastward over the past 20 years deep into Atikaki and as far as Red Lake, Ontario. It usually breeds north of Winnipeg. In all, over 91 species of birds have been recorded within the upper Gammon corridor watershed, and up to 39 species of mammals (27 known). Typical boreal species include lynx, marten, fisher, otter, muskrat, beaver, red squirrel, moose, timber wolf and black bear; uncommon or "elusive" species include woodland caribou, Franklin's ground squirrel (near Manitoba border and west), Heather vole (Haggart River and west), and the occasional sighting of the eastern cougar (rare).

For paddlers taking the south route that leaves the Gammon at Glenn Lake and re-enters Carroll via the Haggart River system, you're in for a real treat. The Haggart has that venerable charm of old precambria; time-worn and glacially scarred, it imbues a story that only Mother Earth could tell.

Continuing along the Gammon the water levels seemed inordinately high for August but by the time we reached the eastern outflow of the river north of Aikens Lake it had obviously decided to take on a more complacent temperament. We wondered, at times, while ploughing through several kilometres of bog horsetail and water lilies, whether the Gammon still actually existed. Once we met up with the west channel the river once again perked up and from here to the junction of the Bloodvein it was pure joy! Not that there were so many rapids to run, in fact most chutes like Lucifer's Boil had to be portaged; it was just the entourage of rock and pine and the beauty of a small river that finds a place in your soul.

Young Ruffed Grouse, Carroll Lake, Ontario

MAP 3

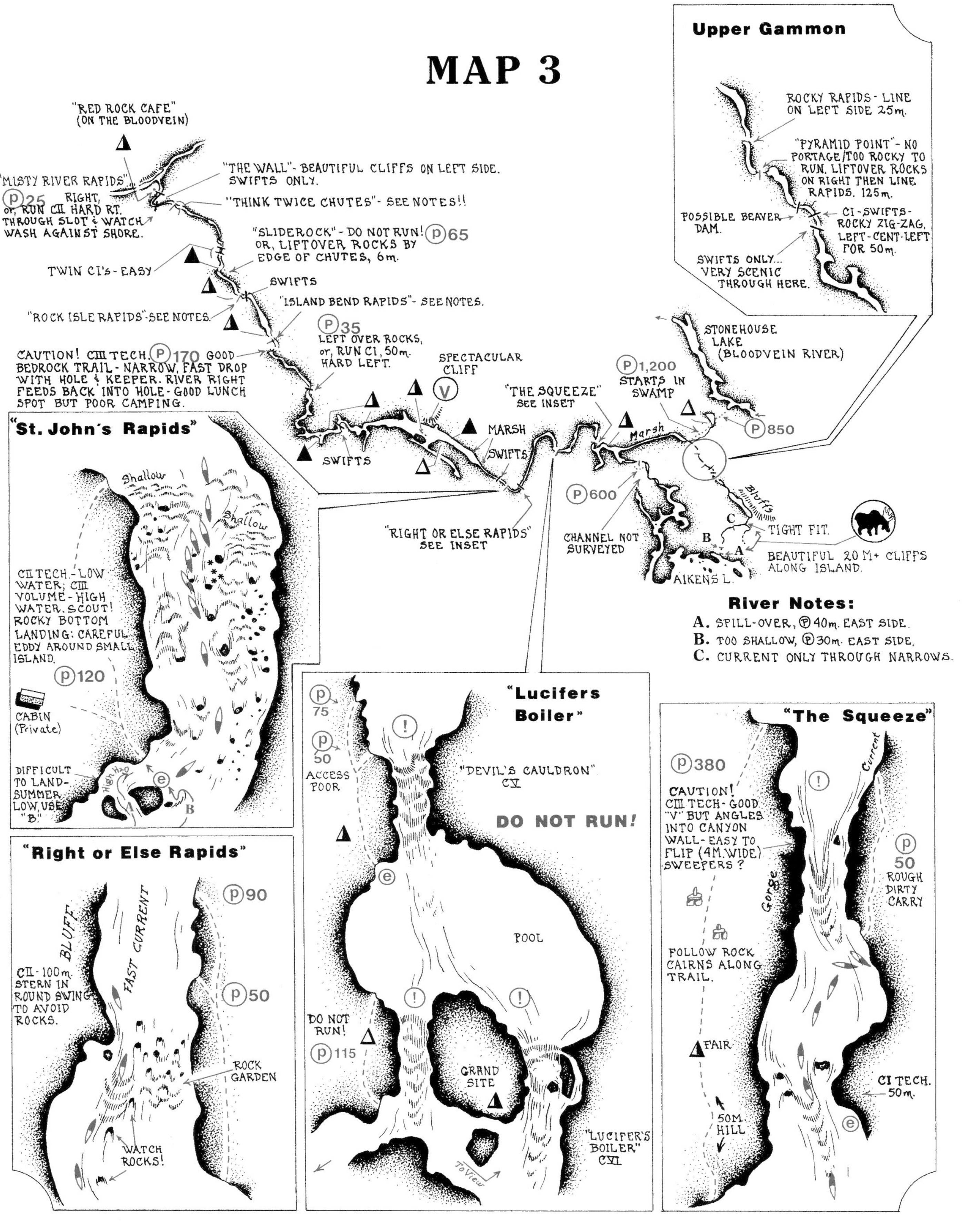

ROCKY RAPIDS - LINE ON LEFT SIDE 25m.

"PYRAMID POINT" - NO PORTAGE/TOO ROCKY TO RUN. LIFTOVER ROCKS ON RIGHT THEN LINE RAPIDS. 125m.

POSSIBLE BEAVER DAM.

SWIFTS ONLY... VERY SCENIC THROUGH HERE.

CI - SWIFTS - ROCKY ZIG-ZAG, LEFT-CENT-LEFT FOR 50m.

STONEHOUSE LAKE (BLOODVEIN RIVER)

"RED ROCK CAFE" (ON THE BLOODVEIN)

"MISTY RIVER RAPIDS" (P)25 RIGHT, or, RUN CII HARD RT. THROUGH SLOT & WATCH WASH AGAINST SHORE.

"THE WALL" - BEAUTIFUL CLIFFS ON LEFT SIDE. SWIFTS ONLY.

"THINK TWICE CHUTES" - SEE NOTES!!

"SLIDEROCK" - DO NOT RUN! (p)65 OR, LIFTOVER ROCKS BY EDGE OF CHUTES, 6m.

TWIN CI's - EASY

SWIFTS

"ISLAND BEND RAPIDS" - SEE NOTES.

"ROCK ISLE RAPIDS" - SEE NOTES.

(P)35 LEFT OVER ROCKS, or, RUN CI, 50m. HARD LEFT.

CAUTION! CIII TECH. (P)170 GOOD BEDROCK TRAIL - NARROW, FAST DROP WITH HOLE & KEEPER. RIVER RIGHT FEEDS BACK INTO HOLE - GOOD LUNCH SPOT BUT POOR CAMPING.

SPECTACULAR CLIFF (V)

"THE SQUEEZE" SEE INSET

(P)1,200 STARTS IN SWAMP

(P)850

MARSH

SWIFTS

Marsh

(P)600

Bluffs

"RIGHT OR ELSE RAPIDS" SEE INSET

CHANNEL NOT SURVEYED

C

B

A

TIGHT FIT.

BEAUTIFUL 20 M+ CLIFFS ALONG ISLAND.

AIKENS L.

River Notes:

A. SPILL-OVER, (P)40m. EAST SIDE.
B. TOO SHALLOW, (P)30m. EAST SIDE.
C. CURRENT ONLY THROUGH NARROWS.

"St. John's Rapids"

Shallow

Shallow

CII TECH - LOW WATER; CIII VOLUME - HIGH WATER. SCOUT! ROCKY BOTTOM LANDING: CAREFUL. EDDY AROUND SMALL ISLAND.

(P)120

CABIN (Private)

DIFFICULT TO LAND - SUMMER LOW USE "B".

High H₂O

(e)

B

"Right or Else Rapids"

(P)90

BLUFF

FAST CURRENT

CII - 100m. STERN IN ROUND SWING TO AVOID ROCKS.

(P)50

ROCK GARDEN

WATCH ROCKS!

"Lucifers Boiler"

(p)75

(p)50 ACCESS POOR

"DEVIL'S CAULDRON" CV

DO NOT RUN!

(!)

(e)

POOL

DO NOT RUN! (p)115

(!)

(!)

GRAND SITE

To View

"LUCIFER'S BOILER" CVI

"The Squeeze"

(P)380

Current

(!)

CAUTION! CIII TECH - GOOD "V" BUT ANGLES INTO CANYON WALL - EASY TO FLIP (4M. WIDE) SWEEPERS?

FOLLOW ROCK CAIRNS ALONG TRAIL.

Gorge

(p)50 ROUGH DIRTY CARRY

FAIR

50M HILL

CI TECH. 50m.

(e)

Wrecked canoe on the Gammon

ROCK ISLE RAPIDS

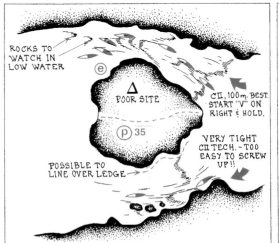

ROCKS TO WATCH IN LOW WATER

ⓔ

△ POOR SITE

ⓟ35

POSSIBLE TO LINE OVER LEDGE →

CII, 100 m. BEST. START "V" ON RIGHT & HOLD.

VERY TIGHT CII TECH. – TOO EASY TO SCREW UP!!

ISLAND BEND RAPIDS

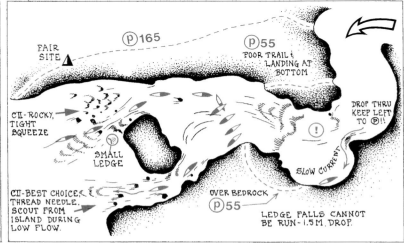

ⓟ165

FAIR SITE △

ⓟ55
POOR TRAIL & LANDING AT BOTTOM

CII - ROCKY, TIGHT SQUEEZE

SMALL LEDGE

DROP THRU KEEP LEFT TO ⓟ!!

CII - BEST CHOICE. THREAD NEEDLE. SCOUT FROM ISLAND DURING LOW FLOW.

SLOW CURRENT

OVER BEDROCK

ⓟ55

LEDGE FALLS CANNOT BE RUN – 1.5 M. DROP.

Think Twice Chutes

!CAUTION!

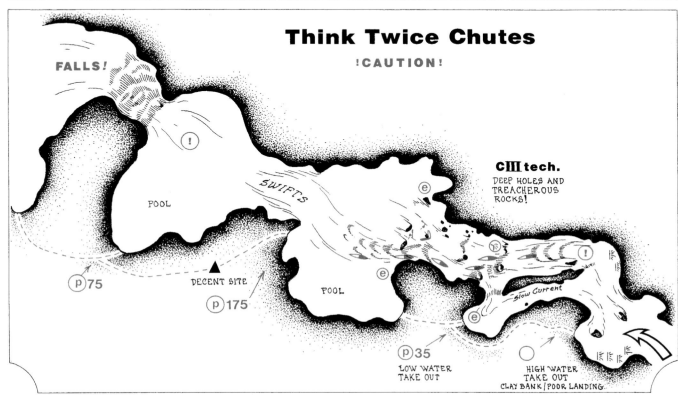

FALLS!

!

POOL

SWIFTS

ⓔ

CIII tech.

DEEP HOLES AND TREACHEROUS ROCKS!

ⓔ

ⓔ

!

ⓟ75

△ DECENT SITE

ⓟ175

POOL

Slow Current

ⓔ

ⓟ35
LOW WATER TAKE OUT

○ HIGH WATER TAKE OUT
CLAY BANK / POOR LANDING

SASAGINNIGAK & LEYOND RIVER
OVERVIEW

SASAGINNIGAK RIVER
LEYOND RIVER

GENERAL INFORMATION

Classification: Experienced Novice
(some difficult portages and technical CI's)
Distance: 200 km. (up the Sasaginnigak and down the Leyond to Lake Winnipeg).
Elevation Rise/drop: SASAGINNIGAK – Rise of 34m. (112')
or 1.36m/km.(4.5'/km)
LEYOND – Drop of 57m.(187') or
.43m/km. (1.4'/km)
*NOTE: 25km. up the Sasaginnigak and 130km. down the Leyond.
Time: 8-10 days
Number of Campsites: 34 or 1 campsite every 6 km.
Number of Runnable Rapids: 19 (100% CI to CII), excluding chutes and falls. Not numbered in sequence.
Portages: 29 (5,270m.)
Season: Late May through September
Maps Required: 62 P/16 62 P/9 52 M/13 52 M/12
Access: Canoeists may add the Leyond sweep to their Bloodvein trip as access and egress leaves and returns from the Bloodvein River. Paddlers also have the option to fly directly to either Katunigan Lake on the Bloodvein, or Sasaginnigak Lake to begin their trip.
Egress: The Leyond rejoins the Bloodvein at mileage 31 and ends in Bloodvein village on Lake Winnipeg where canoeists may catch the ferry back to Matheson Island.
Features: Both rivers are small and intimate with a gentle mix of typical Precambrian rock & jackpine landscape, with the lushness of boreal fenland. It lacks the fluid excitement of the other east Lake Winnipeg rivers but what it doesn't have in moving water magic it certainly makes up for in ecological diversity. The flora and fauna are superb and for the camera buff or nature lover this route is unequalled; fishing for walleye and northern pike is excellent, and campsites are well situated to get optimum enjoyment out of the ambient charm of the small river. There are also several rock art sites which indicate that this route was of particular importance to the aboriginal people.

WHITEWATER CHARACTERISTICS AND GENERAL HAZARDS

The Sasaginnigak can be ascended easily throughout the summer, while paddling downstream on the Leyond in late season may require additional lining and lifting around shallow, rocky rapids. During high flow it may be imperative to scout some of the fast CI's and CII's for possible sweepers. Crossing Sasaginnigak Lake in high winds is not recommended even though the prevailing westerlies may be in your favour.

Portages have been recently cleared by our research group in 1995 and re-marked through the burn near the headwaters; should you encounter heavy growth or recent blowdown, please take the time and help clear the trails.

Sasaginnigak and Leyond River Route

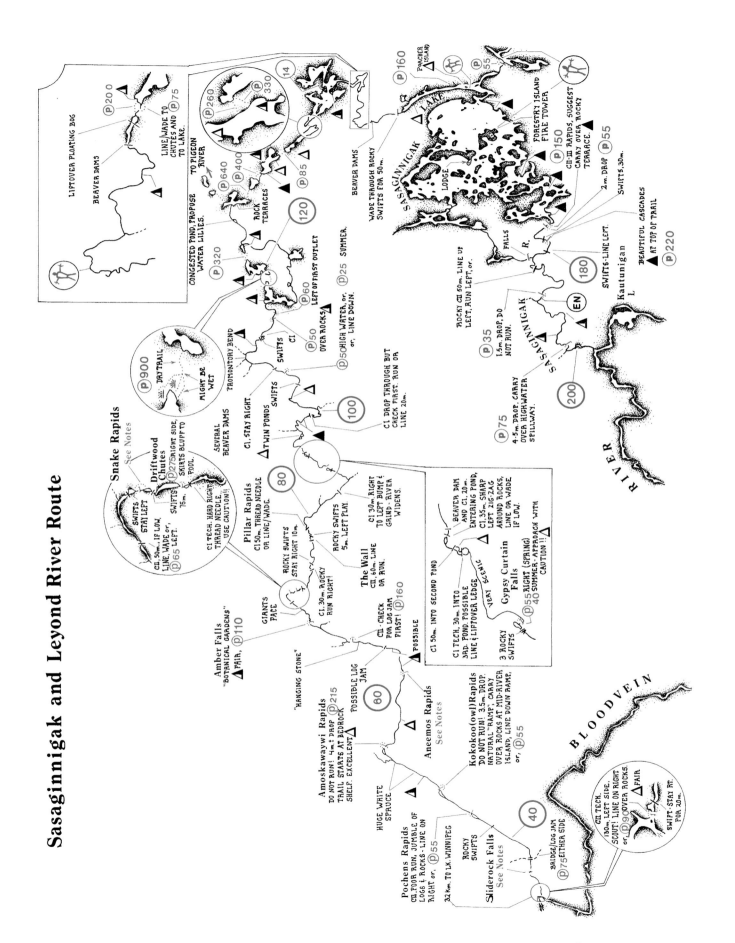

LIFTOVER FLOATING BOG

BEAVER DAMS

(P)200

(P)75

LINE/WADE TO CHUTES AND TO LAKE.

(P)260

330

14

(P)640

(P)400

CONGESTED POND. PROFUSE WATER LILIES.

(P)320

ROCK TERRACES

85

120

(P)160

POACHER ISLAND

55

(P)

SASAGINNIGAK LAKE

FORESTRY ISLAND FIRE TOWER

(P)150

CH-III RAPIDS, SUGGEST CARRY OVER ROCKY TERRACE.

(P)55

2m. DROP.

SWIFTS, 30m.

BEAVER DAMS

LODGE

WADE THROUGH ROCKY SWIFTS FOR 50m.

R.

FALLS

BEAUTIFUL CASCADES AT TOP OF TRAIL

(P)220

(P)50 HIGH WATER, or, LINE DOWN.

LEFT OF FIRST OUTLET

(P)60

(P)25 SUMMER.

(P)50 OVER ROCKS

C1

SWIFTS

ROCKY CH 50m. LINE UP LEFT, RUN LEFT, or.

KAUTUNIGAN L

180

SWIFTS-LINE LEFT.

(P)35

1.5m. DROP, DO NOT RUN.

EN

SASAGINNIGAK

(P)75

4-5m. DROP. CARRY OVER HIGHWATER SPILLWAY.

200

RIVER

(P)900

DRY TRAIL

MIGHT BE WET

PROMONTORY BEND

SEVERAL BEAVER DAMS

C1, STAY RIGHT

Δ TWIN PONDS

SWIFTS

100

C1 DROP THROUGH BUT CHECK FIRST. RUN OR LINE 20m.

Snake Rapids
See Notes

Driftwood Chutes

(P)275 RIGHT SIDE, SWIFTS BLUFF TO POOL.

SWIFTS 75m.

(P)275 RIGHT SIDE, SKIRTS BLUFF TO POOL.

SWIFTS STAY LEFT

CH 50m. IF LOW, WADE or, (P)65 LEFT.

C1 TECH. HARD RIGHT, THREAD NEEDLE. USE CAUTION!!

Pillar Rapids
C1 50m. THREAD NEEDLE OR LINE/WADE.

80

ROCKY SWIFTS 5m. LEFT PLAY.

C1 30m. RIGHT TO LEFT BUMP ξ GRIND - RIVER WIDENS.

BEAVER DAM AND C1 20m. ENTERING POND. C1 35m. SHARP LEFT ZIG-ZAG AROUND ROCKS, LINE OR WADE IF LOW.

Amber Falls
"BOTANICAL GARDENS" (P)110

Δ FAIR,

GIANTS FACE

ROCKY SWIFTS STAY RIGHT

C1 30m. ROCKY RUN RIGHT!

The Wall
C1, 60m. LINE OR RUN.

C1 CHECK FOR LOG JAM FIRST! (P)160

C1 50m. INTO 3RD. POND. POSSIBLE LINE ξ LIFTOVER LEDGE VERY SCENIC

C1 50m. INTO SECOND POND

3 ROCKY SWIFTS

Gypsy Curtain Falls
(P)55 RIGHT (SPRING) 40 SUMMER - APPROACH WITH CAUTION !!

"HANGING STONE"

POSSIBLE

Amoskawaywi Rapids
DO NOT RUN! 4m. ± DROP (P)215 TRAIL STARTS AT BEDROCK SHELF. EXCELLENT.

POSSIBLE LOG JAM

60

Aneemos Rapids
See Notes

Kokokoo(owl)Rapids
DO NOT RUN! 3.5m. DROP. NATURAL "RAMP". CARRY OVER ROCKS AT MID-RIVER ISLAND, LINE DOWN RAMP, or, (P)55

HUGE WHITE SPRUCE

Pochens Rapids
C1. POOR RUN, JUMBLE OF LOGS ξ ROCKS - LINE ON RIGHT or, (P)55

32 km. TO LK. WINNIPEG

ROCKY SWIFTS

Sliderock Falls
See Notes

BRIDGE/LOG JAM (P)75 EITHER SIDE

40

BLOODVEIN

C1 TECH. 130m. LEFT SIDE. SCOUT! LINE ON RIGHT or, (P)90 OVER ROCKS.

Δ FAIR

SWIFT - STAY RT. FOR 20m.

Sliderock Falls ·caution·

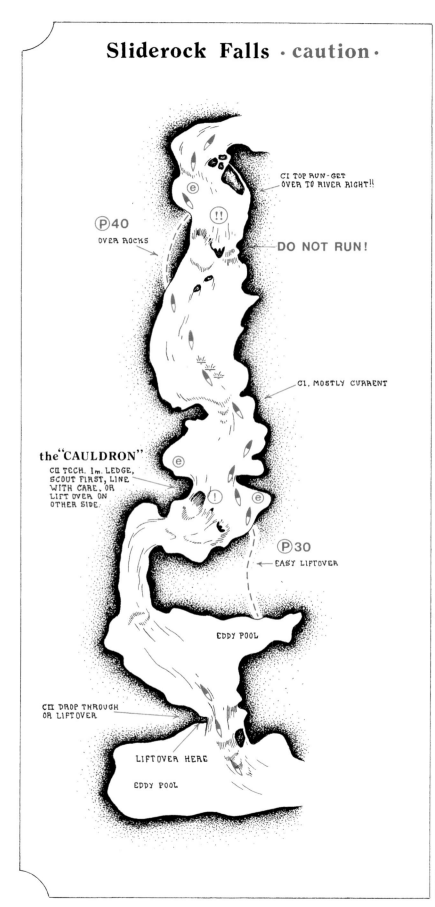

CI TOP RUN - GET OVER TO RIVER RIGHT!!

(P)40
OVER ROCKS

DO NOT RUN!

CI, MOSTLY CURRENT

the "CAULDRON"
CII TECH. Im. LEDGE,
SCOUT FIRST, LINE
WITH CARE, OR
LIFT OVER ON
OTHER SIDE.

(P)30
EASY LIFTOVER

EDDY POOL

CII DROP THROUGH
OR LIFTOVER

LIFTOVER HERE

EDDY POOL

Snake Rapids ·SCOUT!·

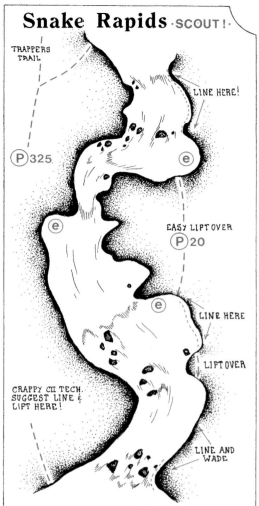

TRAPPERS
TRAIL

LINE HERE!

(P)325

EASY LIFT OVER
(P)20

LINE HERE

LIFT OVER

CRAPPY CII TECH.
SUGGEST LINE &
LIFT HERE!

LINE AND
WADE

Aneemos
Rapids

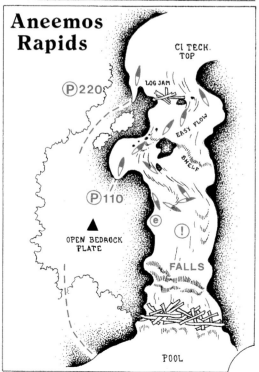

CI TECH.
TOP

LOG JAM

EASY FLOW

SHELF

(P)220

(P)110

OPEN BEDROCK
PLATE

FALLS

POOL

JOURNAL NOTES – SASAGINNIGAK

August '95: The river was 25-30m. across with no appreciable current where even the shore reeds bent upriver; only the first 2.5 km. expressed itself as a mock Bloodvein, almost characterless on its own until we reached a small falls which flowed with great velocity four to five metres over slanted rock. Here we portaged over a high spillway which terminated just above the chutes at a beaver dam that retained the upper river from the precipice.

We entered the *Swamp of the New World* – a four kilometre fenland which envelops you in a common plane, a recumbent blend of terrestrial existence and voidless sky. Water is inconsequential; a pathway through a giant sponge of bulrush, wild celery, sedge-bush and tamarack, backed by a seemingly impervious bastion of trembling aspen.

The swamp emerged into a narrow corridor where the trees drew closer; large looming aspen, blue spruce (which looked too ornamental for such wilderness), white spruce with their outstretched arms and, of course, jackpine and the occasional black spruce and balsam fir (very infrequent).

Bedrock showed itself occasionally in demonstrative but yet overall subtle ways, certainly not dominating the landscape like the Bloodvein, but in disseminated occurrences of vertical slabs and mounds, perched like token watch-dogs over the river. And sometimes the fen would give way to open moss-covered pans of infertile rock, sparsely treed, traipsing off out of eye's path as you paddle by. Where are those Woodland Caribou anyway?

Just before the huge cascades, the river squeezes through a bold cleft between the folds of granite, once again portraying the vast soilless desert, devoid not of life itself but of prime species or marketable commodities sought by the logger. The river is prime for the catching of walleye and for the adventurer.

Sasaginnigak Lake – I wanted to interview Wess and Peggy Klassen who were the long-time caretakers of Sasaginnigak lodge, but at the time of entry into the large crater-shaped lake the wind was gusting at over 90kmh. from the south – a tail wind that whipped up vicious whitecaps and snapped the tops off timber as we paddled by. The spray deck was fastened and we made the last dash to the lodge from behind the lee of a large island. Going was

tough, like riding the back of a violent class IV rapid; nearing the lodge we saw the beaver aircraft take off into the wind, hang motionless for a moment not making any headway at all, then veer north riding the wind in order to gain forward motion. The lodge was quiet and the Klassens extended the kindest hospitality allowing us to spend a much needed rest day in one of the vacant cabins.

JOURNAL NOTES – LEYOND

As I had envisioned, the portages accessing the Leyond headwaters were almost non-existent. To make things worse the entire countryside had undergone a major forest fire about 10 years previous leaving the land bare-rocked and manged with clumps of jackpine so thick as to impede the traffic of rabbits. On reaching Apex Lake (our name), after locating not one but two obscure portage trails shown on the map as a 260m. and 330m. carry, we made camp in a quiet bay at the north end. From here all water descended to Lake Winnipeg. Before the burn we paddled several small pristine lakes but the going was not easy; we would shoulder a load and take the axe across the congested trail and clear a path on the way back. Finally, upon reaching the burn, any indication of a trail had vanished with the previous forest save for a few seemingly misplaced rock cairns. It took us almost 3 hours of heavy axe work to create the 640m. portage through the two-meter high jackpine. It was dry and the sun beat upon us from above and off the rock where we walked. Even the moss crunched into powder when stepped upon; in the rain these wiry clumps would soak up to 20 X's their own weight in water and become as slippery as banana peels underfoot.

The long portage connection to the actual river remained elusive until I took to walking several hundred meters along the shore, finally coming across some old blazes in a tree and a small cairn by the shore. We left the loaded canoe beached by the landing and started clearing with the axe. The first half a kilometre was easy going, through dry upland jackpine and spruce, but this ended abruptly at a flooded footpath and what seemed to be an endless morass of swamp and muskeg...still only halfway to the open water of the next lake. We carried the gear across the freshly cleared portage and loaded the canoe right on the trail which had just enough water to

enable us to slide the boat along with a lot of grunting, moans and choice curse words. This went on for some time, metre by metre, stepping through floating bog, spruce and tamarack sprigs that snagged your legs and the canoe, pinching them between leech infested subterranean clefts.

We walked through spider webs thicker than Irish curtains and picked up several varieties of hitch-hikers as we progressed. Three hours later the lake came into view; gratifying at the least to know we had finally reached the Leyond and far easier paddling. Across the lake at the Leyond River outlet we came across a huge freshly built beaver dam of such magnitude as to back the whole volume of the lake over half a kilometre over the dreaded portage from which we had just come.

Below the beaver dam the river level was at least 2 metres under the high water mark which made the first couple of kilometres of paddling interesting, but once we hauled over a couple more dams it seemed that the water level had evened out some.

We saw geese at every corner of the river and the young would dive under the water while the adults flew off and circled back. On one occasion a young goose came up from the depths so suddenly and, striking the bottom of the canoe, seemed a little dazed by the experience and sat blinking at us as we drifted by. No paddlers had been along this route in some time and it was prime canoeing when you could find more animal and bird shit on the campsites than human. The beautiful marsh environment of the Leyond teemed with activity: river otter, muskrat and beaver, and in one instance a mother cow moose that did not want to vacate the only clear channel in the river. She approached our canoe with hackles raised and head low, unusual I thought until I saw a young calf suddenly stand up on the shore just a few metres away. We kept still until both animals united and walked slowly into the folds of spruce beyond the beaver grass.

The black bear, whose presence along the Leyond is most notable in sightings and unseen activities, and who is almost always full of antics and acrobatics upon confrontation, it being more frightened than we, is often seen along the shores fully extended on its haunches, reaching for berries and pulling them into its maw with its forepaws, quite at leisure with itself in an amusing way.

The Leyond is an intimate embrace with nature; all facets of hardship also have gentle edges, from the sweep of the river bends to the sloping bedrock as it melds with the underwater world. Sounds are passive: the soft staccato of the trembling aspen, the chatter of marsh birds, the applause of gentle rapids, even the falls and chutes seem timid ... all encapsulate a particular visage and river character that is not at all intimidating. Larger rivers are demonstrative by sheer volume and hydrological character alone; the energy pervasive in context with the geology and the forces of nature which moulded it – brassy and defiant, not necessarily serene at all and certainly not forgiving. The Leyond...not for the thrill-seeker but for the lover of nature.   H.W.

PIGEON RIVER
OVERVIEW

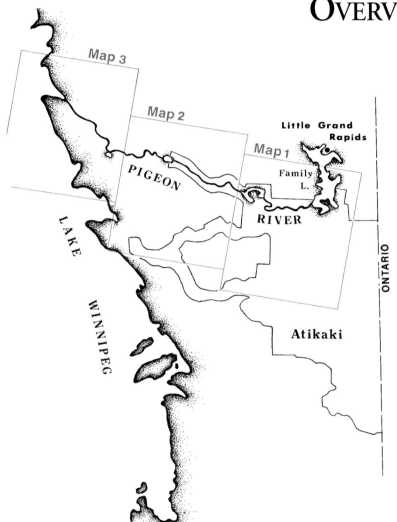

**MONTHLY AVERAGE FLOW
(1957-1992)**

May	76.8 m³/sec.
June	147.0 m³/sec.
July	151.0 m³/sec.
August	115.0 m³/sec.
September	90.9 m³/sec.

PIGEON RIVER

GENERAL INFORMATION

Classification: Intermediate
Distance: 160 km. (Family Lake to Lake Winnipeg) 75 km. (Round Lake to Lake Winnipeg)
Elevation Rise/drop: 79m. (259') or 1/2 m./km. (1.6'/km.)
            *from Family Lake
Time: 10-14 days
Number of Campsites: 58 or 1 campsite every 3 km.
Number of Rapids and Falls: 51 (numbered in sequence)
Number of Runnable Rapids: 42 (65% CI to CII)
Portages: Easy Intermediate – 28 (3,195m.)
            Experienced Intermediate – 22 (2,190m.)
Season: Late May through September
Maps Required: 52 M/13 62 P/16 63 A/1 63 A/2 63 A/3
Access: Access by floatplane from either Matheson Island or Pine Dock to Family Lake for the long trip, or Round Lake for the short trip (5-6 days).
Egress: Prearranged charter pick-up by floatplane from two locations: the wide section of river just north of Windigo Lake (Windigo is not floatplane-friendly); or from the sandy beach at the mouth of the Pigeon on Lake Winnipeg. It is not advisable to paddle the coast unless well experienced on big lakes.
Features: The Pigeon possesses that rogue temperament of being extremely picturesque with an underlying ferocity. Its flow is almost double that of the Bloodvein during the summer but because the physiography of the Pigeon is similar to the Bloodvein, the hydrological character is certainly more spirited. This means greater volume through the runs, less reaction time to manoeuver, bigger standing waves and more of them, and a greater percentage of technical rapids requiring more advanced skills. This is probably one reason why whitewater rafting along the Pigeon has become popular. This river is NOT suitable for canoeists with only novice skills; it is, though, one of the best whitewater rivers in Canada, and probably one of the most scenic. The flow is quite strong along some stretches of the river and because of the wild nature and capricious mood, aboriginal travel was minimal, indicated by the general lack of archaeological findings. Fishing was superb.

WHITEWATER CHARACTERISTICS AND GENERAL HAZARDS

Needless to say, the Pigeon demands respect, and those foolhardy enough to make the run without adequate skills are only tempting fate. Although most of the difficult chutes and rapids can be portaged there are many dangerous approaches to portages especially during high water periods. Experienced novices should have an experienced intermediate paddler with them who is fully aware of all safety procedures.

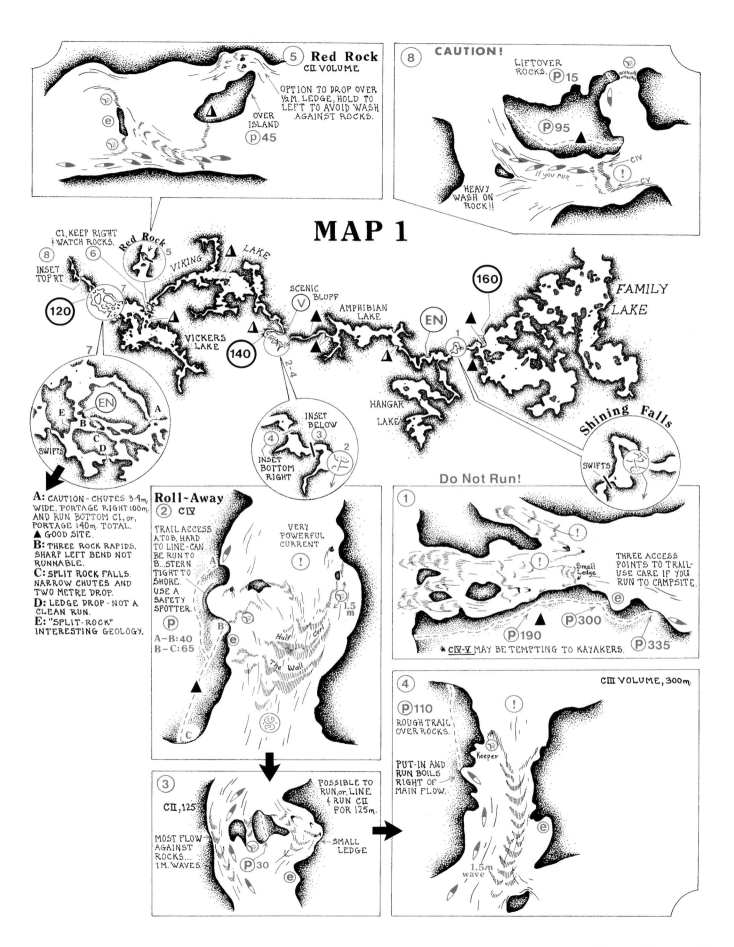

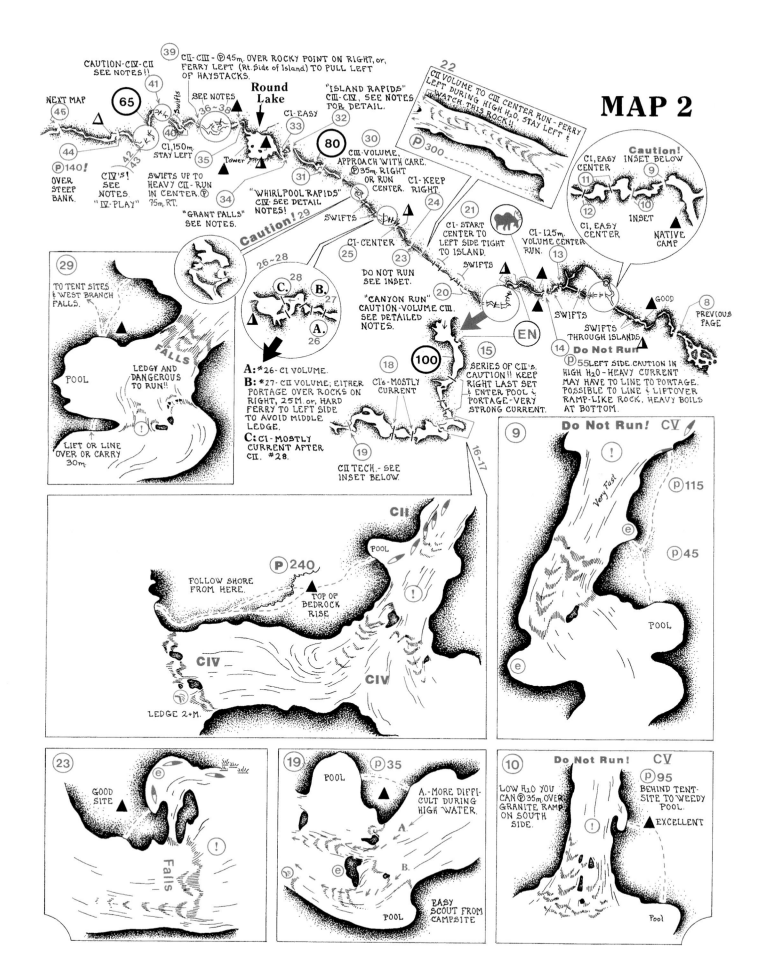

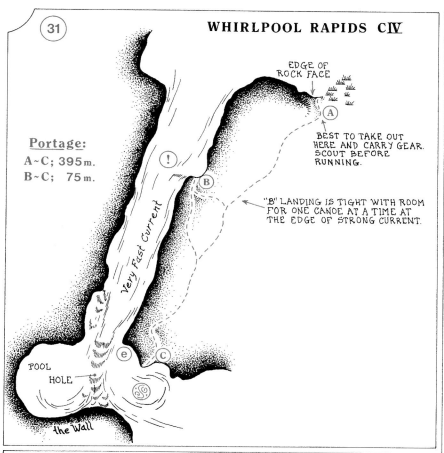

WHIRLPOOL RAPIDS CIV

31

EDGE OF
ROCK FACE

A

BEST TO TAKE OUT
HERE AND CARRY GEAR.
SCOUT BEFORE
RUNNING.

Portage:
A ~ C; 395 m.
B ~ C; 75 m.

!

B

"B" LANDING IS TIGHT WITH ROOM
FOR ONE CANOE AT A TIME AT
THE EDGE OF STRONG CURRENT.

Very Fast Current

POOL
HOLE

e

C

the Wall

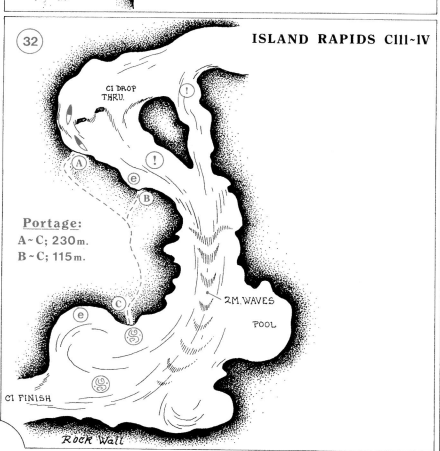

ISLAND RAPIDS CIII~IV

32

C1 DROP
THRU.

!

A

!

e

B

Portage:
A ~ C; 230 m.
B ~ C; 115 m.

C

e

2 M. WAVES

POOL

C1 FINISH

Rock Wall

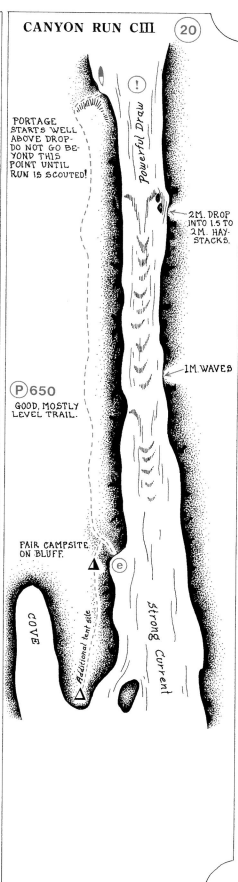

CANYON RUN CIII

20

!

PORTAGE
STARTS WELL
ABOVE DROP·
DO NOT GO BE-
YOND THIS
POINT UNTIL
RUN IS SCOUTED!

Powerful Drop

2 M. DROP
INTO 1.5 TO
2 M. HAY-
STACKS.

1 M. WAVES

P 650

GOOD, MOSTLY
LEVEL TRAIL.

FAIR CAMPSITE
ON BLUFF.

△

e

Additional tent site

△

COVE

Strong Current

PIGEON RIVER JOURNAL

The great British statesman and political philosopher, Edmund Burke, in 1700 once exclaimed that "early and provident fear is the mother of all safety." Perched on a precambrian ledge, I was now gazing down at a course of rapids gnarly enough to swallow a flagship. I was about to heave those very words of wisdom over the precipice into the maelstrom below.

"C'mon Hap, let's see you run this one!" came the prompt from the ranks of the porteurs. NOT on your life, I thought to myself.... But I can't let the others see me buckle and whimper; after all, there comes the moment on every adventure when a whitewater canoe-guide must answer the call, even if it's to maintain integrity as instructor.

But why this one? I whimpered from behind a tree. What would Burke do now if he were in my gumboots? The early and provident fear part greeted us all one kilometre upriver when we first heard the cacophony of tons of water per second being thrashed against the bones of Mother Earth. That should have been ample persuasion for us all to execute the safe yet humble option to portage and show reverence to the water gods.

It was a small canyon that squeezed a respectable river into a narrow yaw that resulted in a series of angry waves... just before it all swelled against a ten-metre granite wall. Typical waterplay along the Pigeon. Gear was portaged. Cameras were extricated from waterproof Pelican cases. Ben, a lawyer from Toronto, along with myself, would pilot the empty canoes down; he was to eddy out right into a safe pool and I'd take the middle track through the viscera of pounding river and provide the audience on shore with the entertainment. Camera lenses were poised to capture the last fleeting moments of my life. I felt like David being cast into the den of lions.

I pushed the canoe off into the excited current and aimed for the vortex of doom. The first wave was a four-metre stationary tsunami that pulsed and heaved and curled at the top like an ocean breaker. I actually made it through that one, and the next, then the third wave, and I thought by God I'm going to make it all the way! Wrong.

It was then that the river entity reached up from the depths of a hidden whirlpool, grabbed the canoe and spun it around 180° and I was suddenly doing one of those impressive, crowd pleasing playboat "enders" only without the thigh-straps to hold me in. I saw a flash of blue sky just before being keel-hauled and assaulted by my own canoe.

Trying to hold on to my paddle was like grasping an angry python.

Luckily, just in time, I managed to get out from between the rock wall and the royalex stallion and wash safely downstream, bruised, humble and very wet. The rescue boat plucked me from the current one kilometre downriver. "Hey, great pictures, Hap. We'll send you one for Christmas!"

Every so often an adventuring canoeist will, serendipitously, happen upon a river route so captivating it defies description. The first thing you don't want to do is share its secrets with anyone else. Manitoba's Pigeon River is no exception to the predications of the "elite" genre of paddler who most often resents the implications projected by guide-books or route descriptions made available to the general masses.

During the two weeks that I spent exploring the Pigeon with my own canoe party we met up with only one other group. Upon learning that I was incorporating the Pigeon into a book on Manitoba's wild rivers, the six paddlers from upstate Michigan (dressed in wrinkle-free and unsoiled L. L. Bean outerwear), who were already distressed at seeing someone else on *their* river, became outwardly unfriendly. Little did they know, or care, that the bureaucrats and resource administrators have a different if not myopic view of a wilderness river, relating its worth by whatever "user-group" generates the highest economic remuneration from its actions. Use it or lose it. Wilderness protection then becomes a sad paradox. Fractured mainstream environmental groups, generally with little assistance from the canoeing fraternity, are no match for the big corporations filling political coffers. If the "green" camp wins a battle it is often too late; since there is far too little wilderness left, the advertised parks become overcrowded while unprotected wildlands are eviscerated by industrial gluttony.

The Pigeon is one of several rivers flowing west into Lake Winnipeg from the highlands of Atikaki Wilderness Park, located 250 kilometres northeast of the city of Winnipeg. Atikaki (pronounced A-tick-akee), is Saulteaux Ojibway meaning "country of the caribou"; the resident herd of 300–500 woodland caribou range the glacially scoured precambrian landscape surviving on boreal lichens, reindeer moss and "oldman's beard" — Spanish moss which hangs in festoons from the branches of mature jackpine and spruce. One of the park's largest herds ranges along the upper Pigeon; another midway downstream and to the north, bisected by the Berens River that parallels the Pigeon.

In opposition to increased timber activities east of Lake Winnipeg in the early 1970's, an activist group calling itself the Atikaki Coalition petitioned the Manitoba government with a proposal to protect the sensitive Atikaki wilderness. Conflicts ensued, arbitrary park boundaries were discussed, excising whole river corridors, including the lower half of the Pigeon, in order to appease the demands of the logging industry. The Bloodvein-Pigeon river region finally became a park in 1985, while the Bloodvein achieved notoriety as one of Canada's celebrated Heritage Rivers in 1991.

Located at the apex of the park is Family Lake, traditional hunting grounds for the migrating Ojibway people or Anishnabeg from the home territory further to the east. It forms the headwaters for the Pigeon, and midpoint of the Pigeon's sister river, the Berens. While the upper course of the Pigeon River is protected within the confines of Atikaki, 80 kilometres downriver to Round Lake, the remaining 80 kilometres to Lake Winnipeg is subject to the development whims of industry. The lower reaches lie within the cutting berths of the Abitibi Paper Company, now controlled by the employee-owned Pine Falls Paper Company residing in Pine Falls, Manitoba. The highest potential forest resource, primarily mature jackpine and spruce, is found along the lower Pigeon and entire Berens river corridor — the very bio-diverse environment required by the resident caribou herds for their survival. All unprotected and subject to displacement, regardless of the 200 metre "good housekeeping" buffer along the river. In real terms "selective" harvesting within the shore veneer through company "sanitization" projects, makes light of any attempt by industry to operate with any environmental or ethical considerations.

For the touring paddler it represents a perplexing contradiction. While the pristine upper reach of the Pigeon enjoys the sanctity and reverence it deserves, the lower half flows abruptly into the political morass monogrammed by visible logging clear-cuts, roads and abandoned camps. Even the government motivated Human Heritage study for the Pigeon was terminated at Round Lake, the upper half where ten new archaeological sites were identified in 1993. It is safe to assume that the potential ten sites of the lower half of the river were conveniently and purposely discounted. For all intent and purpose, the lower Pigeon (as indicated on park maps) does not exist; yet, in the opinion of those who ply its water, all agree that the lower half retains the same ambient charm as its riverhead meandering through the park. The experience of tenting on the driftwood littered beaches of Lake Winnipeg (as opposed to flying out of Round or Wendigo Lake) alone provides unprecedented sunscapes from the edge of the precambrian shield, overlooking the beginning of the great central plains. The consequence of development along the lower river, although visible and unfortunate, did not entirely depreciate the experience.

The Pigeon is an historic anomaly. The two rivers paralleling its course — the Bloodvein and the Berens — were used as important travel corridors by the Lake Winnipeg Saulteaux Ojibwa, "people of the falls or rapids", derived from the French — saulteurs. Both of these rivers share the same elevation drop as the Pigeon (approximately 70 metres or less than .07'/km.) yet, unlike the turbulent and constant flow of the Pigeon, the Bloodview and Berens possess a languorous current by comparison. Early travel and trade up or downstream on either the Berens or Bloodvein proved far easier for the Saulteaux than attempting to battle the Pigeon's tenuous rush. This is one reason why the Pigeon lacks the pre or historic attributes of its sister rivers; it does entice, though, the thrill-seeker who enjoys precipitous, high-volume waterplay; or the adventurer who doesn't mind portaging several of the 55 falls, chutes and rapids, and simply revels in the unprecedented boreal charisma.

The Berens River, prior to the 1800's, was known as the Pigeon, or "omimisipi", referring to the long extinct passenger pigeon which was once found here in great migrating flocks and source of food for the Anishnabeg. The river name was anglicized to Berens, after Joseph Berens Jr., governor of the Hudson's Bay Company from 1812–1822. The river to the south then was given the name Pigeon.

After having paddled most of the 1000 kilometres of connecting canoe routes within Atikaki's boundary over the past two years, I have to admit that the pristine innocence of the Pigeon captured my heart. It wasn't just the tidal rush of adrenaline at each of the whitewater runs coursing through granite chasms, but the apparent "newness" and austere landscape.

Our group took two weeks to fully appreciate the personality of the Pigeon. Campsites were numerous, particularly spectacular at almost all major chutes, at the canyon, Round Lake and at the mystical Windigo Lake. The perception that the cannibal-giants windigowak reside at this shallow lake with its blood-red waters was consolidated during our one night stay on the island campsite. Weather-worn, bleached moose antlers had been propped ceremoniously on the bedrock slope near the shore of the site, surrounded by the scattered bones of fish and small mammals; presumably the lunching spot for either otter or bald eagle — or perhaps the feeding place of the dreaded mythological windigo who grow taller than the tallest trees when they shout. The crimson evening sky illuminated the sanguineous complexion of the lake, eerie yet peaceful it seemed, until windigo's voice conjured up such a violent storm during the darkest hour of night with winds so fierce that our whole camp was almost carried off the island.

The drama of the natural history along the Pigeon is remarkable; the aquatic habitats teem with fish; backshore fenlands support a luxurious growth of spruce, tamarack and floating bogs of sphagnum bedecked with labrador tea, pitcher plants, bog laurel, leatherleaf, willow and wild rice. It is also home of the moose, wolf, bear, lynx and the occasional cougar and wolverine. Caribou are elusive and the actual chance of seeing them is fairly slim. There are over 300 species of birds, whether migrant or resident, including the osprey, bald eagle and pelican.

Waterplay along the Pigeon is pretty serious stuff and many prefer a kayak or raft to the canoe. Canoes require spray-decks for the bigger rapids although we made it down most sensible runs without them. The government park brochure professes that "the Pigeon provides some of the best wilderness whitewater in North America...many consider it to be comparable to the Colorado or Snake rivers in the United States." This is not an exaggeration.

Most of the difficult CIII-CIV ledge-type rapids can be portaged while potentially hazardous hydraulic "souse-holes" require precise scouting and tactical safety measures in place. Lengthy CII and voluminous CIII runs then quell anyone's passion for aqueous excitement. The Pigeon may be Manitoba's premier whitewater wonder, equal in stature to Quebec's Dumoine, Newfoundland's Main, Ontario's Petawawa or British Columbia's Kicking Horse, but it also represents a self-contained but fragile environment supported by an intoxicating melange of boreal life forces animated by the very soul of a great river. H.W.

GRANT FALLS

As is often the case, this falls was nothing more than a heavy volume CII–CIII. It begins with a good entry tongue just right of centre; the first wave may be a good metre in size but everything after that is relatively small. We were able to line carefully down the right side which may become difficult if the sloping rocks are wet. The portage is on the right side, over the rocks for about 45 metres.

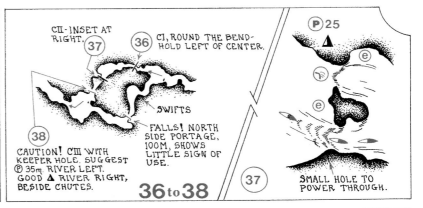

CII-INSET AT RIGHT.
(37)
(36) CI, ROUND THE BEND-HOLD LEFT OF CENTER.
SWIFTS
(38)
FALLS! NORTH SIDE PORTAGE, 100M, SHOWS LITTLE SIGN OF USE.
CAUTION! CIII WITH KEEPER HOLE. SUGGEST (P) 35m. RIVER LEFT. GOOD ▲ RIVER RIGHT, BESIDE CHUTES.

36 to 38

(P) 25
(e)
(e)
(37)
SMALL HOLE TO POWER THROUGH.

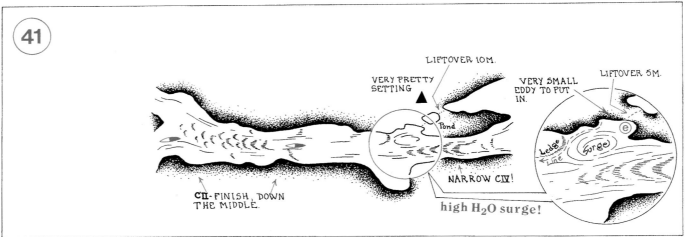

(41)

LIFTOVER 10M.
VERY PRETTY SETTING
Pond
VERY SMALL EDDY TO PUT IN.
LIFTOVER 5M.
(e)
Ledge Line
Surge
NARROW CIV!
high H₂O surge!
CII-FINISH, DOWN THE MIDDLE.

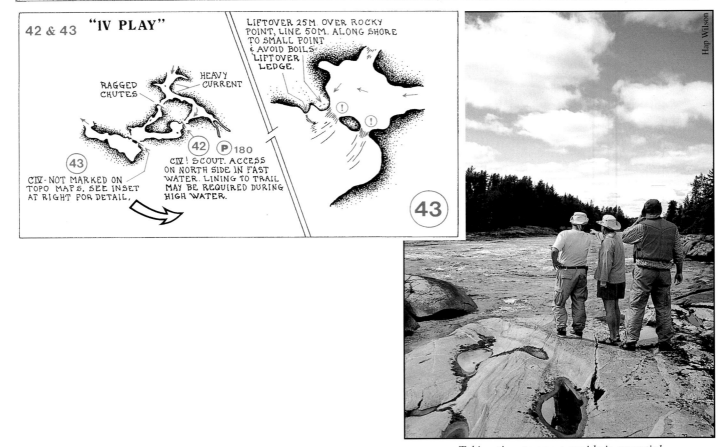

42 & 43 "IV PLAY"

RAGGED CHUTES
HEAVY CURRENT
(43)
(42) (P) 180
CIV - NOT MARKED ON TOPO MAPS, SEE INSET AT RIGHT FOR DETAIL.
CIV! SCOUT. ACCESS ON NORTH SIDE IN FAST WATER. LINING TO TRAIL MAY BE REQUIRED DURING HIGH WATER.

LIFTOVER 25M. OVER ROCKY POINT, LINE 50M. ALONG SHORE TO SMALL POINT & AVOID BOILS-LIFTOVER LEDGE.
(!) (!)
(43)

Hap Wilson

Taking time to scout rapids is essential

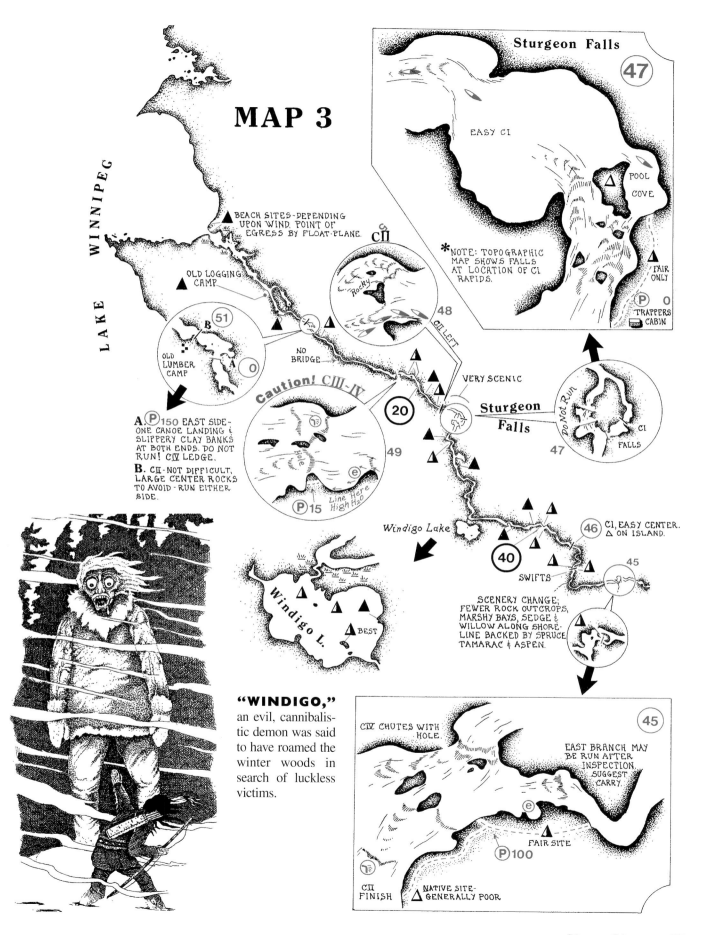

MAP 3

Sturgeon Falls

(47)

EASY CI

POOL COVE

FAIR ONLY

*NOTE: TOPOGRAPHIC MAP SHOWS FALLS AT LOCATION OF CI RAPIDS.

(P) 0 TRAPPERS CABIN

LAKE WINNIPEG

▲ BEACH SITES - DEPENDING UPON WIND. POINT OF EGRESS BY FLOAT-PLANE.

▲ OLD LOGGING CAMP

CⅡ Rocky

48 CⅡ LEFT

51 B

▲ OLD LUMBER CAMP A (0)

NO BRIDGE

A (P) 150 EAST SIDE - ONE CANOE LANDING & SLIPPERY CLAY BANKS AT BOTH ENDS. DO NOT RUN! CIV LEDGE.

B. CⅡ - NOT DIFFICULT, LARGE CENTER ROCKS TO AVOID - RUN EITHER SIDE.

Caution! CⅢ-Ⅳ

Hole

(e)

(P) 15 Line Here High H₂O

(20)

49

VERY SCENIC

Sturgeon Falls

Do Not Run

CI FALLS

47

(40)

46 CI, EASY CENTER. △ ON ISLAND.

45

SWIFTS

SCENERY CHANGE: FEWER ROCK OUTCROPS, MARSHY BAYS, SEDGE & WILLOW ALONG SHORE-LINE BACKED BY SPRUCE, TAMARAC & ASPEN.

Windigo Lake

△

Windigo L. △ △ △ BEST

"WINDIGO," an evil, cannibalistic demon was said to have roamed the winter woods in search of luckless victims.

(45)

CIV CHUTES WITH HOLE.

EAST BRANCH MAY BE RUN AFTER INSPECTION. SUGGEST CARRY.

(e)

▲ FAIR SITE

(P) 100

CⅡ FINISH

△ NATIVE SITE - GENERALLY POOR.

BERENS RIVER OVERVIEW

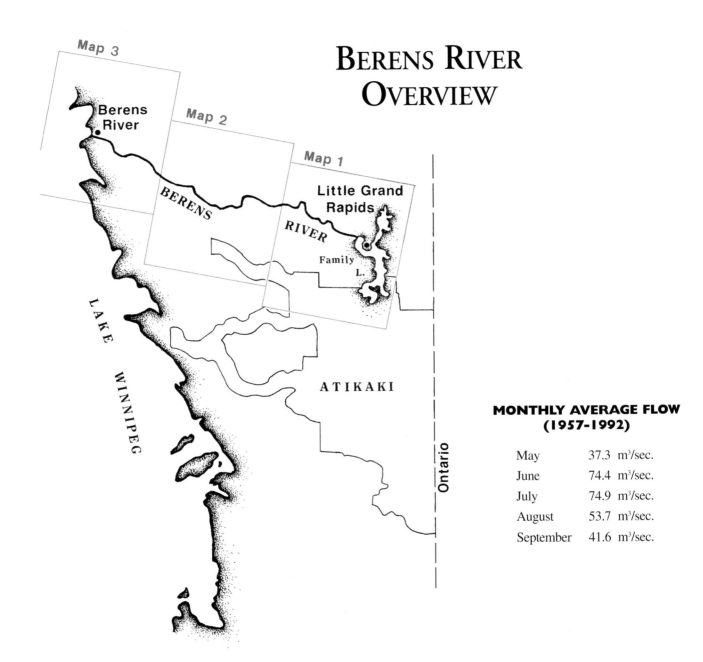

**MONTHLY AVERAGE FLOW
(1957-1992)**

May	37.3 m³/sec.
June	74.4 m³/sec.
July	74.9 m³/sec.
August	53.7 m³/sec.
September	41.6 m³/sec.

BERENS RIVER

GENERAL INFORMATION

Classification: Experienced Novice
(portaging all technical rapids)
Intermediate
(CII tech. to CIII rapids negotiated)
Distance: 175 km. (Little Grand Rapids to Lake Winnipeg)
Elevation Drop: 79m. (259') or 1/2m./km. (1.6'/km.)
Time: 8-10 days
Number of Campsites: 35 or 1 campsite every 5km.
Number of Rapids and Falls: 52 (numbered in sequence)
Number of Runnable Rapids: 31 (68% CI to CII)
Portages: Experienced Novice – 35 (2,700m.)
Creative Intermediate – 21 (1,830m.)
Season: Late May through September
Maps Required: 53 D/4 53 D/3 63 A/1 63 A/2 63 A/7
Access: By floatplane from Pine Dock or Matheson to Family Lake or by charter to Little Grand Rapids.
Egress: By prearranged floatplane charter pick-up at Berens River village. There may be the option to hitch a ride with the local supply boat but the schedule isn't always consistent.
Features: The Berens River was one of our favourites, for many reasons, probably most of all because of the sense of remoteness and sheer beauty of the Precambrian mantle – a mix of open rock, a lush lichen and moss carpet and a generous overstory of jackpine and spruce. It also showed some aboriginal use for hunting, fishing and spiritual ceremony at Big Moose Falls. The Berens should be done slowly as there is much to see and experience, and it wouldn't be difficult to spend at least two weeks plying the backchannels and hidden coves along the way. Campsites are exceptional and we found it hard sometimes to break camp and get back on the move again.

WHITEWATER CHARACTERISTICS AND GENERAL HAZARDS

The Berens flow pattern is quite similar to that of the Bloodvein except for the month of May. It only seems like a small river until you start riding some of the volume rapids through narrow cuts in the dramatic geology. The rapids of the Berens are easier than those along the Bloodvein, not subject to steeply pitched ledges and dangerous souse holes. That doesn't mean that the canoeist should be less wary; this river can catch you up if you aren't prepared. Follow the route descriptions and the detailed rapid drawings carefully and you'll be guaranteed a wonderful journey. Tobacco offerings are a requirement.

MAP 1

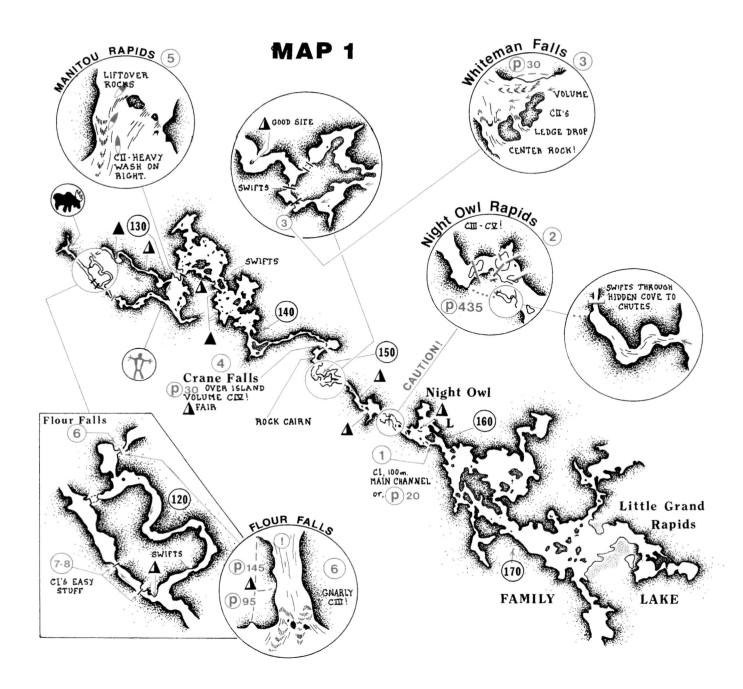

MANITOU RAPIDS ⑤
LIFTOVER ROCKS
CII-HEAVY WASH ON RIGHT.

▲ GOOD SITE
SWIFTS
③

Whiteman Falls ③
ⓟ30
VOLUME
CII's
LEDGE DROP
CENTER ROCK!

▲⑬⓪
SWIFTS
⑭⓪

Night Owl Rapids ②
CIII - CIV!
ⓟ435

SWIFTS THROUGH HIDDEN COVE TO CHUTES.

④ ⑮⓪
Crane Falls
ⓟ30 OVER ISLAND
VOLUME CIV!
▲FAIR

ROCK CAIRN

CAUTION!

Night Owl
▲
L ⑯⓪

Flour Falls ⑥

①
CI, 100m.
MAIN CHANNEL
or, ⓟ20

Little Grand Rapids

⑫⓪
SWIFTS

⑺-⑻
CI'S EASY STUFF

FLOUR FALLS
ⓟ145 ⑥
▲
ⓟ95 GNARLY CIII!

⑰⓪

FAMILY **LAKE**

BERENS RIVER JOURNAL

We arrived at the end of Matheson Island road where William, owner-pilot of WamAir, flew us in to Family Lake at the headwaters of the Manitoba portion of the Berens River. From there we promptly headed downstream. It was almost a shock to be alone and surrounded by the things we love; such peace after the insane rush to prepare for the trip, madly dashing about in the whirlwind and dust of downtown Winnipeg. And now, suddenly, we found ourselves paddling furiously as if to shake the grime of the city out of our souls. After a while the natural rhythms of the river took over and we could finally relax.

It was sunny, and the heat intense as we paddled through a recently burned-over landscape; the charred hills exposed rocks and the heat waves rose in visible streams like hot pavement. The 500 metre portage around Night Owl Rapids was hot work although we were grateful for an easy trail, a cool breeze near the end and the lack of mosquitoes and blackflies. This was a bit of an anomaly for this time of year and for old burns where biting bugs are hungry for new blood.

It felt good to be on the river again, able to move at our own pace and bask in the stillness and cheer of each other's company. We continued paddling until we reached a veritable island oasis a short distance past "Whiteman's Falls." Not actually a falls but an easy run through, it made me wonder if whoever named it had a rather inane sense of humour. The island was beautiful. It had a sheltered area treed on one side and we pitched our tent under a canopy of jack-pine; on the other side of the island was a natural flat rock terrace with large boulders at the water's edge that resembled a pre-arranged Native petroform.

Dinner was eaten in peace without the incessant biting and buzzing of the myriad flies that normally descend upon an evening campsite at this time of year. Was this good tripping karma or what? The moments of bugless bliss were thoroughly enjoyed while they lasted.

The river past Crane Falls continued with a vibrant current and a shorescape that now seemed to be happily leaving a boneyard of sun-dried and blackened timber behind. It was here that we were entertained by the carefree and playful antics of the river otter. Upon seeing us they dove full tilt into the cool springtime water, not that it was really cold to them, and proceeded to follow us along the shore before tiring of the game. Logs and shore rocks often displayed painted turtles basking in the sun and fish broke the stillness of the surface, scooping up May flies that had fallen into the river. Fishing for walleye was quite good along the Berens, and that probably explained why there were so many otter, and the continuous sighting of Bald eagle. Other river denizens included muskrat, mink, beaver, moose, great blue heron, and somewhere...the elusive woodland caribou.

The wildflowers that added fragrance and beauty to the Berens trip included wild roses, wood lilies (*lilium philadelphicum*), pink lady's slipper (*cypripedium acaule*), found mostly among the trees alongside of the portages; bluebells and even clumps of blue flag (*iris versicolor*), which graced the shoreline between Flour Falls and Big Moose Falls.

At this point of our journey the river took on a changing aura, probably accentuated in part simply upon the absence of fire, but most of all because of the rock walls along the river here that seemed to channel some kind of spiritual energy. At the entrance to Flour channel we saw the first rock painting which never ceases to fill me with a sense of wonder and excitement. It was easy to locate the second pictograph site at Big Moose Falls, so called for the inordinate size of the moose image painted on the rock face above the chutes. This drawing, among others, was situated quite high above the river's edge and the shaman artist must have climbed up to a

ledge in order to paint the spirit-images. This was the only rock art site we've seen yet in Manitoba where there were any recent offerings left by members of the First Nations. A gift of a tin of chewing tobacco and some cigarettes had been left there sometime last year. Red ochre figures seemed to dance in the warm light of the afternoon sun; mythical figures in canoes, disembodied hands and many other ancient symbols came alive, prompted by the majesty of moose medicine and the roar of the falls below. We left some tobacco and gave our own prayer to the resident spirits.

Big Moose Falls splits into two channels enveloping a dome-shaped island, and being hemmed in on one side with a very steep canyon wall, the rush of water and the pull of current made it a rather dangerous place if you weren't careful on the approach to the portage. It was too grand a place to paddle right by so we camped at a fabulous site that faced the falls and planned to take a rest day in which to explore the local area fully.

The fishing for pike and walleye was excellent, almost sinful, but we kept enough for a healthy feast and dined that night in the bliss of a Berens River sunset and the music of the falls. The extra

Hap Wilson

Night Owl Rapids

day here was not nearly enough and I thought how easy it would be to spend the rest of the summer right here.

We left Big Moose Falls with reluctance but with a great feeling of peace that to put into words would simply trivialize the power and influence of such a place. The beauty of the river continued: through glacially-gouged channels, past noisy chutes that at least drowned out the sound of the flies that buzzed around our heads; over exciting rapids and over steep ledges where it was unsafe to run and where our gear was hauled to the quiet pools below.

The water felt colder here than some of the other rivers, perhaps because it was deeper, or because of the late spring ice breakup, but swimming was, to say the least, refreshing on the hot June days of late spring. The rapids were deep and not overly technical and we enjoyed many a good ride through mini-canyons and small chutes where the river shores came together and inspired the water to move a little more quickly.

On reaching the village of Berens River it stormed. It was one of those wild and capricious wind storms that often plague the east shore of such a large ocean-like lake, and we camped high up on a rock bluff, somewhat protected from the cold chill off Lake Winnipeg. The next day we walked around the Ojibway village, listened to the barking of dogs, the happy sounds of children playing, and chatted with locals coming in and out of town by way of the government dock.

In a way it was a bit sad, leaving such a grand river behind as it had left such an indelible impression upon the both of us.

I wondered too, if many or any of the present day residents here at the village had seen the river upstream, or if the spirit of the river is only a memory to most, of stories told by elders about Windigo, the memgwishiwok and of a giant moose that now resides on the face of a forgotten cliff along a river almost too wonderful to put into words. S.A.

Campsite at Big Moose Falls – a magical place

Typical hydrology along the Berens

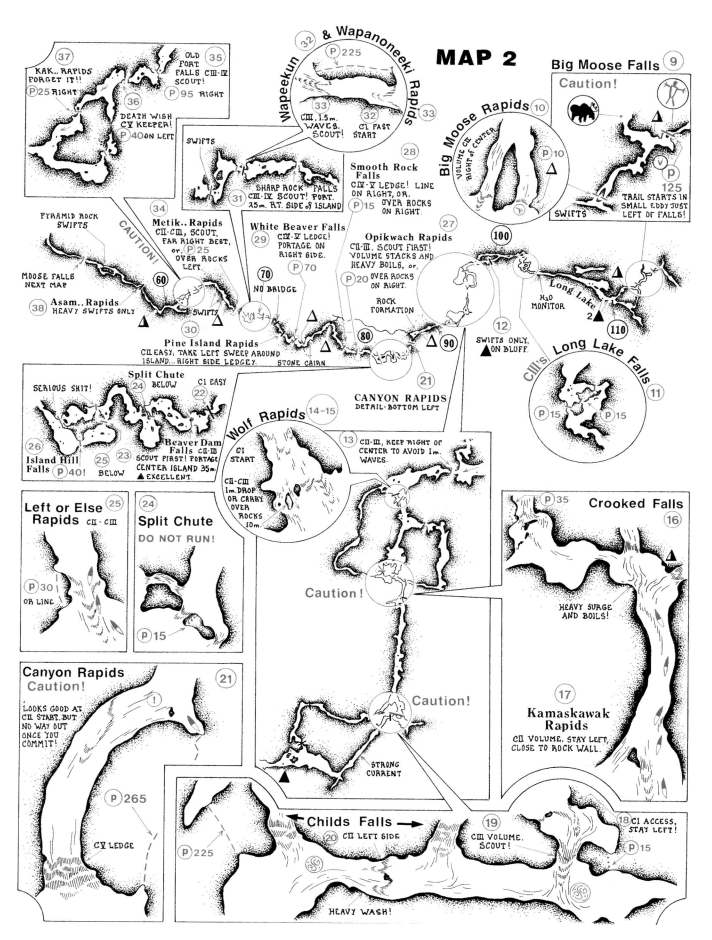

MAP 2

Wapeekun & Wapanoneeki Rapids

32 P 225

33 CIII, 1.5m. WAVES. SCOUT!

33

32 CI FAST START

37 KAK.. RAPIDS FORGET IT!! P 25 RIGHT

35 OLD FORT FALLS CIII-IV SCOUT!

P 95 RIGHT

36 DEATH WISH CV KEEPER! P 40 ON LEFT

SWIFTS

31 SHARP ROCK FALLS CIII-IV SCOUT! PORT. 25m. RT. SIDE of ISLAND

28 Smooth Rock Falls CIV-V LEDGE! LINE ON RIGHT, OR, OVER ROCKS ON RIGHT.

P 15

Big Moose Falls 9

Caution!

▲

v P 125

TRAIL STARTS IN SMALL EDDY JUST LEFT OF FALLS!

Big Moose Rapids 10

VOLUME CIII RIGHT OF CENTER

P 10 ▲

SWIFTS

34 Metik.. Rapids CII-CIII, SCOUT, FAR RIGHT BEST, or, P 25 OVER ROCKS LEFT.

PYRAMID ROCK SWIFTS

CAUTION!

MOOSE FALLS NEXT MAP

38 Asam.. Rapids HEAVY SWIFTS ONLY

60

29 White Beaver Falls CIV-V LEDGE! PORTAGE ON RIGHT SIDE.

P 70

70

NO BRIDGE

30

SWIFTS

Pine Island Rapids CII EASY, TAKE LEFT SWEEP AROUND ISLAND...RIGHT SIDE LEDGEY.

STONE CAIRN

27 Opikwach Rapids CII-III, SCOUT FIRST! VOLUME STACKS AND HEAVY BOILS, or, P 20 OVER ROCKS ON RIGHT.

ROCK FORMATION

80

100

90

21

12 SWIFTS ONLY, ON BLUFF. ▲

H₂O MONITOR

Long Lake

2 ▲

110

CIII's

Long Lake Falls 11

P 15 P 15

CANYON RAPIDS DETAIL- BOTTOM LEFT

SERIOUS SHIT!

24 **Split Chute** BELOW

22 CI EASY

26

25 BELOW

23 **Beaver Dam Falls** CII-III SCOUT FIRST! PORTAGE CENTER ISLAND 35m. ▲ EXCELLENT.

Island Hill Falls P 40! BELOW

Wolf Rapids 14-15

CI START

CII-CIII 1m. DROP OR CARRY OVER ROCKS 10m.

13 CII-III, KEEP RIGHT OF CENTER TO AVOID 1m. WAVES.

25 **Left or Else Rapids** CII-CIII

P 30 OR LINE

24 **Split Chute** DO NOT RUN!

P 15

Caution!

Caution!

STRONG CURRENT

▲

Canyon Rapids Caution!

LOOKS GOOD AT CII START, BUT NO WAY OUT ONCE YOU COMMIT!

21

!

P 265

CV LEDGE

P 225

← **Childs Falls** →

20 CII LEFT SIDE

19 CII VOLUME. SCOUT!

18 CI ACCESS, STAY LEFT!

P 15

HEAVY WASH!

P 35 **Crooked Falls** 16

▲

HEAVY SURGE AND BOILS!

17 **Kamaskawak Rapids** CII VOLUME, STAY LEFT, CLOSE TO ROCK WALL.

MAP 3

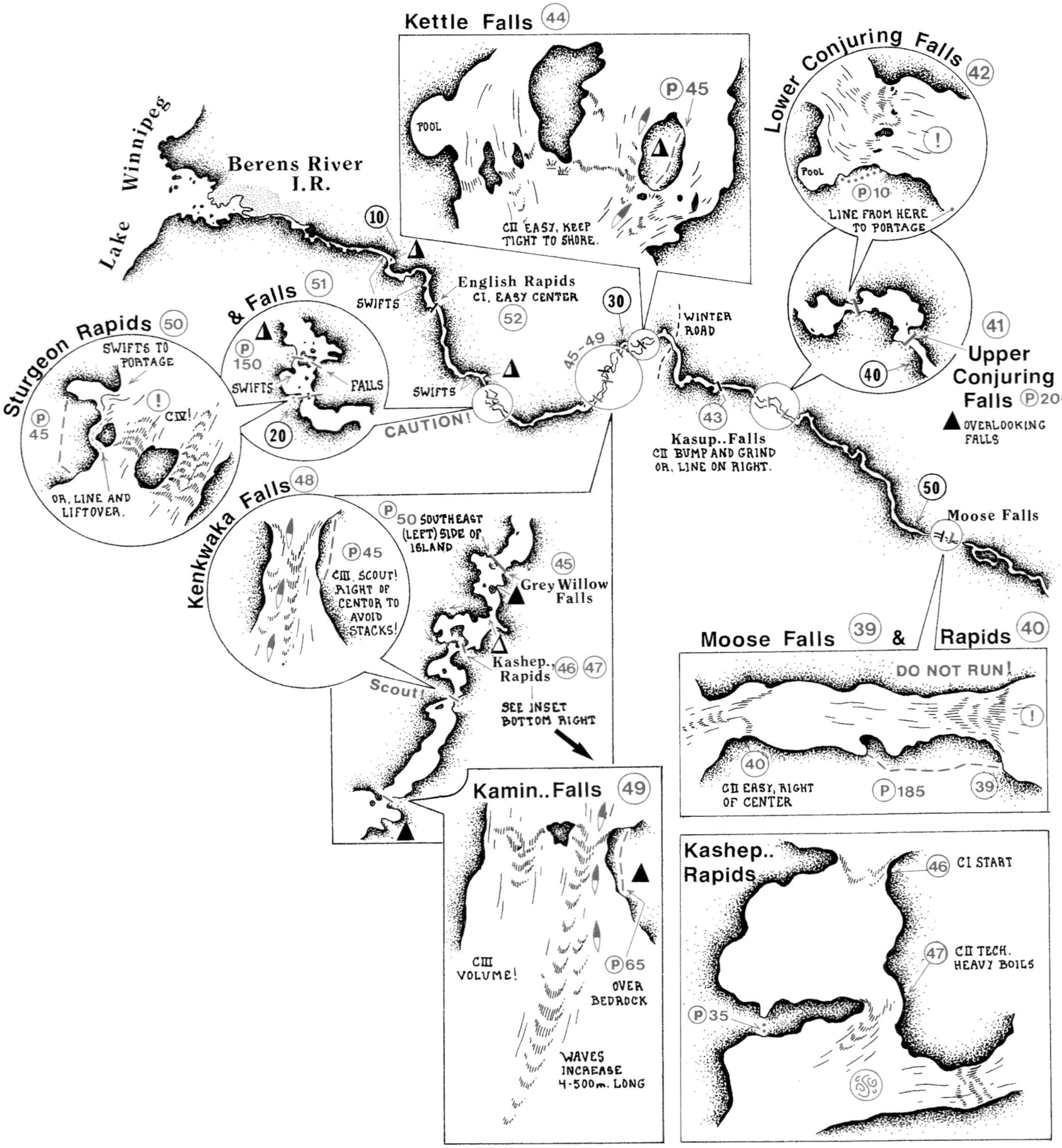
Kettle Falls 44
POOL
P 45
CII EASY, KEEP TIGHT TO SHORE.
Lower Conjuring Falls 42
POOL
!
P 10
LINE FROM HERE TO PORTAGE
Lake Winnipeg
Berens River I.R.
10
SWIFTS
English Rapids
CI, EASY CENTER
(52)
30
WINTER ROAD
45–49
41
Upper Conjuring Falls P 200
40
OVERLOOKING FALLS
Sturgeon Rapids 50
SWIFTS TO PORTAGE
!
CIV!
P 45
OR, LINE AND LIFTOVER.
& Falls (51)
P 150
SWIFTS
FALLS
SWIFTS
20
CAUTION!
43
Kasup..Falls
CII BUMP AND GRIND OR, LINE ON RIGHT.
50
Moose Falls
Kenkwaka Falls 48
P 45
CIII, SCOUT! RIGHT OF CENTER TO AVOID STACKS!
Scout!
P 50 SOUTHEAST (LEFT) SIDE OF ISLAND
45
Grey Willow Falls
Kashep.. Rapids 46 47
SEE INSET BOTTOM RIGHT
Moose Falls 39 & Rapids 40
DO NOT RUN!
!
40
CII EASY, RIGHT OF CENTER
P 185
39
Kamin..Falls 49
CIII VOLUME!
P 65
OVER BEDROCK
WAVES INCREASE 4-500m. LONG
Kashep.. Rapids
46 CI START
47 CII TECH. HEAVY BOILS
P 35

Rivers of Atikaki

Waterplay on the Bloodvein River

Polyphemus moth, Berens River

Stephanie Aykroyd

Hap Wilson

Hap Wilson

Leyond moose encounter

Hap Wilson

Stephanie Aykroyd

Wood Lily

Berens River sunburst

Whitewood Falls, Grass River

Hap Wilson

Tobacco offering at the Tramping Lake pictographs

Hap Wilson

Grass River sunset

Grass River reflections

Hap Wilson

Hap Wilson

Hap Wilson

Lining rapids on the Hayes

Shad Fly sunset, Swampy Lake on the Hayes

Night fires — Great Island campsites

Tadoule village youths — nonchalent about the approaching fires

The world takes on an amber glow as the wildfires intensify

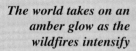

Smiling child, Tadoule village

Beyond the conflagration — tranquil sunset

Land of Little Sticks
Cochrane, Thlewiaza
Caribou Rivers

Waymarker and caribou antlers — Wolverine River

"Head" stone along the Caribou — an ancient "waymarker" for travelling Dene

Waymarker and caribou antlers — Wolverine River

A brief moment of rest while lining up the East River

Caribou crossing at Long Lake on the Caribou River

The Middle Track

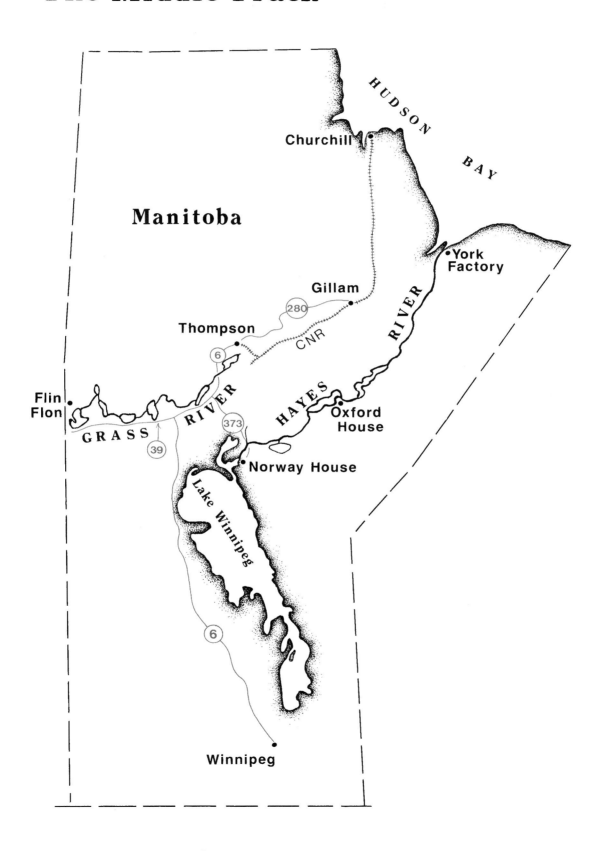

THE MIDDLE TRACK

THREE CENTURIES OF EXPLORATION

The Grass and the Hayes Rivers are featured within this section. Although the "Middle Track" technically once referred to the Fox River route, the track lying between the Nelson in the north and the Hayes in the south, we've chosen to use this location to depict those representative rivers lying within the same cultural and geophysical middle provincial region.

Both routes were important prehistorically and archaeological findings attest to the importance of these waterways in Native ideology and survival. Today, the rivers remain important to the First Nations people for the same reasons, including a growing tourist trade that envelops tradition and wise use of the land. Some of the province's most celebrated rock art sites, located at their most northerly limit, can be found at Tramping Lake on the Grass, Molsen Lake just south of the Hayes, and at Oxford and Knee Lakes.

Historically, the Hayes was first established as a major fur trade route, explored by the likes of Radisson in 1682, Henry Kelsey in 1690, David Thompson in 1784, Franklin in 1819, and Tyrrell in 1892. Thompson, Samuel Hearne and J.B. Tyrrell plied the waters of the Grass, opening "middle" Canada to exploration, trade and mineral discovery.

One of the most remarkable historical feats took place on the Hayes between the years 1811 and 1815 when the river was used for transporting supplies and settlers establishing a colony in the Canadian interior along the Red River. Even farm equipment and livestock were hauled 650km upstream to Lake Winnipeg by York Boat to supply the flourishing farms of the Red River colony, now present day Winnipeg and Selkirk.

Tyrrell's explorations at the turn of the century opened up a new spirit of development along the Grass watershed when geological surveys discovered gold and copper. Several mines are still operating today. The upper reaches of the Grass is unique as it marks the natural boundary between the rugged granite outcroppings of the Precambrian Shield and the limestone lowlands that represent the northern extent of the great vast central plains.

The Grass River resides within the Boreal Shield Ecozone which is typified by pretentious displays of granite and greenstone bedrock and a gracious spread of coniferous forests. Black spruce and jackpine are most common but we have yet to witness a greater white spruce forest than that which we viewed along the shores of the Grass; magnificent and stately, home to a myriad of songbirds, its shade cooled us during the heat of the day, and at night, from its somber depths could be heard the industry of creatures both known and unverified.

The largest swath of metamorphosed sedimentary bedrock, or "greenstone", found in Manitoba, traces a path across the river corridor. This bedrock anomaly has biological significance in that it happens to be less acidic than normal Shield granite and this gives rise to several provincially rare floral species including: Northern Beech-fern (*Pheopteris connectilis*); Prairie Cliff-brake (*Pellaea occidentalis*); Large-leaved Pondweed (*Potamogeton amplifolius*); Northern Spikemoss (*Selaginella selaginoides*); and Smooth Woodsia (*Woodsia glabella*).

The Hayes, like the Grass, remains in its wild, unaltered state with few noticeable developments. The natural and human heritage resources of the Hayes, combined with an unspoiled environment, provide an outstanding wilderness experience. The Hayes is also unique because it shares with us two diverse ecological zones – both the Precambrian Shield along its upper reaches, and the Hudson Bay Lowlands. The upper river is resplendent in character with its miles of exciting whitewater stretches, drama of landscape etched by the artistry of time and geological process, while the lower river enters that austere morass of boreal slough that terminates at the edge of the Arctic Ocean.

While the Grass River is easily accessed and would appeal to all levels of outdoor enthusiasts, the Hayes remains aloof and whimsical in its total isolation, alluring and taunting with a vitality that remains undaunted through centuries of use.

THE HAYES RIVER

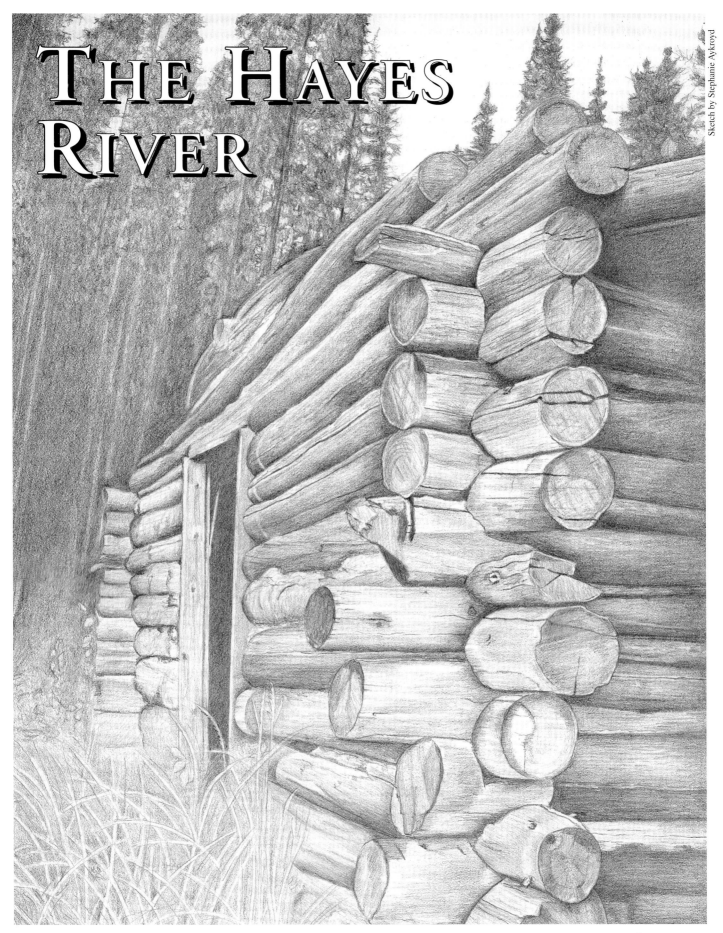

Sketch by Stephanie Aykroyd

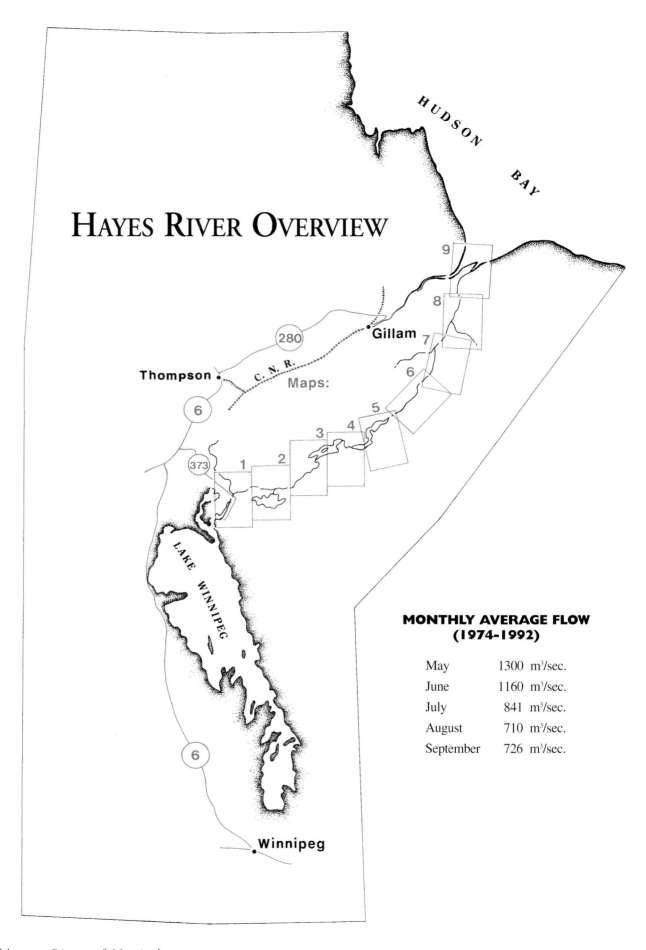

HAYES RIVER OVERVIEW

HUDSON BAY

9

8

280

Gillam

7

Thompson

C. N. R.

6

Maps:

6

5

373

3   4

1   2

LAKE WINNIPEG

6

Winnipeg

MONTHLY AVERAGE FLOW (1974-1992)

May	1300	m³/sec.
June	1160	m³/sec.
July	841	m³/sec.
August	710	m³/sec.
September	726	m³/sec.

HAYES RIVER

GENERAL INFORMATION

Classification: Intermediate (long technical CII's and isolation)

Distance: The Hayes River route is divided into 3 sections:
  Norway House to Painted Stone Portage – 105 km.
  Painted Stone Portage to Oxford House – 125 km.
  Oxford House to York Factory/Hudson Bay – 380 km.
  Total trip length: 610 km.

Elevation Drop: Beginning @ Painted Stone Portage @ 218 m.
  (715'), or .4m./km. (1.4'/km).

Time: Norway House to Oxford House – 8 to 10 days
  Oxford House to York Factory – 14 to 18 days

Number of Campsites: 94 or 1 campsite every 6.5 km.

Number of Rapids and Falls: 45 (numbered in sequence)

Number of Runnable Rapids: 43 (80% CI to CII tech.)

Portages: Easy Intermediate – 15 (3,245 m.)
  Creative Intermediate – 11 (2,395 m.)

Season: Early June through September

Maps Required: 63 H/13 63 I/4 63 I/5 63 I/6 63 I/7 63 I/8 63 I/9
53 L/12 53 L/13 53 L/14 53 L/15 53 M/2 53 M/1 53 M/8 53 N/5
53 N/12 53 N/11 53 N/14 54 C/3 54 C/6 54 C/7 54 C/10 54
C/15 54 C/16 54 F/1

Access: *By vehicle:* Starting at Norway House or Sea River Ferry
  Crossing on the Nelson; take hwy #373 (improved gravel road) off route #6 from Thompson. Outfitters services
  available in Thompson or Norway House.
  By Air: Charter flight from Thompson to Oxford House
  or Norway House.

Egress: Air charter pick-up (floatplane) and return to either
Thompson or Gillam. Via Rail from Gillam to Thompson.
Paddling the coast from York Factory and up the Nelson River to
Gillam is *not* recommended.

Features: Once a link from Hudson Bay to Canada's new territory beyond Lake Winnipeg, the Hayes tells a story of endurance,
hardship and perseverance. Historically, the river knows no equal
in the founding and exploration of this country. Oddly enough
there is far less traffic along this Heritage River candidate waterway than there was 200 years ago. Past history combined with the
thrill of whitewater and an ever-changing scenery make the Hayes
an excellent choice for the discriminating paddler.

The Hayes is the largest naturally flowing river in Manitoba
and drains the third largest watershed. Earth-science, flora and
fauna are typical of northern Shield eco-zones while the lower
reaches near Hudson Bay exhibit lowland features and its own
micro-climate resulting from a proximity to the cold Arctic weather mass.

WHITEWATER CHARACTERISTICS AND GENERAL HAZARDS

The majority of the Hayes route is under the influence of weather
borne by the prevailing westerlies; this is a plus when travelling the
larger lakes such as Oxford and Knee. These lakes can also get
very rough and additional travelling time should be built into your
schedule. The influence of Hudson Bay creates cooler air, fog and
winds from the north and east which could also hinder progress
nearing York Factory. Weather is unpredictable and changes quickly so be prepared.

There are many technical class II rapids with ledge-type
drops; some can be run while others should be lined. Lining skills
are a requirement although running with spray decks is optional.
The chance of broaching rocks is quite high, especially during
periods of reduced flow; this means safety and rescue skills are
crucial. This river also demands good skills involving ferries and
eddy turns as there are many cross-channel manoeuvers requiring
quick judgement calls.

MAP 1

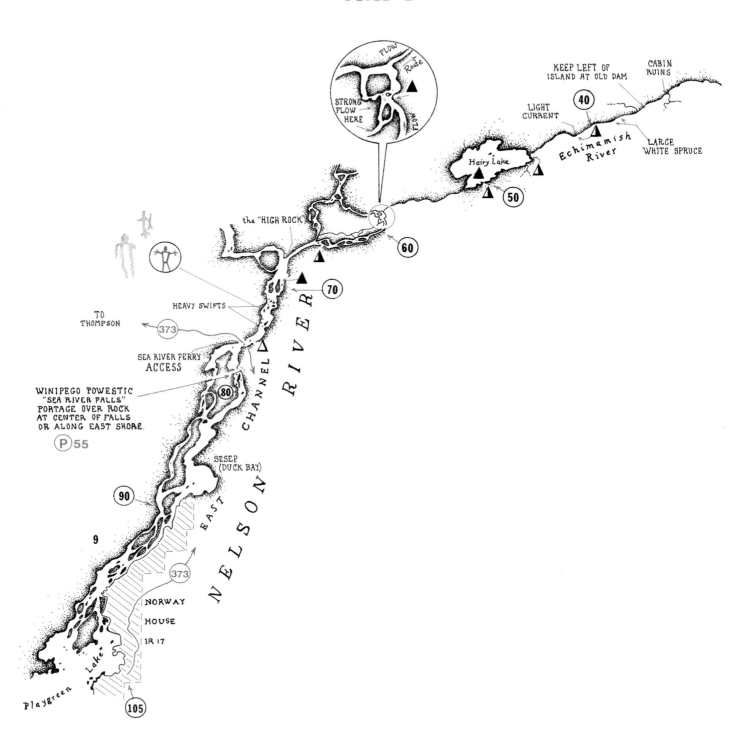

FLOW

Route

STRONG FLOW HERE

FLOW

KEEP LEFT OF ISLAND AT OLD DAM

CABIN RUINS

LIGHT CURRENT

40

Echimamish River

LARGE WHITE SPRUCE

Hairy Lake

50

the "HIGH ROCK"

60

70

HEAVY SWIFTS

TO THOMPSON

373

SEA RIVER FERRY ACCESS

WINIPEGO POWESTIC "SEA RIVER FALLS" PORTAGE OVER ROCK AT CENTER OF FALLS OR ALONG EAST SHORE.

(P)55

EAST CHANNEL

NELSON RIVER

80

SESEP (DUCK BAY)

90

9

373

NORWAY HOUSE

1R 17

Playgreen Lake

105

MAP 2

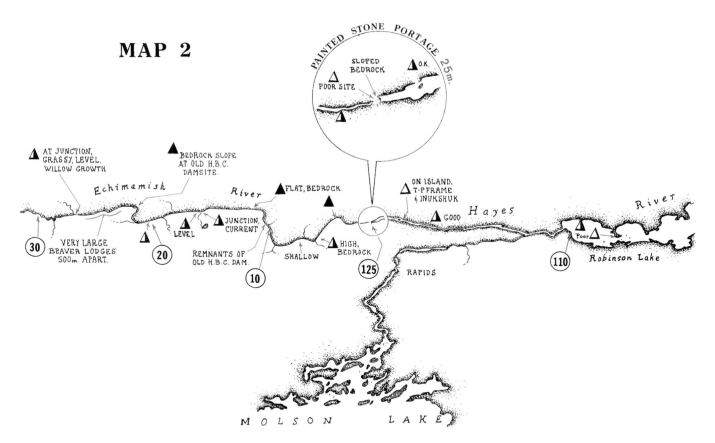

PAINTED STONE PORTAGE 25m.

POOR SITE

SLOPED BEDROCK

O.K.

AT JUNCTION, GRASSY, LEVEL. WILLOW GROWTH

BEDROCK SLOPE AT OLD H.B.C. DAMSITE.

Echimamish

River

FLAT, BEDROCK

ON ISLAND, T-P FRAME & INUKSHUK

Hayes

River

LEVEL

JUNCTION, CURRENT

GOOD

(30)

VERY LARGE BEAVER LODGES 500m. APART.

(20)

REMNANTS OF OLD H.B.C. DAM.

SHALLOW

HIGH, BEDROCK

(110)

Poor

Robinson Lake

(10)

(125)

RAPIDS

MOLSON LAKE

An uncommon moment – crossing Knee Lake during a calm

Hap Wilson

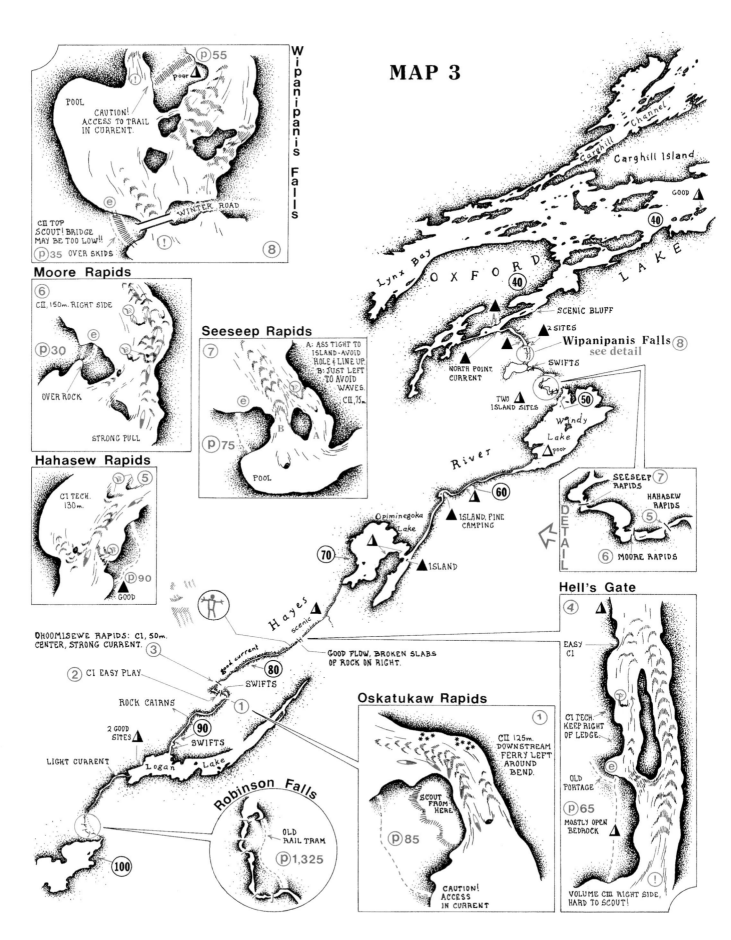

MAP 3

Wipanipanis Falls

(p)55

Poor △

POOL

CAUTION!
ACCESS TO TRAIL
IN CURRENT.

(t)

(e)

WINTER ROAD

CII TOP
SCOUT! BRIDGE
MAY BE TOO LOW!!
(p)35 OVER SKIDS

(!)

(8)

Moore Rapids

(6)

CII, 150m. RIGHT SIDE

(p)30 (e)

OVER ROCK

STRONG PULL

Seeseep Rapids

(7)

A: ASS TIGHT TO
ISLAND-AVOID
HOLE & LINE UP.
B: JUST LEFT
TO AVOID
WAVES.
CII, 75m.

(e)

(p)75

B   A

POOL

Hahasew Rapids

(5)

CI TECH.
130m.

(p)90

GOOD

OHOOMISEWE RAPIDS: CI, 50m.
CENTER, STRONG CURRENT.

(2) CI EASY PLAY

(3)

ROCK CAIRNS

good current

(80)

(1)

SWIFTS

2 GOOD
SITES △

(90)

SWIFTS

LIGHT CURRENT

Logan   Lake

(100)

Robinson Falls

OLD
RAIL TRAM

(p)1,325

Carghill Channel

Carghill Island

GOOD △

(40)

Lynx Bay   OXFORD   (40)   LAKE

SCENIC BLUFF

2 SITES

Wipanipanis Falls (8)
see detail

NORTH POINT,
CURRENT

SWIFTS

TWO △
ISLAND SITES

(50)

Windy
Lake
△ poor

River

(60)

Opiminegoka
Lake

△

(70)

△ ISLAND, PINE
CAMPING

△ ISLAND

DETAIL

SEESEEP (7)
RAPIDS

HAHASEW
RAPIDS

(5)

(6) MOORE RAPIDS

Hayes   scenic

GOOD FLOW, BROKEN SLABS
OF ROCK ON RIGHT.

Hell's Gate

(4) △

EASY
CI

CI TECH.
KEEP RIGHT
OF LEDGE.

(e)

OLD
PORTAGE

(p)65

MOSTLY OPEN
BEDROCK

△

(!)

VOLUME CIII RIGHT SIDE,
HARD TO SCOUT!

Oskatukaw Rapids

(1)

CII 125m.
DOWNSTREAM
FERRY LEFT
AROUND
BEND.

SCOUT
FROM
HERE

(p)85

CAUTION!
ACCESS
IN CURRENT

HAYES RIVER JOURNAL

It's not as if I hadn't paddled at night before. After all, there does arise the occasion when a guide must make a decision that may challenge common practice through circumstance. What's a river expedition without the element of risk? Without due hardship, trepidation or uncertainty? All components of high adventure.

Three weeks into a 630 kilometre trip toward Hudson Bay, our stalwart group of ten paddlers had survived the more than 75 rapids – which translates into 750 opportunities to mess up. There were a couple of token swampings, nothing serious, a few laughs, some tense moments playing in the shelves and eddies of the high water current. It wasn't until I mentioned we were entering polar bear country that the general mood changed.

Past "the rock" there were no more rapids, just fast current for the remaining 170 kilometres to York Factory and Hudson Bay. We had to make up some time in order to catch our flight from York Factory to Gillam where we would hook up with the train and return to Thompson. There were three days left to do it in, but I knew that the winds off Tu Cho, the "big water" of Hudson Bay as the Dene called it, would be pounding our canoes from the north. We were also saving an extra day for exploring the estuary of the Hayes near York Factory.

The only plausible solution was to raft through the night — lash the five canoes together and let the current carry us downriver as we slept. I elected myself as the night watch and rudderman while the others nestled in their sleeping bags to ward off the sub-Arctic chill.

Few of us slept. It was one of those portentous nights, seldom experienced by normal people who, logically, travel by day only; the canoes drifted in lazy circles under a canopy of a million stars and the most spectacular display of northern lights any of us could recall.

"Waussnodae" — *illumination ... dance of the deadmen:* known to the First Nations as a phenomenon caused by the waves splashing against the rocky shores of the northern seas, producing a reflected glow. None needed any other explanation. A caribou followed us along the shore for over a kilometre but could not keep up with the current speed of our Huck Finn craft.

Completely entranced by the light-show we almost unknowingly floated past "Quiche matauang," the big fork where the Gods River joined the Hayes. Our float speed increased dramatically between ever-widening banks but as suspected, the wind appeared with the first light of day. We soon had to dismantle the rafted canoes and opted to paddle against the relentless wind until midday when we just couldn't make any headway — even with the strong current. We slept on the rocky beach still 35 kilometres short of York Factory, unable to go any further.

The wind calmed at dusk and once again we paddled through the night under the soft fluorescent glow of stars and northern lights, totally entranced by the experience. We stopped briefly on two occasions to rest, working our way northeast in current and tidal flow towards the great sea.

Reaching the estuary during peak tidal draw the canoes were almost propelled even faster, uncontrollably towards the yellow beacon of the rising sun — past the security of the diminishing shoreline.

We stopped, built a warming fire, kept watch for polar bears, drank toxic coffee and waited for the infamous Bay fog to break. We were only 200 metres from the landing at York Factory.

———— 🐚 ————

No other Canadian river flowing into the great northern sea bestows as colourful a history as does Manitoba's Hayes River.

The Churchill and the Nelson, the only two watercourses larger than the Hayes flowing into Hudson Bay, have been silenced by hydro-electric development; the Hayes has escaped this fate and remains, to this day, virtually as pristine as it was when Hudson's Bay Company traders first plied its waters in the 1680's.

Although this eminent "gateway" corridor to Canada's interior was known to the indigenous people by many names, it was anglicized formally by Pierre Radisson in 1684 as the Hayes River after Sir James Hayes, secretary to Prince Rupert.

York Factory post was established at the estuary at this time and would gainfully serve the Hudson's Bay Company as a central collection and dispatch centre for the fur trade over the next 150 years, continu-

York Factory – a step back into the fur-trade era

ing to operate as a base for surveyors and geologists – the likes of Bell and Tyrrell, until it finally closed its doors in 1957.

The Hayes was selected as the choice water route to the interior chiefly because of the difficult and dangerous current that characterized both the Nelson and Churchill rivers; the current of the Hayes, although strong, could still be navigated upstream by trade canoe and later York boats, simply by the ability to line or track along the open shore or by lifting over the shelves of bedrock at the many falls and rapids.

Not only was the Hayes River used for exploring Canada's interior and securing trade with the Cree, it was also used

MAP 4

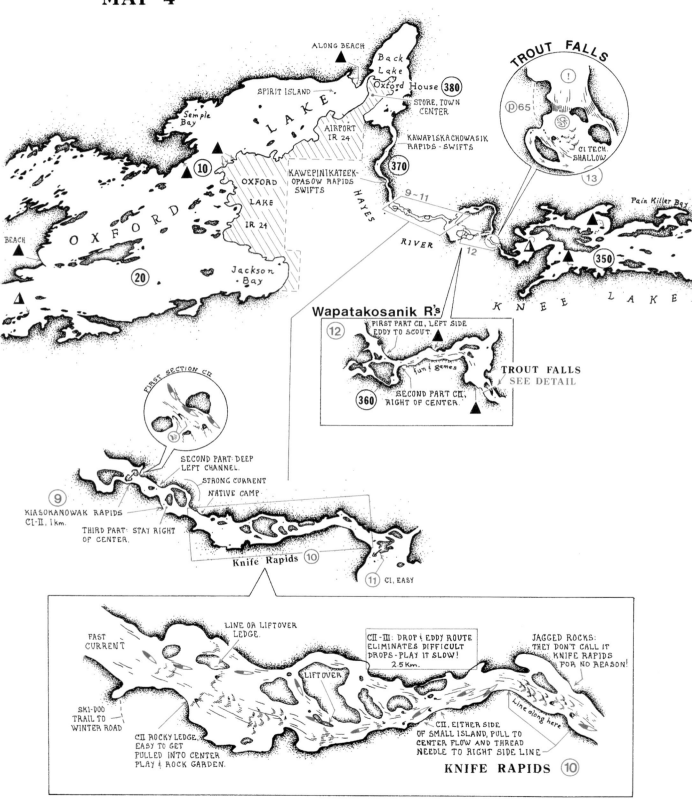

ALONG BEACH

Back Lake

Oxford House (380)

SPIRIT ISLAND

STORE, TOWN CENTER

Semple Bay

L A K E

AIRPORT IR 24

KAWAPISKACHOWASIK RAPIDS - SWIFTS

(370)

(10)

KAWEPINIKATEEK-OPASOW RAPIDS SWIFTS

BEACH

OXFORD LAKE IR 24

O X F O R D   L A K E

(20)

Jackson Bay

HAYES

RIVER

9~11

12

TROUT FALLS

(p)65

!

CI TECH. SHALLOW.

(13)

Pain Killer Bay

(350)

K N E E   L A K E

Wapatakosanik R's

(12) FIRST PART CII, LEFT SIDE EDDY TO SCOUT.

fun & games

(360) SECOND PART CII, RIGHT OF CENTER.

TROUT FALLS SEE DETAIL

FIRST SECTION CII

SECOND PART: DEEP LEFT CHANNEL.

STRONG CURRENT

NATIVE CAMP

(9)

KIASOKANOWAK RAPIDS CI-II, 1km.

THIRD PART: STAY RIGHT OF CENTER.

Knife Rapids (10)

(11) CI, EASY

FAST CURRENT

LINE OR LIFTOVER LEDGE.

CII-III: DROP & EDDY ROUTE ELIMINATES DIFFICULT DROPS - PLAY IT SLOW! 2.5 Km.

JAGGED ROCKS: THEY DON'T CALL IT KNIFE RAPIDS FOR NO REASON!

LIFTOVER

SKI-DOO TRAIL TO WINTER ROAD

CII ROCKY LEDGE, EASY TO GET PULLED INTO CENTER PLAY & ROCK GARDEN.

Line along here

CII, EITHER SIDE OF SMALL ISLAND, PULL TO CENTER FLOW AND THREAD NEEDLE TO RIGHT SIDE LINE

KNIFE RAPIDS (10)

MAP 5

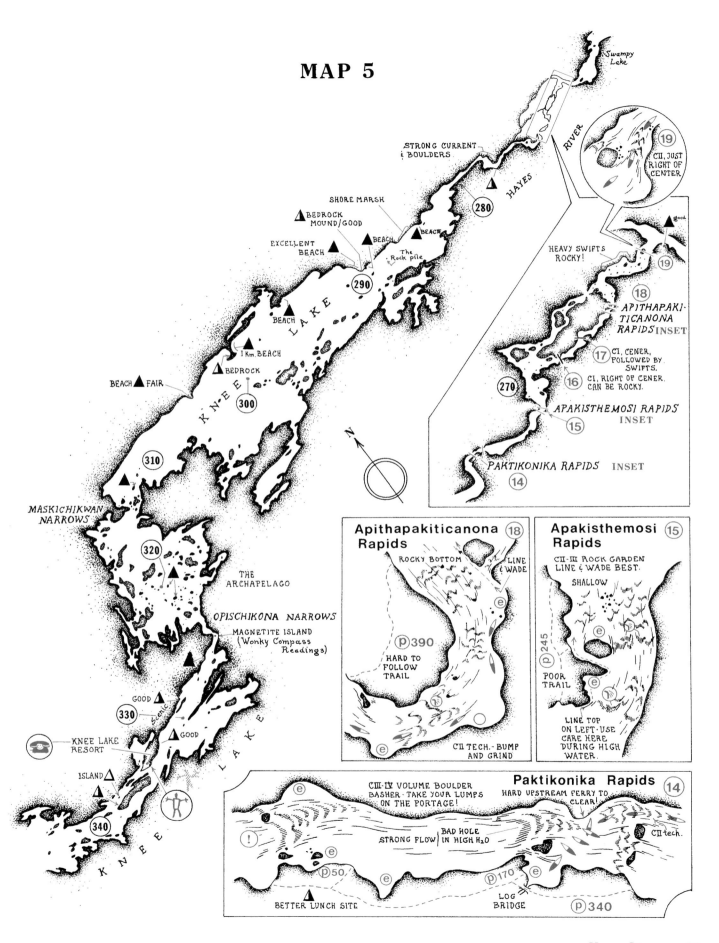

Swampy Lake

STRONG CURRENT & BOULDERS

HAYES RIVER

(280)

19 CII, JUST RIGHT OF CENTER

SHORE MARSH

BEDROCK MOUND/GOOD

BEACH

BEACH

good

19

HEAVY SWIFTS ROCKY!

EXCELLENT BEACH

The Rock pile

(290)

18

APITHAPAKI-TICANONA RAPIDS INSET

BEACH

17 CI, CENER, FOLLOWED BY SWIFTS.

1 Km. BEACH

16 CI, RIGHT OF CENER. CAN BE ROCKY.

BEDROCK

(270)

APAKISTHEMOSI RAPIDS INSET

BEACH FAIR

(300)

KNEE LAKE

15

(310)

PAKTIKONIKA RAPIDS INSET

14

MASKICHIKWAN NARROWS

(320)

THE ARCHAPELAGO

N

OPISCHIKONA NARROWS

MAGNETITE ISLAND (Wonky Compass Readings)

Apithapakiticanona Rapids 18

ROCKY BOTTOM

LINE & WADE

e

p 390

HARD TO FOLLOW TRAIL

Apakisthemosi Rapids 15

CII-III ROCK GARDEN LINE & WADE BEST.

SHALLOW

e

p 245

POOR TRAIL

e

LINE TOP ON LEFT-USE CARE HERE DURING HIGH WATER.

GOOD

Scenic

(330)

GOOD

KNEE LAKE RESORT

CII TECH.- BUMP AND GRIND

ISLAND

(340)

KNEE LAKE

Paktikonika Rapids 14

e

CIII-IV VOLUME BOULDER BASHER- TAKE YOUR LUMPS ON THE PORTAGE!

HARD UPSTREAM FERRY TO CLEAR!

!

e

BAD HOLE STRONG FLOW IN HIGH H₂O

CII tech.

p 50

e

p 170

e

BETTER LUNCH SITE

LOG BRIDGE

p 340

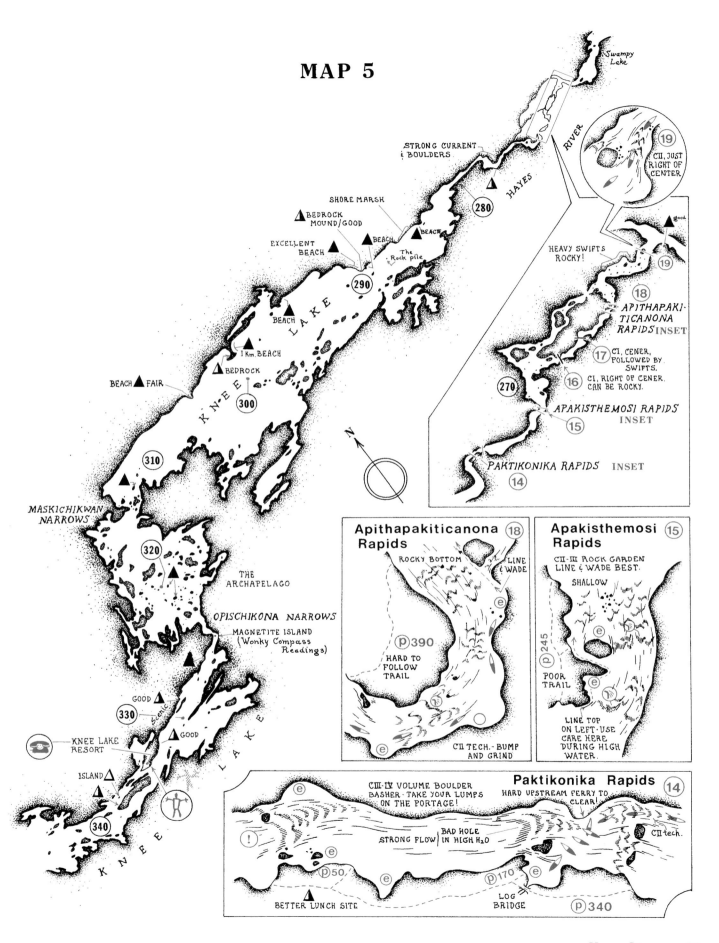

MAP 6

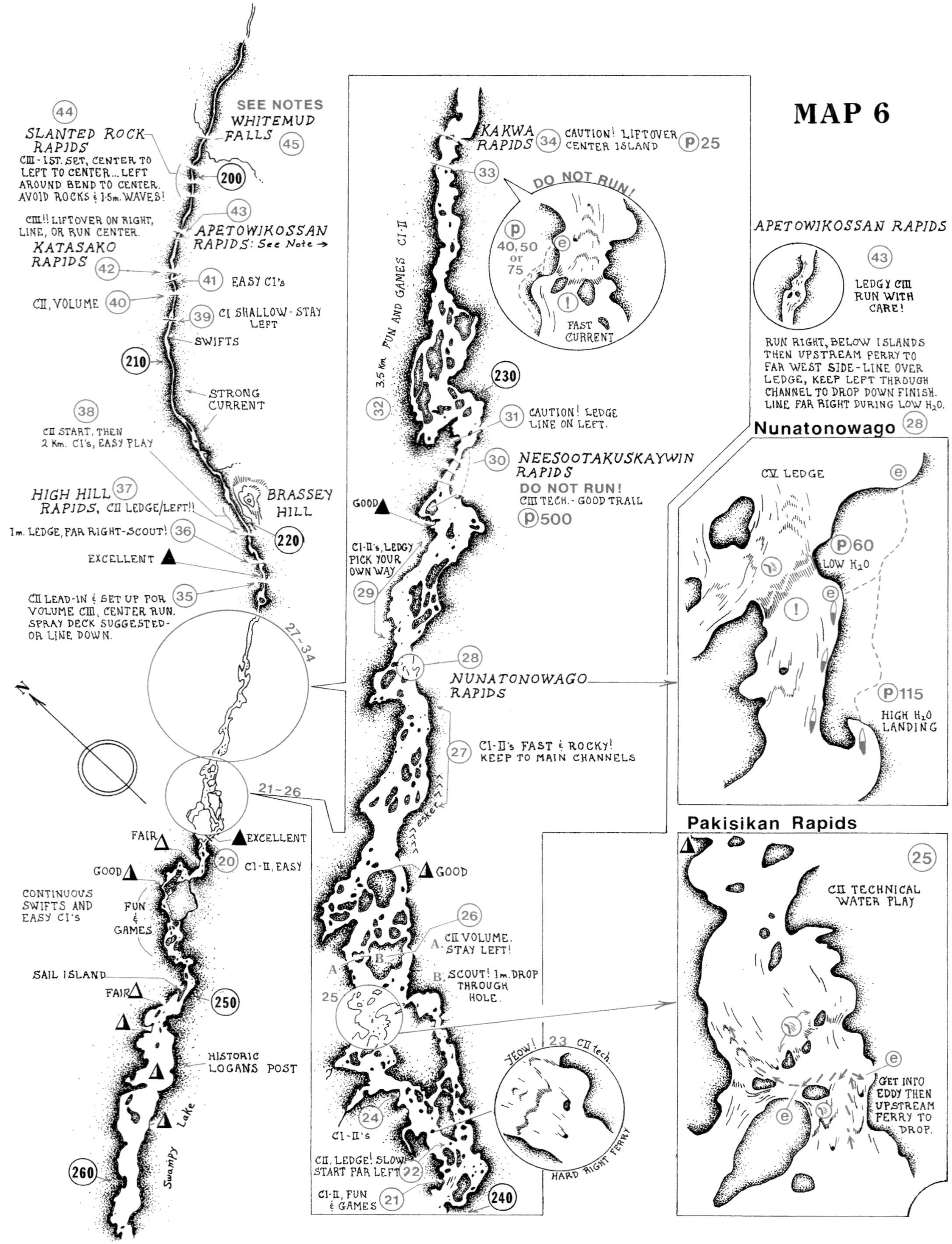

SEE NOTES
WHITEMUD FALLS
45
44
SLANTED ROCK RAPIDS
CIII - 1ST. SET, CENTER TO LEFT TO CENTER... LEFT AROUND BEND TO CENTER. AVOID ROCKS & 1.5m. WAVES!
200
43
CIII!! LIFTOVER ON RIGHT, LINE, OR RUN CENTER.
APETOWIKOSSAN RAPIDS: See Note →
KATASAKO RAPIDS
42
41
EASY CI's
CII, VOLUME
40
39
CI SHALLOW - STAY LEFT
SWIFTS
210
STRONG CURRENT
38
CII START, THEN 2 Km. CI's, EASY PLAY
BRASSEY HILL
HIGH HILL RAPIDS, CII LEDGE/LEFT!!
37
220
1m. LEDGE, FAR RIGHT-SCOUT!
36
EXCELLENT
CII LEAD-IN & SET UP FOR VOLUME CIII, CENTER RUN. SPRAY DECK SUGGESTED- OR LINE DOWN.
35
27-34
21~26
N
FAIR
EXCELLENT
20
CI-II, EASY
GOOD
CONTINUOUS SWIFTS AND EASY CI's
FUN & GAMES
SAIL ISLAND
FAIR
250
HISTORIC LOGANS POST
Swampy Lake
260
KAKWA RAPIDS
34
CAUTION! LIFTOVER CENTER ISLAND
P 25
33
DO NOT RUN!
P 40,50 or 75
FAST CURRENT
3.5 Km FUN AND GAMES CI-II
32
230
31
CAUTION! LEDGE LINE ON LEFT.
30
NEESOOTAKUSKAYWIN RAPIDS
DO NOT RUN!
CIII TECH. - GOOD TRAIL
P 500
GOOD
CI-II's, LEDGY PICK YOUR OWN WAY
29
28
NUNATONOWAGO RAPIDS
27
CI-II's FAST & ROCKY! KEEP TO MAIN CHANNELS
esker
GOOD
26
A. CII VOLUME. STAY LEFT!
B. SCOUT! 1m. DROP THROUGH HOLE.
25
Yeow!
23 CII tech.
HARD RIGHT FERRY
24
CI-II's
CII, LEDGE! SLOW START FAR LEFT
22
CI-II, FUN & GAMES
21
240
APETOWIKOSSAN RAPIDS
43
LEDGY CIII RUN WITH CARE!
RUN RIGHT, BELOW ISLANDS THEN UPSTREAM FERRY TO FAR WEST SIDE-LINE OVER LEDGE, KEEP LEFT THROUGH CHANNEL TO DROP DOWN FINISH. LINE FAR RIGHT DURING LOW H₂O.
Nunatonowago 28
CV LEDGE
P 60
LOW H₂O
P 115
HIGH H₂O LANDING
Pakisikan Rapids
25
CII TECHNICAL WATER PLAY
GET INTO EDDY THEN UPSTREAM FERRY TO DROP.

by Lord Selkirk to transport settlers, animals and equipment up the dangerous rapids to Lake Winnipeg via the Hayes, Echimamish and upper Nelson River. Selkirk was determined to establish the Red River Settlement by any means possible. From then on, until the completion of the railroad connecting Manitoba with eastern Canada in 1870, the Hayes served as an entry port and travelway for interior settlers including the military.

The Hayes, although a candidate Heritage River since 1987, is still unprotected; Manitoba Hydro has identified nine potential sites for dam construction and two sites for flow diversion (into the Nelson). A video crew from CITY-TV in Toronto, including Bob Hunter, an ecology specialist and co-founder of Greenpeace, would join our expedition at Oxford House for the final two weeks of the trip. The video production would be used to help secure a foundation of public support for the protection of the Hayes.

Four of us started the trip at the Sea River Falls ferry crossing at the mouth of the Nelson River, about 15 kilometres downstream of Norway House. A driver was hired out of Thompson to shuttle us the 200 kilometres to the start point, then return with my vehicle to Thompson. We would have 22 days to cover the 630 kilometres and that included three rest days. That translated into 32 kilometres per travel day. In 1828, Sir George Simpson on his way to the Peace River made the same trip, upstream, in less than a week — over 100 kilometres per day! River current and technogear were to our advantage so in relative terms it all seemed feasible. At Oxford House Indian Reserve we would team up with the rest of the party for the final leg of the expedition. Flights were pre-booked with Gillam Air Service for the pick-up at York Factory. At Gillam we would catch the train back to Thompson.

The river is divided into six reaches (CHRS background study, Dodds, 1987), each with its own particular resource characteristic, heritage value and physiography. Two thirds of the trip would follow the heavily glaciated Precambrian shield topography while the last third empties through typical Hudson Bay Lowland slough, terminating at the tidal flats in the geologically young estuary.

Reach One: The Nelson River

The power of the "sea river" was felt as soon as we put our canoes into the green silt-laden waters of the Nelson. It didn't help that we also had a 40 kilometre per hour headwind to contend with and little leecover. Just upriver at the actual "sea falls," chief factor Belanger and at least one other Hudson's Bay Company employee had drowned back in the 1800's, setting a rather sombre tone to our expedition departure.

White and black spruce dominated the backshore swamps along the Nelson; surprisingly, though, the bugs were tolerable. Aspen, birch and willow grew along the irregular shoreline. One rock outcrop in a set of swifts sported a distinct native pictograph that could have been easily by-passed had we not taken that particular channel through a small archipelago of islands.

By the end of the day we had reached a historic campsite overlooking a large bedrock fracture zone and rapids at the confluence of the Echimamish River — the same campsite used by the Franklin expedition in the early 1800's. Heavy rain set in overnight and we used up one of our precious "rest" days waiting for decent travel weather.

Reach Two: The Echimamish River

More of a glorified creek — it was marked on David Thompson's map prepared for the Northwest Company in 1813 as "each a way mak mus brook"; in fractured Cree "ehkinum mumanis", or "the water drains away in different directions," depicting a more hydrological explanation. As a vital 67 kilometre link between the Hayes and the Nelson, this thin ribbon of brackish water lined with alder, bog and rock outcroppings was dammed at various locations in the early 1800's so as to provide enough water to float the heavily laden York boats.

Painted Stone Portage, barely 50 metres long, is a hydrological anomaly in that the narrow band of rock disperses the water in opposing directions. The Cree once worshipped a "spirit manitou" rock that was erected like an altar on the portage but white traders destroyed it claiming "the savages spent too much time loitering here and not attending to their duties." Unlike other typical bog environments the Echimamish offered several good camping sites along the corridor.

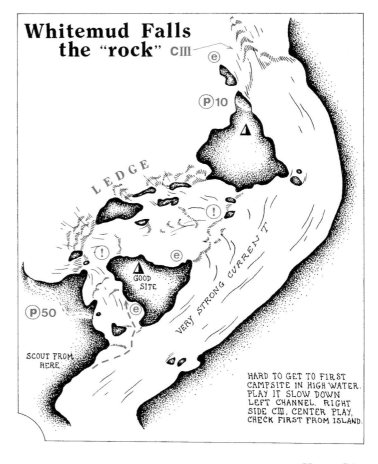

Whitemud Falls
the "rock"

HARD TO GET TO FIRST CAMPSITE IN HIGH WATER. PLAY IT SLOW DOWN LEFT CHANNEL. RIGHT SIDE CIII, CENTER PLAY, CHECK FIRST FROM ISLAND.

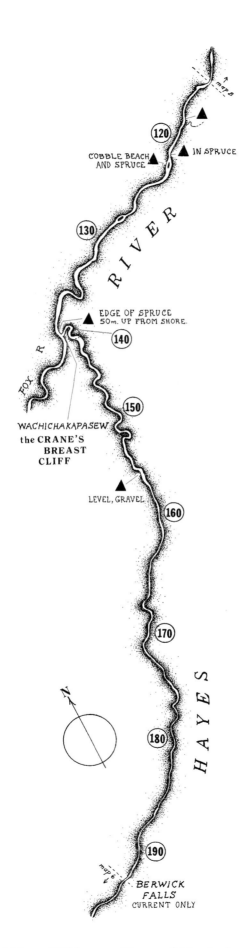

MAP 7

COBBLE BEACH AND SPRUCE

IN SPRUCE

RIVER

EDGE OF SPRUCE
50m. UP FROM SHORE.

FOX R

WACHICHAKAPASEW
the CRANE'S
BREAST
CLIFF

LEVEL, GRAVEL

N

HAYES

BERWICK
FALLS
CURRENT ONLY

Reach Three: The Upper Hayes

I shall long remember the rude and characteristic wilderness of the scenery which surrounded those falls; rocks piled on rocks hung in rude and shapeless masses over the agitated torrents which swept their bases, whilst the bright and variegated tints of the mosses and lichens, that covered the face of the cliffs, contrasting with the dark green of the pines, which crowned their summits, added both beauty and grandeur to the general effect of the scene.

So taken by the beauty of Robinson Falls, the first of a series of whitewater drops, Sir John Franklin actually slipped and almost disappeared along the wild chutes in 1819.

The river descent for us was thus initiated: a 220 metre drop to the Bay, starting off through a melange of precambrian lakes (all windy); a 1500 metre portage at Robinson Falls (easy walk alongside a dilapidated historic tramway used to haul York boats); a 10 kilometre gorge at Hell's Gate (insanely beautiful); a paddle past ancient dolmen stones (markers at native campsites); and our first semi-serious whitewater that required some serious scouting and bushwhacking to locate old portages.

Reach Four: Lake Country

Treacherous rapids (according to most written accounts) connect three lakes: Oxford, Knee and Swampy which span the next 175 kilometres. Luckily there was no wind on Oxford Lake and we crossed the 45 kilometre expanse under a searing 30° Celsius sunblast. There were few campsites on the lake save for a few isolated rocky clearings, but the fishing was excellent. On reaching the reserve settlement of Oxford House we were told that it might be to our advantage to camp along the beach across the lake from the village.

Good advice. It was a little unsettling to learn that the Indian kids sometimes pilfer tentsites and lob rocks at white visitors. I don't think this is too common an occurrence and most villagers seemed friendly and obliging. The bay was heavily littered and so full of garbage that it was piled high along the beach where we tried to search out a place to camp. Despite the presence of the 2,000 person settlement (and the localized refuse) the surrounding land maintained much of its original wild character.

The video crew arrived at the airport and we were soon paddling on our way once supplies had been replenished.

The next ten sets of rapids leaving Oxford Lake were tricky. Huge blocks of gneiss littered the river creating irregularly patterned rapids that were very hard to scout or read. The fractures of rock at Knife Rapids memorialized a previous canoeing party's attempt at running the rapids by permanently pin-

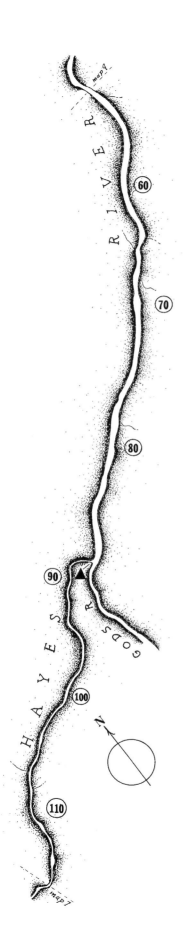

MAP 8

ning their broken canoe against a centre channel boulder. We navigated safely by combining running, ferrying and lining. At Oxford and Knee Lake we marvelled at the artistry of ancient rock paintings, located fragments of clay pipes at Trout Falls (a rest stop for the York boat oarsmen and one of five major portages along the route), and spent two gruelling days battling headwinds across Knee Lake. Unlike Oxford, the 65 kilometre expanse of Knee Lake provided several choice bedrock or beach campsites. Wind was our only nemesis. On exiting Knee Lake we passed a grave site along a portage, the marker dating back to 1868, and we camped at the south end of Swampy Lake in time to witness an amazing occurrence of mating shadflies. They streamed in the millions over our camp, wings aglow in the golden hue of the setting sun.

Reach Five: Shield Transition

We now entered a distinct and exciting river valley, dropping off the slope of the prehistoric Tyrrell Sea into a series of broken channels and unending bouldery rapids that flowed in a pool-and-riffle sequence. It was hard to fathom how early traders, land settlers in York boats, made their way upstream in the strong current. Brassey Hill, the highest point between Lake Winnipeg and Hudson Bay, affords an unprecedented view of over 36 surrounding lakes. At Whitemud Falls, or the "Rock" as it was once called, we took a much needed rest before the final drop to Hudson Bay. The charter of the river changed here; there were no more rapids and the steep 30 metre clay banks indicated that we were now in the lowland bay bio-region.

Reach Six: Hudson Bay Lowlands

From The Rock it should have been an easy four days to York Factory if one didn't hit any Bay winds. It remained as a spectacular "float" trip, easing our way down the steady current, building at the Fox River and again at the junction of the God's River, doubling the magnitude and greatness of the Hayes. The estuary, ever-changing, constantly bombarded by wind and mist off Hudson Bay, should be explored by any river traveller, as well as York Factory which remains intact as one of Canada's oldest settlements. Parks Canada operates a radio-phone for use by visitors requiring transportation back to Gillam, the only other service being a private commercial lodge adjacent to the post. Although we didn't see any polar bears, they do frequent the post. The lodge owner's dog was attacked by a young male bear....inside the porch, just last year.

The magnificence of the Hayes was felt by all...especially the experience of travelling by star and northern lights. The history, beauty and the silence of the Hayes River remain in our souls as a journey through time. Remarkably neither words nor film can capture its pure essence. H.W.

MAP 9

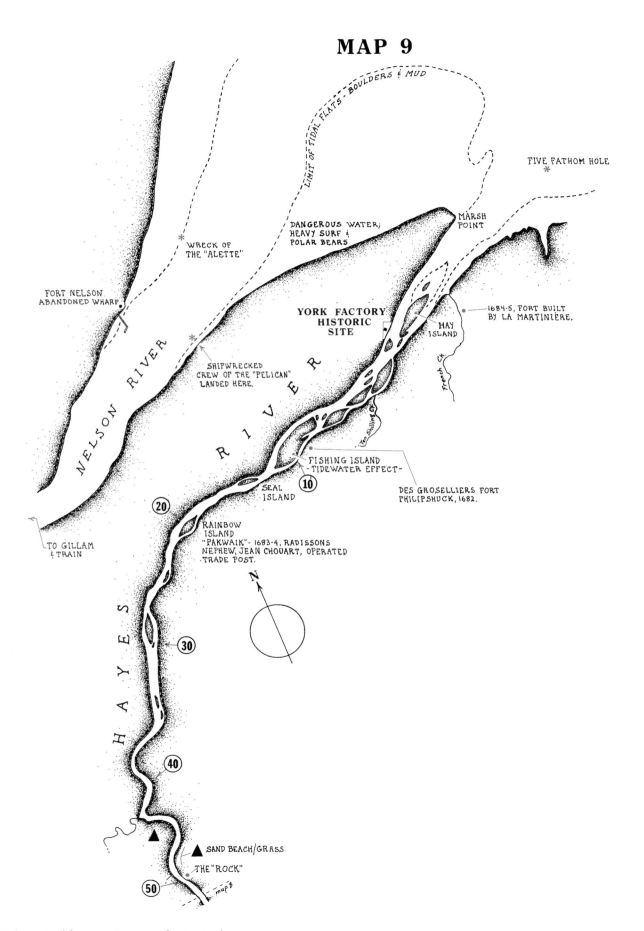

FIVE FATHOM HOLE

LIMIT OF TIDAL FLATS - BOULDERS & MUD

DANGEROUS WATER;
HEAVY SURF &
POLAR BEARS

MARSH
POINT

WRECK OF
THE "ALETTE"

FORT NELSON
ABANDONED WHARF

YORK FACTORY
HISTORIC
SITE

1684-5, FORT BUILT
BY LA MARTINIÈRE.

HAY
ISLAND

French Ck.

SHIPWRECKED
CREW OF THE "PELICAN"
LANDED HERE.

NELSON RIVER

RIVER

Ten Shilling Ck.

FISHING ISLAND
-TIDEWATER EFFECT-

SEAL
ISLAND

10

DES GROSELLIERS FORT
PHILIPSHUCK, 1682.

20

TO GILLAM
& TRAIN

RAINBOW
ISLAND
"PAKWAIK"- 1683-4, RADISSONS
NEPHEW, JEAN CHOUART, OPERATED
TRADE POST.

N

H A Y E S

30

40

▲

▲ SAND BEACH/GRASS

THE "ROCK"

50

map 8

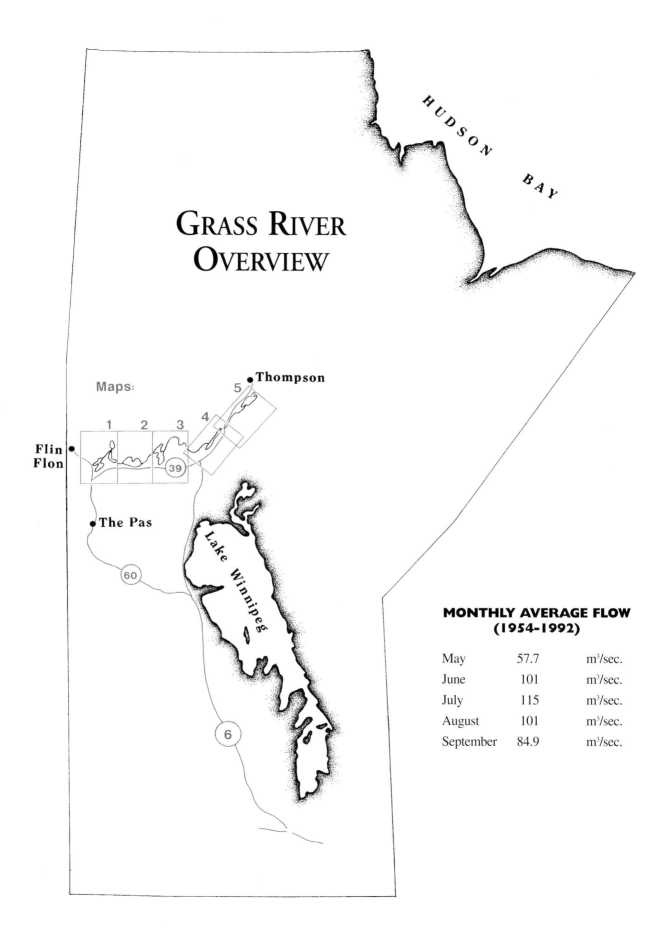

GRASS RIVER
OVERVIEW

HUDSON BAY

Maps:

1 2 3 4 5

39

Thompson

Flin Flon

The Pas

60

Lake Winnipeg

6

MONTHLY AVERAGE FLOW
(1954–1992)

May	57.7	m³/sec.
June	101	m³/sec.
July	115	m³/sec.
August	101	m³/sec.
September	84.9	m³/sec.

GRASS RIVER

GENERAL INFORMATION

Classification: Novice to Experienced Novice (some technical CI-CII's)

Distance: 370 km.
(From Cranberry Portage to Paint Lake Provincial Park)

Elevation Drop: 112 m. (367') or .3 m/km. (1'/km.)

Time: 21-24 days (can be paddled in various sections)

Number of Campsites: 42 or 1 campsite every 9 km.

Number of Rapids and Falls: 33 (not numbered)

Number of Runnable Rapids: 21 (95% CI–CII's)

Portages: 24 (4,790 m.)

Season: Late May through September

Maps Required: 63 K/9, 10, 11, 12, 15, 16 63 J/13, 14, 15 63 O/1, 2, 8 63P/5, 12

Access & Egress: Both access and egress are made easy by the existence of hwy #39 and hwy #6. Self-shuttles between Provincial Parks may be an option, or hire the services of outfitters located in Thompson or Wekusko.

Features: With the aid of Cree guides, David Thompson and Peter Fidler mapped the Grass River in 1794. Other notable explorers including Samuel Hearne travelled up the Grass in search of minerals, fur and personal glory. It is a river of history, both pre-historic and of whiteman's intrusion and exploitation of wealth. One of the finest pictograph sites in Manitoba is located at Tramping Lake but you had better not pass by without leaving some tobacco.

The Grass empties into the huge Nelson basin, both rivers acting as part of the "middle track" system of fur-trade and travel routes to the interior. Black spruce, balsam fir and tamarack are abundant along the forested wetlands bordering the Grass, and healthy stands of white spruce tower high above, creating both shade along the shore for canoeing, and for the forest denizens within the confines of this Boreal Shield Ecozone. Typical fauna is varied: an abundance of otter and beaver; a high density of woodland caribou, lynx, marten, moose, timber wolf, common loon, white pelican, osprey, bald eagle, boreal chorus frog, boreal owl, red-sided garter snake and least chipmunk, to name only a few.

WHITEWATER CHARACTERISTICS AND GENERAL HAZARDS

The Grass is not a difficult river, but it does have some very large lakes which demand some respect. Do not attempt any lake crossing in windy conditions. There is a shuttle boat service available at Wekusko Lake Falls Lodge; otherwise it is a long paddle along the north shore and some wide bay crossings. Add extra time to your trip for bad weather and wind delays. Rapids are generally shallow and should be scouted carefully before any attempt is made at running.

MAP 1

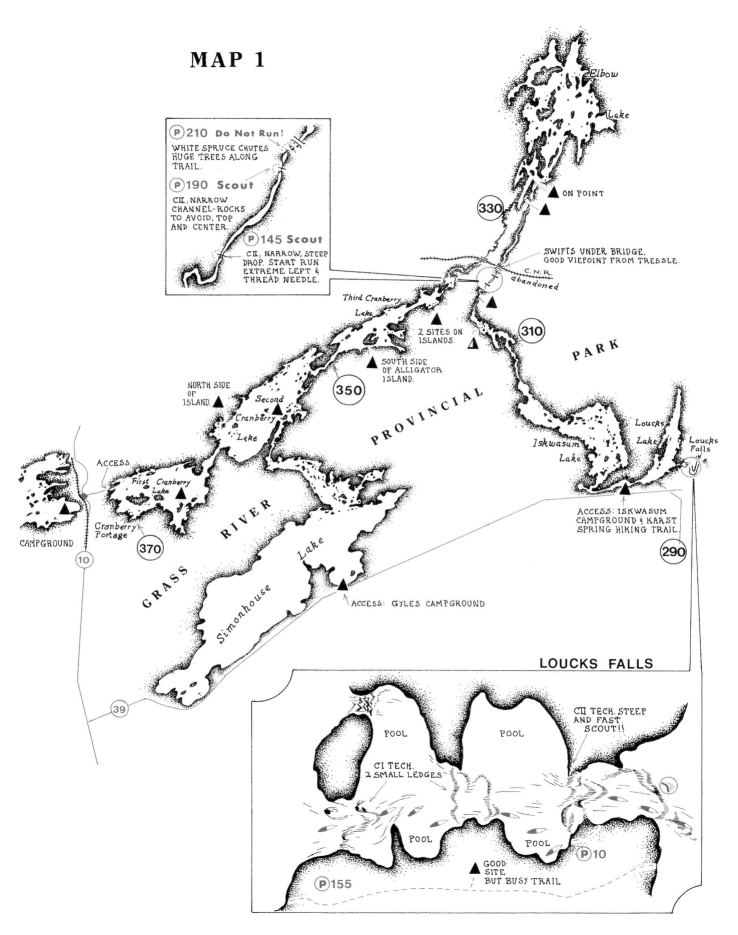

P 210 **Do Not Run!**
WHITE SPRUCE CHUTES HUGE TREES ALONG TRAIL.

P 190 **Scout**
CII, NARROW CHANNEL-ROCKS TO AVOID, TOP AND CENTER.

P 145 **Scout**
CII, NARROW, STEEP DROP. START RUN EXTREME LEFT & THREAD NEEDLE.

Elbow Lake

ON POINT

330

SWIFTS UNDER BRIDGE, GOOD VIEPOINT FROM TRESSLE.

C.N.R. abandoned

Third Cranberry Lake

2 SITES ON ISLANDS.

SOUTH SIDE OF ALLIGATOR ISLAND.

310

NORTH SIDE OF ISLAND.

Second Cranberry Lake

350

PROVINCIAL

PARK

Loucks Lake

Iskwasum Lake

Loucks Falls

ACCESS

First Cranberry Lake

370

Cranberry Portage

10

RIVER

GRASS

Simonhouse Lake

ACCESS: ISKWASUM CAMPGROUND & KARST SPRING HIKING TRAIL.

290

CAMPGROUND

ACCESS: GYLES CAMPGROUND

39

LOUCKS FALLS

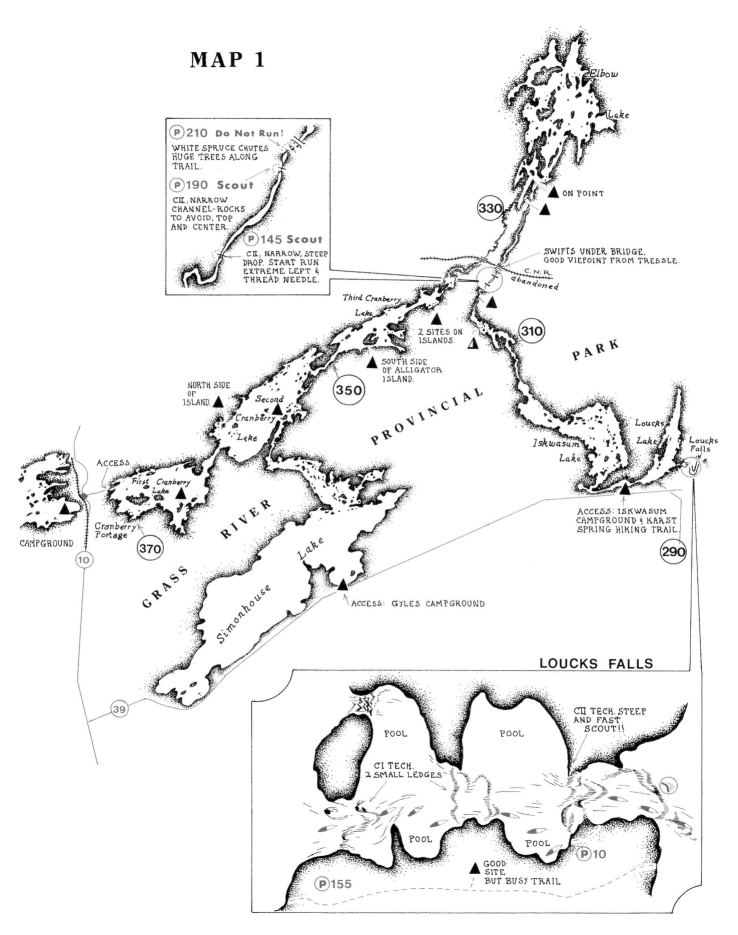

CII TECH. STEEP AND FAST. SCOUT!!

POOL

POOL

CI TECH. 2 SMALL LEDGES

POOL

POOL

P 10

P 155

GOOD SITE BUT BUSY TRAIL

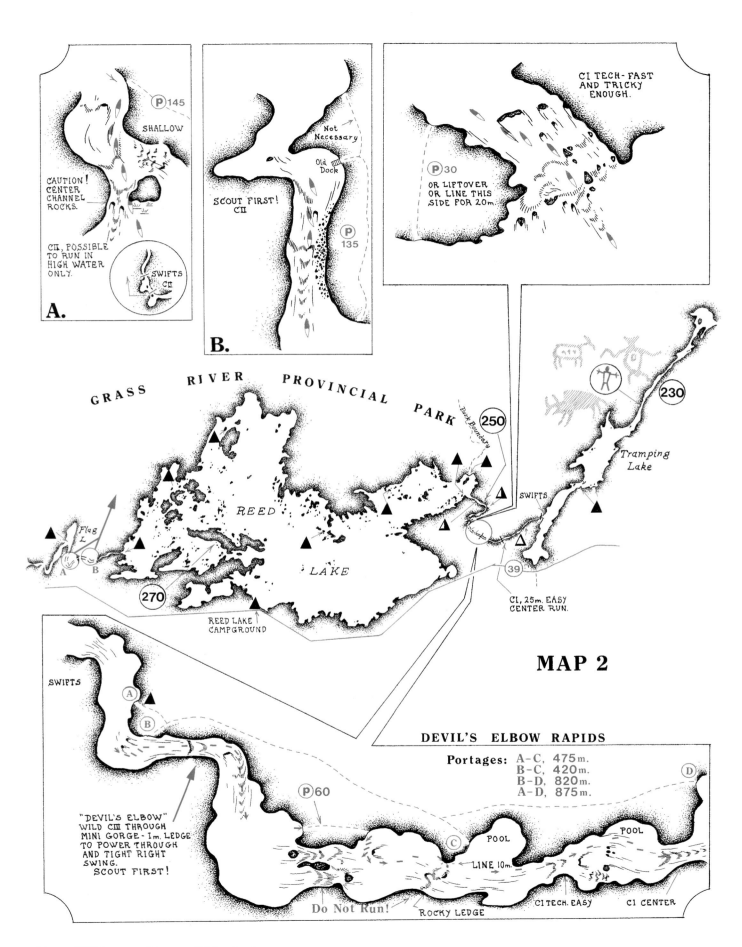

A.

SHALLOW

(P)145

CAUTION!
CENTER CHANNEL
ROCKS.

CII, POSSIBLE TO RUN IN HIGH WATER ONLY.

SWIFTS CII

B.

Not Necessary

Old Dock

SCOUT FIRST!
CII

(P)135

CI TECH- FAST AND TRICKY ENOUGH.

(P)30
OR LIFTOVER OR LINE THIS SIDE FOR 20m.

GRASS RIVER PROVINCIAL PARK

Park Boundary

(250)

(230)

Tramping Lake

SWIFTS

REED

Flag L.

A   B

LAKE

(270)

REED LAKE CAMPGROUND

(39)

CI, 25m. EASY CENTER RUN.

MAP 2

SWIFTS

(A)

(B)

(P)60

(C)   POOL

(D)

POOL

DEVIL'S ELBOW RAPIDS

Portages: A–C, 475 m.
B–C, 420 m.
B–D, 820 m.
A–D, 875 m.

"DEVIL'S ELBOW"
WILD CIII THROUGH
MINI GORGE - 1 m. LEDGE
TO POWER THROUGH
AND TIGHT RIGHT
SWING.
SCOUT FIRST!

LINE 10 m.

Do Not Run!   ROCKY LEDGE

CI TECH. EASY   CI CENTER

JOURNAL NOTES

At first we were hesitant about the inclusion of the Grass into a book that delineaed "wilderness-class`" rivers only. Reservations about the proximity of PTH #39, 392 and the Thompson Hwy. #6 made us think about the obtrusion of access and the effect it would have upon the experience. As it turns out, our fears were unfounded.

Like many northern rivers, the extent of travel by canoe today is only a faint whisper of what it was over a century ago. Albeit, the reasons for travel then were strictly for commerce and exploration, but the Grass River has assumed that rare dignity of having survived the intrusions of enterprising humankind despite the ease with which one can access the water.

The presence of roadside or larger scale Provincial Parks as a preferred measure of development is not as pervasive as hydro development, a fate that has befallen the mighty Churchill and Nelson rivers, but easy access does change the persona of a river nonetheless...and to some, that isn't necessarily a bad thing. The existence of mines along the route is unobtrusive, while those that have been abandoned now lend themselves to the discussion of "boom and bust" resource methodology, and artistic motifs for the camera buff. The occasional wayside park and motorboat are reminders to us canoeheads that road accessible wilderness is an ever-occurring "phenomenon" of multiple-use strategy. On the Grass, however, there are ample opportunities to leave the world behind and bask in the privacy of a river environment between the lakes, so to speak — a place reserved to those individuals with a soul for adventure.

The Grass River is, in fact, lined with grass. It's as peculiar as the clear water that comes through such a headstream of boreal morass and fen that one would quite expect the turbidity to resemble the complexion of root beer. The willow, alder and sedge landscape of the Manitoba dolomite lowlands blends well with the boreal Shield environment; this was evident during our first week's travel along the series of lakes forming the headwaters of the Grass. Because the river water is filtered through the vast substrata of peat, it carries very little silt or pollutants, natural or otherwise; in fact, the Clean Environment Commission designated the Grass as a protected "High Quality Surface Water" resource.

Historic Cranberry Portage marks the height of land between the Grass and Saskatchewan drainage basins. The H.B.C. ascended the Nelson and Grass from York Factory post over 200 years ago. Samuel Hearne was whisked up the Grass by his native guides in 1774, 5 & 6, whereupon he established the first H.B.C. inland post at Cumberland House, just west of the Manitoba border. Others followed.

Of the many posts built during the 1790s, only Weggs Post at Setting Lake has actually been found. The famous "standing chimney" (as shown on the map) is an example of early fur-trade architecture.

We reached an abandoned railway trestle south of Elbow Lake. The decrepit structure spanned a small canyon where the Grass split into two channels and a set of swifts washed gently at its log footings. The bridge was yet another monument of the "gold" boom, its aging timbers now feeling the pangs of time and the unrelenting elements of nature.

It wasn't until we reached Reed Lake that wind became a particular concern. For the most part, the prevailing westerlies allowed us to cruise comfortably along, taking shelter when needed along a shoreline, or pausing in the lee of an island; now, the 25 km. expanse of Reed Lake stretched out before us and storms were moving in from the southwest.

With the help of a spray deck we rode the swells which often topped two metres. In time we rounded the entrance to the northeast bay and eventually the shelter of the river once again. Paddling the lakes you get the chance to really see the changes in landscape. The glacially scoured upland, typical of the Shield area, now replaced the recumbent grass veld of the Cranberry chain of lakes; eskers, kames and drumlins — isolated glacial debris in the form of sinewy ridges, domes and forest-covered gravel mounds, made up part of the melange of new scenery along the Grass. In the confines of the river channel itself, where the world is linear and close, it was a Tolkien world, lost in the shadows of giant white spruce, balsam fir and poplar.

Woodland Caribou range throughout much of the upper reaches of the Grass; in fact, the islands on Reed Lake provide predator-free calving grounds and it is not unusual to get a glimpse of both cow and calf enjoying their island solitude as you quietly glide by.

We ran the top chute that marks the beginning of the long portage which Berard had marked on his early maps as a 2,110 m. carry. It was only just over 800 m, but most of the total distance can be lined or shot depending on the height of the water.

TRAMPING LAKE PICTOGRAPHS

"The two guys are both dead now," Tony told us, "violent deaths too...one in a car wreck, the other in a mining accident!" Tony, the owner of Wekusko Falls Lodge let us in on a local secret; apparently, the two white men had painted graffiti on the native rock art site and had paid for their disrespect, with their very lives. Earlier that day, before arriving at Wekusko, we had visited the site revered as one of Manitoba's best pictograph displays. Of all sites Stephanie and I had explored, this one definitely was the most magnificent. The shaman's journey depicted animals, birds and mythical figures, horned serpents and the fabric of which only the dream world of the artist could relate. The paintings were several tiers high, unusual when compared with most other rock art sites, as the majority of drawings were rendered from the canoe and not from the vantage of the rock face, although this site lent itself well to "perching." Upon scanning the shoreline further up the lake we found another small drawing that to our knowledge had yet to be recorded. A gift of tobacco was left and we made our own apologies for the thoughtlessness of the graffiti artists.

Wekusko Lake was the most intimidating body of water along the Grass string of lakes. The open expanse of capricious lakewater had to be crossed, somewhere, either straight across (which was foolhardy), or by following the north shore which could take some time and still present some angst. Tony offered to shuttle us across in his boat. "What a great idea," I praised myself for the money well spent and dispensed with the personal tradition of not accepting help. After all, this was a different kind of trip for us.

The course of river between Wekusko and Setting Lake is as fine a stretch of water as one could aspire to paddle. Muskrat Country, or "Pays du Rat" as the Grass was known during the early fur-trade days, did support a variety of not-so-shy river critters which either followed us along the shore (mink), or played head-bob beside the canoe (otter).

There was a great variety of fauna on the Grass, precipitated by the dual geographic harmony of transitional lowland plain with the ancient upland folds of the Canadian Boreal Shield. There were caribou, but also moose and a recent resurgent white-tailed deer population moving up from the south; and there were wolf, lynx, wolverine, double-crested cormorants, white pelicans, herons, loons, Boreal owls and terns. Beaver, muskrat, mink and otter are commonly observed doing daily commerce along the river, and in such numbers that I would tend to believe that any trapping of furs is only an incidental pastime.

The Grass River is endowed with the most resplendent waterfalls in all of Manitoba. Kanisota, White Forest and Whitewood Falls lay testimony to the art of Nature, each place demanding so much of your time, and it is not very hard to give in to the whim of such alluring beauty, to sit by the precipice and listen to the river sing. Not to camp over is to betray your senses and deprive your soul of the music of the river.

Whitewood Falls, in our opinion, far surpasses the much praised Pisew Falls for its inherent charisma and vibrant character and display...and there are no roads here carrying noisy motorists who care little that their pop tins and gum wrappers find sanctuary amongst the starflower and Indian pipe. The fishing for walleye here was exemplary of those places untrod by mechanized sportsmen.

A storm passed through which further added to the drama, but like the water coursing over the granite ledges of the falls, it didn't stay long, and the sun appeared shortly after and lacquered the rocks and beached timber in evening brilliance...we lingered another day.

We ended our journey at Wabowden. It seemed appropriate to do so after having enjoyed the last segment of river so much; the long stretch of lake travel up Setting wasn't appealing, nor were the motorboats that plied the water a pleasant finale to a great trip. We would paddle the Grass again — no question about it.   H.W.

The Grass River is endowed with the most resplendent waterfalls in all of Manitoba

MAP 3

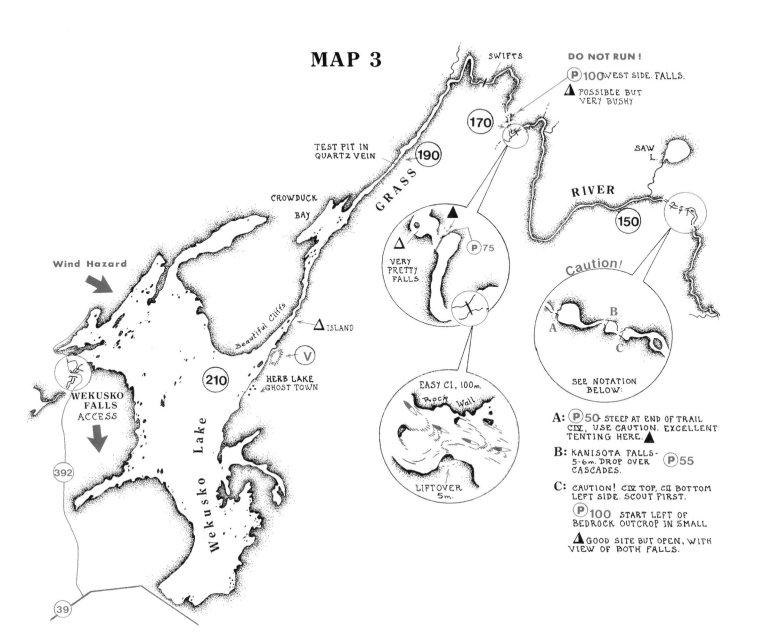

SWIFTS

DO NOT RUN!

(P)100 WEST SIDE. FALLS.

▲ POSSIBLE BUT VERY BUSHY

(170)

TEST PIT IN QUARTZ VEIN

(190)

SAW L.

RIVER

GRASS

CROWDUCK BAY

(150)

Beautiful Cliffs

▲ ISLAND

Wind Hazard

(V)

HERB LAKE GHOST TOWN

(210)

VERY PRETTY FALLS

(P)75

Caution!

A   B

C

SEE NOTATION BELOW:

EASY CI, 100m.

Rock Wall

LIFTOVER 5m.

A: (P)50 STEEP AT END OF TRAIL CIV, USE CAUTION. EXCELLENT TENTING HERE. ▲

B: KANISOTA FALLS- 5-6m. DROP OVER CASCADES. (P)55

C: CAUTION! CIV TOP, CII BOTTOM LEFT SIDE. SCOUT FIRST.

(P)100 START LEFT OF BEDROCK OUTCROP IN SMALL

▲ GOOD SITE BUT OPEN, WITH VIEW OF BOTH FALLS.

Wekusko Lake

WEKUSKO FALLS ACCESS

(392)

(39)

Wekusko Falls

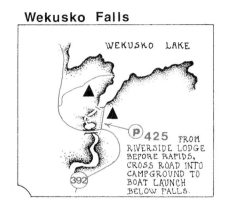

WEKUSKO LAKE

(P)425 FROM RIVERSIDE LODGE BEFORE RAPIDS, CROSS ROAD INTO CAMPGROUND TO BOAT LAUNCH BELOW FALLS.

(392)

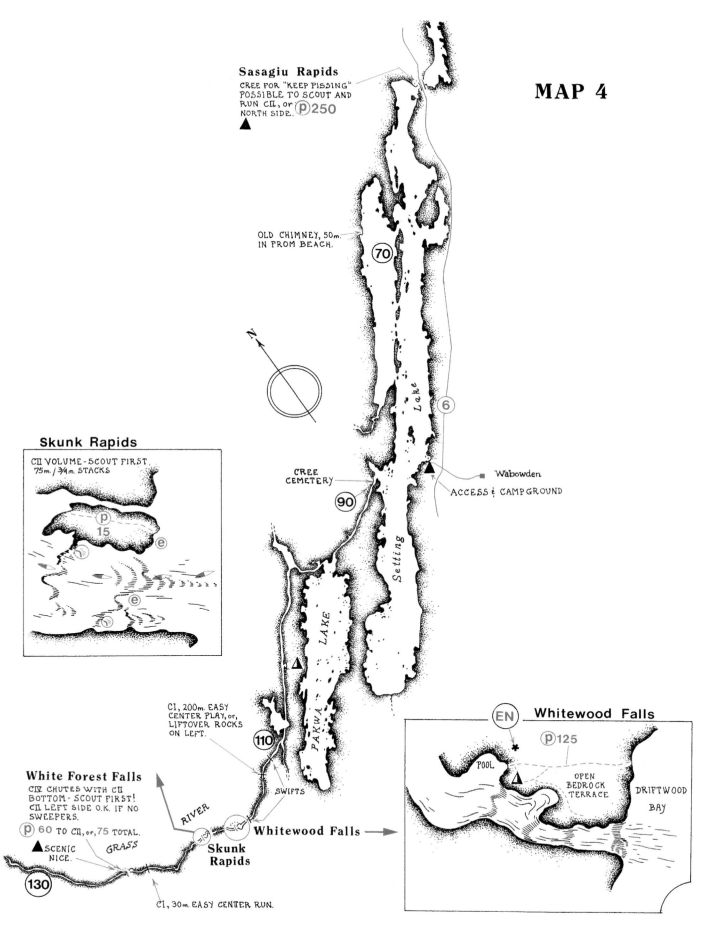

Sasagiu Rapids

CREE FOR "KEEP PISSING"
POSSIBLE TO SCOUT AND
RUN CII, or (p)250
NORTH SIDE. ▲

MAP 4

OLD CHIMNEY, 50m.
IN FROM BEACH.

70

N

6

Skunk Rapids

CII VOLUME-SCOUT FIRST.
75m./¾m. STACKS

(p) 15

(e)

(e)

CREE
CEMETERY

Wabowden

ACCESS & CAMPGROUND

90

Setting   Lake

Δ

PAKWA   LAKE

CI, 200m. EASY
CENTER PLAY, or,
LIFTOVER ROCKS
ON LEFT.

110

SWIFTS

(EN) **Whitewood Falls**

(p)125

POOL

Δ

OPEN
BEDROCK
TERRACE

DRIFTWOOD
BAY

White Forest Falls

CIV CHUTES WITH CII
BOTTOM- SCOUT FIRST!
CII LEFT SIDE O.K. IF NO
SWEEPERS.

(p) 60 TO CII, or, 75 TOTAL.

▲ SCENIC
NICE.

RIVER

GRASS

Whitewood Falls

**Skunk
Rapids**

130

CI, 30m. EASY CENTER RUN.

MAP 5

This section of the Grass
was not surveyed

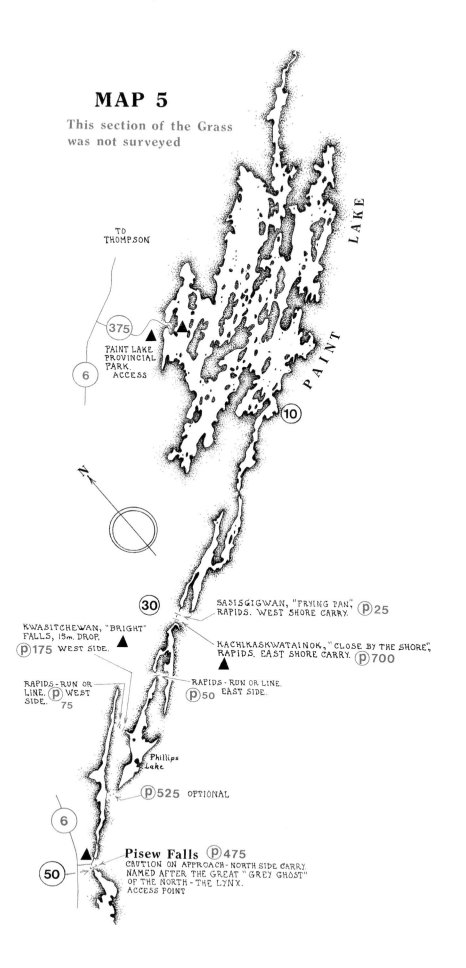

TO
THOMPSON

(375)

PAINT LAKE
PROVINCIAL
PARK.
ACCESS

(6)

PAINT LAKE

(10)

N

(30)

SASISGIGWAN, "FRYING PAN",
RAPIDS. WEST SHORE CARRY. (p)25

KWASITCHEWAN, "BRIGHT"
FALLS, 15m. DROP.
(p)175 WEST SIDE.

KACHIKASKWATAINOK, "CLOSE BY THE SHORE",
RAPIDS. EAST SHORE CARRY. (p)700

RAPIDS - RUN OR
LINE. (p) WEST
SIDE. 75

RAPIDS - RUN OR LINE.
(p)50 EAST SIDE.

Phillips
Lake

(p)525 OPTIONAL

(6)

(50)

Pisew Falls (p)475
CAUTION ON APPROACH - NORTH SIDE CARRY.
NAMED AFTER THE GREAT "GREY GHOST"
OF THE NORTH - THE LYNX.
ACCESS POINT

Land of Little Sticks
Rivers of the Tundra

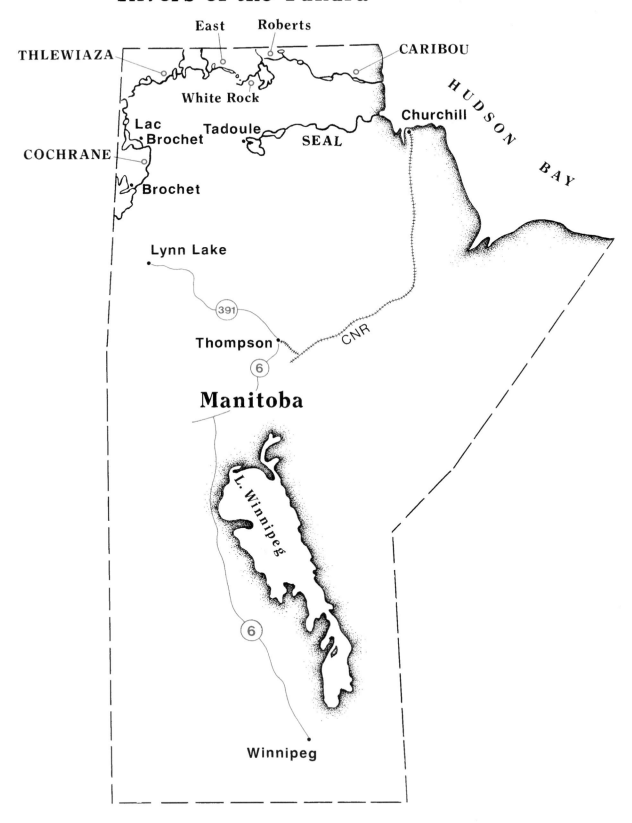

East

Roberts

THLEWIAZA

CARIBOU

HUDSON BAY

White Rock

Lac Brochet

Tadoule

SEAL

Churchill

COCHRANE

Brochet

Lynn Lake

391

Thompson

CNR

6

Manitoba

L. Winnipeg

6

Winnipeg

LAND OF LITTLE STICKS

The "Land of Little Sticks," as referred to by the locals, is that sub-arctic region or tractless void of space where the sky embraces an ever-changing and scabrous landscape that time seemed to forget. It is also known as the Taiga Shield Ecozone by the academic society. Here, the terrain takes on the "edge of the world" visage where a confusing mosaic of land and life-forms constitute such a hodge-podge of shapes and eye-treats that one is mystified and tantalized at the same time.

The Land of Little Sticks is represented by a rolling, undulating Precambrian plain, almost pastoral in some places, with a thin mantle of glacial, morainic material overtopping a scoured and scarred bedrock foundation. "Parkland" vegetation, comprised of black spruce and larch, is sporadic; interspersed with lichen barrens, sinewy sand and gravel eskers, and interlaced with thousands of caribou trails. As one travels towards Hudson Bay, or Tu-cho ("big water"), clumps of stunted spruce are confined to depressions and the arctic climate is clearly experienced.

These are the barrenlands, home of the "people under the sun," the Dene or Chipewyan. It is a crude land were rivers run fast, cold and shallow; where arctic grayling dance and flit amongst the underwater boulders and in quiet pools; a heath-rich tundra that has recorded the movements of ancient peoples and uncountable caribou in a gridwork of time-worn paths, bleached bones and old graveyards perched on top of eskers – the only place where the summer sun melts the permanently frozen biomass enough to bury the dead.

The land is harsh, the weather unpredictable, and in no other place will you feel so insignificant as you will in the barrenlands. Here, you are no longer on the top of the food chain, and inexperience and foolishness is not tolerated...outcome of such disrespect for place can be swift and sure and permanent. Skills are required, and the right attitude and temperament will outlast any hyperborean wind, deluge of biting insects or feeling of total isolation. The Land of Little Sticks glows with a primal beauty, fresh and alluring, and it will capture your soul and change the way you view your place in the wilderness.

Both the Seal River, and the Cochrane, Thlewiaza and Caribou River routes, resound with the magic of the sub-arctic. Each has a character and personality so different that you wouldn't believe they shared the same eco-zone. Anyone travelling here is required to plan carefully, assess their skills accordingly, and to paddle smart.

Nueltin Lake Beach

May	389 m³/sec.
June	762 m³/sec.
July	693 m³/sec.
August	521 m³/sec.
September	465 m³/sec.

* Has been noted as high as 1800 m³/sec.

Maps:

1   2   3   4   5

SEAL RIVER OVERVIEW

"Long ago, people played handgames to bond in friendship. When different tribes gathered together, the game got exciting as teams of up to forty players started betting everything they owned. Games start with two people playing to determine which team will go first. The players take an object small enough to hide in their hand and put both hands behind their backs. Then they put their closed hands in front again, hiding the object in one hand. Both players guess in which hand the other holds the object. The one who guesses the wrong hand loses the chance for his side to start first.

"The game is played to the drum, and drummers on the team hiding the bones beat their drums faster and faster as guesses are made by the other team. Some players wave their hands wildly and dance around to tease and confuse the guessers. When a player continues to outsmart his opponents, his movements become wilder and wilder as his team racks up winning points, and onlookers laugh at his antics.

"Throughout all the laughter and high energy, someone always manages to keep score with sticks. Shouts and whoops raise the roof when a team's losing streak is interrupted by an incorrect guess by the other team. When just one of their players manages to outfox his opponents, the sticks are gathered up and the losers are back in the game.

"There are stories of handgames that lasted for three days, during which players stopped only long enough to eat. People would start out betting small things like arrows and slingshots, and then move up to bigger things like spears and sleds. Later, trade goods like matches and gunshells were bet, and some people lost all of their clothes, traps, and dogteams. Today, we bet small amounts of money."
Excerpt from *Yamoria the Lawmaker – Stories of the Dene* by George Blondin.
(see page 119)

SEAL RIVER

GENERAL INFORMATION

Classification: Advanced (isolated with long, difficult rapids).
Distance: 315 km. (Tadoule village to Hudson Bay)
Elevation Drop: 247 m. (741') or .8m/km. (2.35'/km).
Time: 18-21 days
Number of Campsites: 35 or 1 campsite every 9 km. (includes established sites only; actual possible campsites exceeds 50)
Number of Runnable Rapids: All 42 sets are runnable (numbered in sequence); 80% high volume or technical rapids.
Portages: No established portages, although lining or portaging is possible along the shore of most difficult rapids.
Season: Late June through early September
Maps Required: 64 J/9 64 J/16 64 I/13 64 I/14 64 I/15 64 I/16 54 L/13 54 M/4 54 L/14 54 M/3 54 M/2
Access: Charter flight can be arranged from Thompson to Tadoule village (land base airport). The canoeist also has the option to begin this trip at Leaf Rapids on the Churchill River via hwy #391 north of Thompson. Shuttles can be arranged with outfitters in Thompson. Add 7-8 days travel time. For those paddling the Cochrane/Thlewiaza route, and water levels are low, it is suggested that the Caribou River be avoided and canoeists may take the Wolverine south and join on to the Seal where water levels are generally good throughout the season.
Egress: IT IS NOT RECOMMENDED TO PADDLE THE HUDSON BAY COAST. Pick up by water transport can be arranged through outfitters in Churchill; from Churchill canoeists have the option of flying back to Thompson or taking the train (Via Rail). See listing of general services and outfitters in the back of the book.
Features: The Seal River provides an unprecedented journey through the land of the Dene people. Of the four major river systems in Manitoba, only the Seal remains completely undeveloped. Prehistory dates back 7,000 years and the corridor is still used by the Churchill/Tadoule Band of Dene for the hunting of harbour seals which travel upriver over 200 km. Native culture combined with earth-science features made it an easy choice for selection into the Heritage River System in 1992. Hiking along eskers at midnight, the exhilaration of the best whitewater one can imagine, the excitement of polar bear encounters, and paddling in a still-developing estuary filled with beluga whales all make the Seal River one of the best wilderness trips available in this hemisphere.

WHITEWATER CHARACTERISTICS AND GENERAL HAZARDS

This trip is not for the faint-hearted or timid. It is remote. It is demanding, and it is not kind to the foolish. People have died on this route before because they put themselves above the power of the river. For the unprepared a paddle on the Seal could prove disastrous.

Just because there are no portages it doesn't mean that each rapid can be safely run without proper circumspection. Spray decks are recommended for the Seal, otherwise you'll be doing a lot of lining, bailing or drying your gear around the campfire every night.

Tadoule and Shethanei Lakes are big, often windy, and the water is damn cold. Remember this. Build in extra days for being windbound or be prepared to paddle in the late evening to avoid the wind.

Most rapids are much easier if you play the shores and stay out of the middle flow. This is easy during higher water but when the river flow diminishes you can expect to dodge boulders. It's great fun and some runs are quite long so you may want to pack gravol or sea-bands in your med-kit to combat sea-sickness! Watch the ledge at 9-Bar Rapids and try to hit Deaf Rapids at high tide or soon after. Take flares and an air-horn to ward off polar bears at the coast (there is a shelter on the north side of the estuary). DO NOT ATTEMPT TO PADDLE DOWN THE COAST TO CHURCHILL.

SEAL RIVER JOURNAL

"Let's get the hell out of here NOW!" Hodding was yelling at Mike to get back into the canoe. "LOOK AT THE FIRE...WE'VE GOTTA MOVE OR WE'RE TOAST!" Russell and I were 200 metres beyond in our canoe taking pictures of the fire while Mike had pulled his canoe up to shore at the end of the rapids to take a piss — that's when we heard Hodding screaming at the top of his lungs for Mike to get moving.

We had just finished running 9-Bar Rapids, a notorious 3.5-kilometre-long, hair-raising roller-coaster ride, classed as a class V rapid by Parks Canada, running the left side, eddying out twice to scout the bends and finishing by dropping over a two-metre ledge, very nearly getting stuck in the hydraulic backwash. If that wasn't tense enough, the entire north shore of the river was being engulfed in a conflagration the size of Prince Edward Island!

Russ and I sat in our canoe, completely enthralled by the towering flames that crowned at least two kilometres of river horizon forming the leading edge of the wildfire; that's when we heard the roar...or rather felt it — even above the din of the rapids. The fire was consuming forest at an alarming rate, judging that in this wind it was moving almost twice as fast as we could possibly paddle...and coming straight toward us!

It wasn't the fire so much as the threat of the smoke engulfing us before we could get downriver to safety. For days now we had been dodging wildfires, so bad at times that we had to brush burning and smoking debris off our clothing and canoe-skirts, running rapids while the shore vegetation burst into columns of fire and smoke. But each day the wind miraculously carried the debris straight up or away from the river, allowing us to sneak by unscathed, at worst having to soak our bandanas and tie them across our faces to make it easier to breathe. The pungent smoke was only irritating, but luckily so far, not life-threatening.

And now, with the fire burning so fiercely, the air became saturated with burnt debris and a choking, black smoke descended on the water below the rapids where only moments ago we had beached our canoes. We paddled hard to keep just ahead of the deadly wall of smoke while being showered with scorched spruce needles, and the river became coated with a greasy slick of soot, the sun was blotted out and the day was transformed into an eerie orange twilight.

We stopped 3 kilometres downriver at the Environment Canada water-monitoring shack so we could catch our breath. Once inside the cabin we sat for only two minutes before hearing the explosions upriver. We couldn't believe that the fire had already reached the 1950's mining exploration camp located at the extreme east end of Great Island; it was obviously the dynamite storage shed that was being razed...remnant blasting-caps and charges igniting, adding sharp retorts above the low rumble of the not-so-distant fire. We snatched up the two "visitor's journals" before high-tailing it back to the canoes. The log-books, as far as we were concerned, were the only valuable items worth saving from the quickly approaching fire.

Once again we leaned on our paddles to put distance between us and the fire, covering another 18 kilometres before we felt that is was safe enough to pitch camp. Clear of the smoke, which now painted an ominous scene to the western horizon, resembling a nuclear oblation, we realized that we were finally outside the gauntlet of wildfires that seemed to be consuming all of Manitoba's northern boreal forests. Perils that still lay ahead, like "Deadly Rapids," and "Deaf Rapids," polar bears and the run down the Hudson Bay coast would now seem anti-climactic in comparison to what we'd been through already...or so I thought at the time.

———— ❦ ————

Mike and I were to guide a writer and photographer from *Men's Journal Magazine* on a "classic" Canadian wilderness canoe trip for a feature story to be published in the spring of '95. *Men's Journal* was the most recent of magazines published by *Rolling Stone* out of New York City and the editor wanted the river article to appeal to the new genre of armchair outdoor enthusiasts...the executive jocks in their BMWs, with their 6-figure incomes and cottages up in the Adirondacks. How this was going to figure into the trip I didn't have the faintest clue; I did know that I wasn't about to wear a tux while serving Arctic grayling on the lid of my wannigan!

The two of us drove the 3000 kilometres to Thompson, with the canoes and gear and met Hodding and Russell at the airport the next day. It was June 30th and the river would still be running high. Neither Hodding, a part-time postmaster from Thermond, West Virginia, or Russell, a downtown Brooklyn photographer, had any previous whitewater experience and this added to the complexity of emotions about the trip in general... it was an assignment for them; for myself, the Seal River offered a trip down one of Manitoba's wildest rivers, and unlike the Nelson and the Churchill that had been dammed for hydro-power, the Seal remained unscathed, virtually untrammeled and truly pristine. As for Mike, well...Mike's just plain crazy!

We met with Tom Ellis at the Burntwood diner in downtown Thompson. Tom, a Chipewyan, was a fountain of knowledge about the cultural features along the Seal. Our biggest concern was whether to sail down the Hudson Bay coast to Churchill, or hire Jackie Bastone to pick us up with his barge. We were better equipped to do the trip than any other canoeist who had made the attempt previously. Some locals asserted grimly that no one had ever done it yet and lived to tell the

Dene family at Tadoule before evacuation

tale! An over-exaggeration perhaps; nonetheless, anyone travelling down the bouldery Hudson Bay coast would have to face the unpredictable nature of Tu Cho — the great body of water.

We boarded Skyward Aviation's "Bandit," a twin-engine E-110 Bandeirante. It would take just over an hour to make the 300 kilometre trip north to the native village of Tadoule. Once in the air, at 10,500 feet, we could immediately see the smoke haze from at least a dozen wildfires burning unchecked. The Manitoba government just allows them to burn because there isn't any marketable timber. If the smoke gets bad enough they'll evacuate a reserve, elders and childern first, as they were now doing at North Indian Lake and as they did two days later at Tadoule itself while we were there. The burnt spruce smell clung to our nostrils as the Bandit pitched through a wall of smoke against a strong northeast headwind. The land itself resembled a mosaic puzzle of sand eskers, patches of spruce and fenland, interspersed with lakes that comprised at least half of the visible landscape. We had entered the northwestern Boreal Uplands region where the land was in a state of transition between the boreal forest and the Arctic tundra. This bio-region extends far into the Northwest Territories and envelops sections of the Coppermine, Thelon, Kazan and Dubawnt Rivers — land of little sticks and caribou in the sub-Arctic region of Canada.

At Tadoule we met up with Alan Code and his wife Mary (a Dene native) who together had recently produced a video about the Seal and the Sayisi Dene history. Long before white European imperialist influence, the Edthen-El-Deli Dene, the most eastern of the Dene people, or "Caribou Eaters" (an ethnological/anthropological label; the Sayisi dene prefer to be known as the "people under the sun") travelled the barren-grounds along the eskers following the caribou migrations. The great caribou herds have since changed their travel patterns, much to the dismay of the Sayisi Dene. The caribou hunt even took precedence over the fur trade with the Hudson's Bay Company at Fort Prince of Wales in Churchill.

The village was built on an esker only a short while ago, after the government had herded the Dene together and forced them to live in Churchill. Without connection to the land, they had had enough of urban life and moved back to their homeland of their own volition and without initial compensation from the government. They are a very proud people with close ties to the land around them. The men still engage in traditional "hand games" and talk about the old days and the caribou hunt, and of battles with their enemies the Inuit and Cree. The few canoeists who paddle the Seal usually spend little time at the village. This is a shame because the Sayisi Dene are friendly people who enjoy talking with outsiders – although one year a native elder did come down to the beach-landing to place a curse on a couple of kayakers, thinking they were Inuit enemies!

We helped three visiting Navajo healers at the village cut and peel 20 foot spruce poles for their large ceremonial smoke-lodge. The government at this time was evacuating elders and children because of the encroaching fire. The main Dene ceremonies were postponed so we lost the opportunity to participate, although Hodding and I managed to coerce the healers into giving us a private-ceremony during which we asked the river spirits permission to allow us to pass safely. Our somewhat meagre cash and tobacco offering wasn't quite sufficient to include a chew of peyote which the Navajo still use in their healing and vision-quest ceremonies. *Lophophora williamsii* is a cactus native to Texas and Mexico. Collected by Indians, the tops are dried into "buttons" and chewed to release a hallucinogenic drug similar in nature to LSD. The Navajo and Sayisi Dene are closely

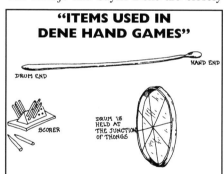

aligned in culture and language, having the same Paleo-Indian background.

Alan told us that the private ceremony was a good idea. It also showed the Dene our respect for both their culture and the power of the river. It is something that I have taken very seriously over the past several years as part of my own standard pre-trip preparations which generally include various types of tobacco or smoke rituals. The Seal is a complex waterway with many dangers and we would be paddling into the worst of the Manitoba wildfires in a short time.

Aside from 1:50,000 topographic charts, we were using the Canadian Heritage River System's (Parks Canada) background study information which was compiled in 1986 when the Seal became a candidate for CHRS designation. The study indicated 42 rapids up to class VI — right off the international scale! The resource study, although informative, was not very accurate.

It was 385 kilometres from Tadoule to Churchill, with an elevation drop of 247 metres (741 feet); 240 kilometres would be river travel with 80% technical rapids as well as 85 kilometres of runnable fastwater and a steady current running between 5-15 km/h. We were heavily loaded: three weeks of provisions, "traditional" gear including two wannigans and reflector oven and close to 100 kg of photo-related equipment. The canoes were rigged with spray covers, mandatory for the bigger rapids along the Seal. At least half of the two dozen river travellers each year prefer rafts to canoes because of the large volume rapids and few if any portages.

Unlike Canadian Shield rivers to the south, the Seal waterflow peaks in June instead of May and recedes quickly after that, generally exposing shallow, bouldery rapids. The prevailing wind is also out of the north and east and that's what makes any travel down the Bay coast particularly hazardous. "If you guys sail the Bay... don't try and cross Button Bay whatever you do," Alan warned us as we pushed off from Tadoule against a stiff southeast wind. It was early July...the water was cold...the wind had an Arctic edge to it and blew in our faces for the first three days, and like the mosquitoes and black flies, it seemed that all the forces of nature were putting us through an initial test of endurance.

Right off the bat, the CHRS map was wrong. The cartographer had drawn the east Shethanei Lake entrance upside down, reversing the north and south Seal river entrances. One of the wildest rapids, not marked on any maps, was a serious class IV rapid with 2-metre swells that would have certainly swamped any open canoe. Russell, who was getting a "crash" course in whitewater paddling, disappeared momentarily as we lunged through a huge roller. As we broke out on the other side he turned to look at me with an almost pleading expression and asked if it was okay to go home now.

Shethanei (Sheth-than-nee) Lake to the Dene refers to "the hill going into the lake" – a large esker that literally disappears into the north shore narrows. The

MAP 1

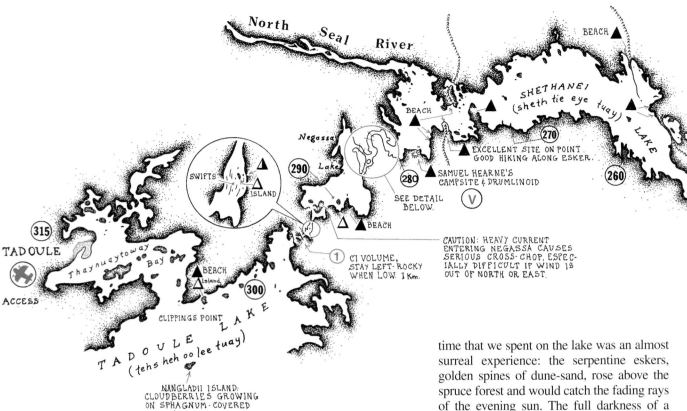

North Seal River

BEACH

SHETHANEI
(sheth tie eye tuay) LAKE

BEACH

Negassa Lake

SWIFTS ISLAND

290

280

270

260

EXCELLENT SITE ON POINT. GOOD HIKING ALONG ESKER.

SAMUEL HEARNE'S CAMPSITE & DRUMLINOID

SEE DETAIL BELOW.

V

315

TADOULE

ACCESS

Thaynuaytoway Bay

BEACH Island

BEACH

1

CI VOLUME, STAY LEFT - ROCKY WHEN LOW. 1 Km.

CAUTION: HEAVY CURRENT ENTERING NEGASSA CAUSES SERIOUS CROSS-CHOP, ESPECIALLY DIFFICULT IF WIND IS OUT OF NORTH OR EAST.

300

CLIPPINGS POINT

TADOULE LAKE
(tehs heh oo lee tuay)

NANGLADII ISLAND:
CLOUDBERRIES GROWING ON SPHAGNUM-COVERED GROUND.

CAUTION! VOLUME CIII, 1.5m. STACKS, LARGE BOULDERS BUT NO LEDGE - NOT MARKED ON TOPO MAP - USE SPRAY SKIRT. 500m.

3

MORE ROCK & SHALLOWER THAN SOUTH BRANCH.

DENE CAMPSITE

2   1.2 Km.

CII ROCK STREWN, MOSTLY CI HEAVY FLOW AT TOP - STAY LEFT OF CENTER AWAY FROM STACKS - SIDESLIP TO RIGHT BY ISLAND TO AVOID ROCK GARDEN.

time that we spent on the lake was an almost surreal experience: the serpentine eskers, golden spines of dune-sand, rose above the spruce forest and would catch the fading rays of the evening sun. The full darkness of a deep summer night, familiar in southerly regions, was never attained.

The eskers on Shethanei and along the upper reaches of the Seal were prehistoric travelways for the Dene during caribou migrations. Today you can see still tracks of caribou, wolf, black bear, fox, moose and the occasional barrenland grizzly. We hiked all of the better eskers that snaked their way inland off the river, exploring sand "blowouts," animal trails and observed the many traces of pre and historic use of the river along the dunes. This included: old grave sites, discarded stone implements, fire rings and rolls of birch bark intended for use in canoe construction.

Samuel Hearne was commissioned by the Hudson's Bay Company out of Fort Prince of Wales (Churchill) to explore the barrenlands in quest of the fabled coppermines that were said to exist "12 to 24 months near a permanently frozen sea," Both his 1769 and 1770 trips were unsuccessful; however, he did spend considerable time camped on Shethanei Lake and gave us our first European account of the Seal River environment.

The midnight treks along the eskers

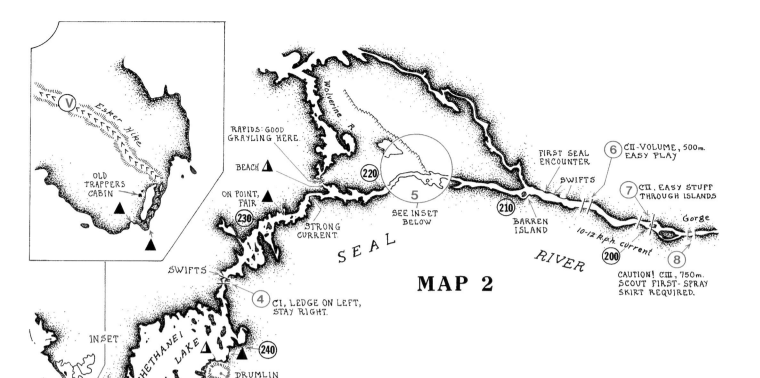

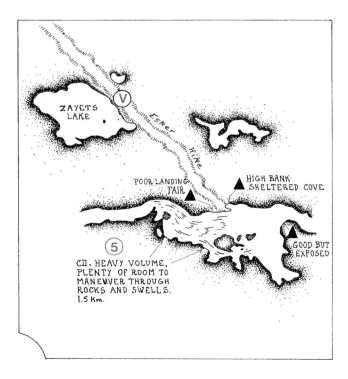

MAP 2

Map labels (Map 2, top):
- V — Esker Hike
- OLD TRAPPERS CABIN
- Wolverine R.
- RAPIDS: GOOD GRAYLING HERE.
- BEACH ▲
- ON POINT, FAIR ▲
- (230)
- (220)
- STRONG CURRENT.
- SEAL RIVER
- 5 — SEE INSET BELOW
- FIRST SEAL ENCOUNTER
- SWIFTS
- (210)
- BARREN ISLAND
- (200)
- 10-12 kph current
- 6 — CII-VOLUME, 500m. EASY PLAY
- 7 — CII, EASY STUFF THROUGH ISLANDS
- Gorge
- 8
- CAUTION! CIII, 750m. SCOUT FIRST- SPRAY SKIRT REQUIRED.
- SWIFTS
- 4 — CI, LEDGE ON LEFT, STAY RIGHT.
- INSET
- SHETHANEI LAKE
- (240)
- DRUMLIN V
- (250)

Inset map labels (bottom left):
- ZAYETS LAKE
- V — Esker Hike
- POOR LANDING FAIR ▲
- HIGH BANK SHELTERED COVE ▲
- 5 — CII, HEAVY VOLUME, PLENTY OF ROOM TO MANEUVER THROUGH ROCKS AND SWELLS. 1.5 Km.
- GOOD BUT EXPOSED

afforded an unprecedented look at the surrounding boreal landscape and animal activity as well as an opportunity to explore the boreal bio-region away from the river. On one occasion I came face to face with a rather large tundra wolf as I stepped over an embankment into a blowout. I reached slowly behind me for my camera on its sling but the movement inspired the wolf to dash along the opening, stopping just long enough to look back, allowing me just enough time to get off a couple of quick shots.

Pioneer lichens and mosses grew over the eskers in circular and polygonal mosaic designs in a struggle to stabilize the eroding dunes. The view from the eskers gave an unrestricted view over the endless plain of spruce and bog veneers, while scattered clumps of dwarf birch and jackpine clung to the edges of the dunes. It was a week before we reached the east end of Shethanei Lake from Tadoule. The prevailing winds have a 40 kilometre opportunity to whip up healthy whitecaps although we were fortunate to have an almost mirror-perfect crossing during a break in the seemingly ever-present wind.

It was a 240 kilometre paddle to the Bay from Shethanei, dropping 700 vertical feet without one waterfall to eat up the bulk of the drop. This translated into a lot of long, steep descents over the next week and a half. We stopped briefly at the Wolverine River ("Nah yah eye desay" to the Dene, or "river that drains soaked-through lake"), and we caught our first

MAP 3

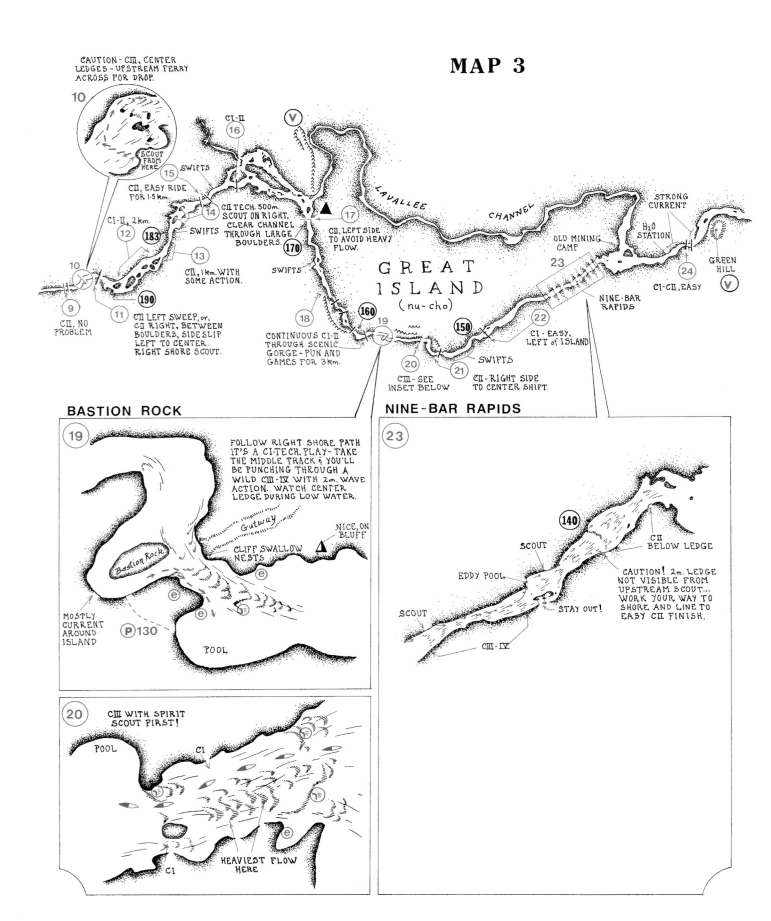

CAUTION - CIII, CENTER LEDGES - UPSTREAM FERRY ACROSS FOR DROP.

10

SCOUT FROM HERE

CI-II

16

(V)

15 SWIFTS

CII, EASY RIDE FOR 1·5 km.

14

CII TECH. 500m. SCOUT ON RIGHT, CLEAR CHANNEL THROUGH LARGE BOULDERS.

170

17 CII, LEFT SIDE TO AVOID HEAVY FLOW.

CI-II, 2 km.

12 (183)

SWIFTS

13

CII, 1 km. WITH SOME ACTION.

10

9

CII, NO PROBLEM

11 (190)

CII LEFT SWEEP, or, CII RIGHT, BETWEEN BOULDERS, SIDESLIP LEFT TO CENTER. RIGHT SHORE SCOUT.

SWIFTS

18

160

19

20

CIII - SEE INSET BELOW

CONTINUOUS CI-II THROUGH SCENIC GORGE - FUN AND GAMES FOR 3 km.

21

SWIFTS

CII - RIGHT SIDE TO CENTER SHIFT.

150

LAVALLEE CHANNEL

G R E A T
I S L A N D
(nu-cho)

STRONG CURRENT

H₂O STATION

OLD MINING CAMP

23

GREEN HILL

24 (V)

CI-CII, EASY

22

CI - EASY, LEFT of ISLAND

NINE-BAR RAPIDS

BASTION ROCK

19

FOLLOW RIGHT SHORE PATH - IT'S A CI-TECH. PLAY - TAKE THE MIDDLE TRACK & YOU'LL BE PUNCHING THROUGH A WILD CIII-IV WITH 2m. WAVE ACTION. WATCH CENTER LEDGE DURING LOW WATER.

Gutway

NICE, ON BLUFF

CLIFF SWALLOW NESTS

Bastion Rock

(e)

(e)

(e)

MOSTLY CURRENT AROUND ISLAND

(P) 130

POOL

NINE-BAR RAPIDS

23

140

SCOUT

CII BELOW LEDGE

EDDY POOL

SCOUT

STAY OUT!

CAUTION! 2m. LEDGE NOT VISIBLE FROM UPSTREAM SCOUT... WORK YOUR WAY TO SHORE AND LINE TO EASY CII FINISH.

CIII-IV

20

CIII WITH SPIRIT SCOUT FIRST!

POOL

CI

(e)

HEAVIEST FLOW HERE

CI

Arctic grayling at the foot of the rapids. It was here, also, that we spotted our first harbour seals playing near some centre-channel boulders.

We stopped just shy of the fires and made camp at the esker site shortly past an easy set of class III rapids. The 30-metre dune would give us a clear view of where the fire was spreading so I could plot it onto our topo map. I was concerned with which direction the smoke would blow with tomorrow's wind. All day, since leaving Shethanei, we had been following the sheer-line of smoke managing to keep it out of our faces by less than half a kilometre....tomorrow we would be right into it.

It had been unseasonably hot the past few days in marked contrast to the first three on leaving Tadoule. We feasted on grayling that evening under the shadow of the esker behind us and the looming cloud of smoke downriver. In the morning we didn't have to paddle far before getting a good view of the fire burning along the river. With a current pulling at 10 km/h., interspersed with long sets of rapids, we had little chance of back-tracking if the fire and smoke proved to be intolerable. We had played our cards, betting that the wind had forced the smoke to rise vertically, and it did, instead of hanging in a deadly shroud over the Seal.

At one point we stopped along shore to photograph the forest fire but the intense heat seared our bare skin and showers of glowing sparks and airborne cinders fell like rain on top of the canoes forcing us to continue down into the raging inferno. At least it was safer to stay out in the centre of the river away from the flames and heat, playing the rapids cautiously as we rounded river-bends not knowing what waited past the corners.

We ran 12 sets of rapids over 44 kilometres that day, often shooting difficult runs while the forests on both sides of the river were fully ablaze. Camp was set up at the west end of Great Island (Nu cho or "big island"), a 100-metre rise in the elevation where the Seal split into two diverse channels. This was a spiritual place for the Sayisi Dene where certain rocks were once collected for ceremonial purposes.

It was the narrowest section of the Seal River and the fire burned close to camp through the night. If the wind had changed direction, the fire would have easily "jumped" the river necessitating a quick departure off the beach. The next day we had decided to rest-over, allowing the fire to move downriver and give us an opportunity to hike along one of the most fascinating esker ridges that terminates at the escarpment overlooking the north Seal channel.

The fire had completely gutted "Bastion Rock," a vertical fortress of rock circled by one calm channel and a rather energetic class IV rapid through the main channel. We made early camp here pitching our tents over recently scorched earth and took time to play in the rapids and enjoy the remarkable beauty of the location.

Our CHRS information guide had marked many of the rapids as class IV's and even class V rapids when most were actually rather simple II's and III's. One of the inherent problems with the international grading system for rapids is contingent on inexperienced people setting rather vague standards to identify them. Much of the volume on the runs kept centre profile but we always seemed to manage to find easier slots on either side, usually with a few minor ferrys and a shitload of bracing. Everyone we had talked to said that we would have to portage 9-Bar Rapids but we ran it in its gruesome entirety. Luckily, as it turned out, because any hesitation would have put us in, or behind the most frightening of all the fires we encountered en route. For over 100 kilometres the fires burned along the Seal, but we were never actually clear of the smoke at any point during our trip, and were always in sight of the huge flames in the near horizon that resembled massive thunderhead clouds.

Past Great Island, as we were entering a new bio-region of treeless heath and peat plateaus, the river dropped steadily through long rapids and boulder trains known as Felsenmeer. There was an endless stretch of rapids 13 kilometres long, mostly class II's and III's, including Tambanay rapids. Mike and Hodding dumped in a small hole over a ledge near the end of the run which added a little tense excitement to the already high level of adrenalin-pumping thrills.

At the last campsite before Hudson Bay, I cut poles for a sailing rig to be used along the coast run — tomorrow we would be in the tundra flats of the Seal estuary with no opportunity to find good wood of any dimension. We stopped briefly at "the stone," a huge, monolithic granite outcropping propped in the middle of an expanse of tundra. It was used by Dene as a way-marker across the tundra.

"Deaf Rapids" loomed ahead of us as the biggest whitewater challenge. The CHRS guidebook rated the run as a class VI rapids, top of the scale, but we were intent on completing the Seal without a single portage carry. The canoes were lashed together 20 kilometres ahead of Deaf Rapids and the sail was hoisted to try out the rigging. The wind had finally shifted to the west, which carried us downriver, running various rapids fully under sail, pulling up just shy of the pitch-off to Deaf Rapids and the Bay.

From the head of the rapids we could see Hudson Bay (but not the bottom of the rapids!); it was 3 kilometres away yet, and we still had about 50 vertical feet to drop before getting there. The canoes were disassembled and we scouted the rapids, shotgun in hand just in case we met up with a polar bear. The rapid was doable, down the left side, and was no more than a wily class III rapid with a few boulders to dodge and some sideslipping to keep the canoe on the inside edge of the heavy centre-channel rollers. After a few moments of anxiety, both canoes made it down to the bottom eddy and we celebrated with a few hearty hurrahs. A few more ledge drops and we met the tide going out at the bottom of the very confusing estuary. We had to backtrack when we realized we had gone too far, and made camp on a small sedge-bush island. We would wait for tomorrow's high tide and make a quick dash down the coast until the next low tide, playing the winds which were now safely blowing off shore.

Our last camp was so bug-infested that we were forced to eat our dinner inside the tent. We still had the coastline ahead of us. Others had tried it, some turned back while others had even perished in the violent storms off the Hudson Bay coast. The final night we slept in trepidation of polar bear visits. We kept a vigilant watch through the night while on the coast and didn't let any bear approach too closely. Our bear-blasters, "cherry bomb"-type firecrackers, were kept on hand to keep any bears out of camp. Flares and yelling while shaking your tent in the air will also work in most cases. For us, thankfully, it was a quiet night.

The tide came in around 11:00 a.m.

the next morning, so we pushed off into the very calm water of the estuary, passing at least two dozen harbour seals before reaching the open water of Hudson Bay. Two hundred metres past the shoreline boulders we encountered the first Beluga whales. We heard them first, blowing air and water and making the typical sonar-like noises. Soon we were paddling amongst hundreds of white whales that would break surface alongside the canoes. Mothers with young attached to their backs gazed at us from slitted eyes.

As the tide went out (5-6 metres), we found ourselves an uncomfortable distance out from shore, eventually allowing ourselves to become beached on the flats while the tide went out completely. It was

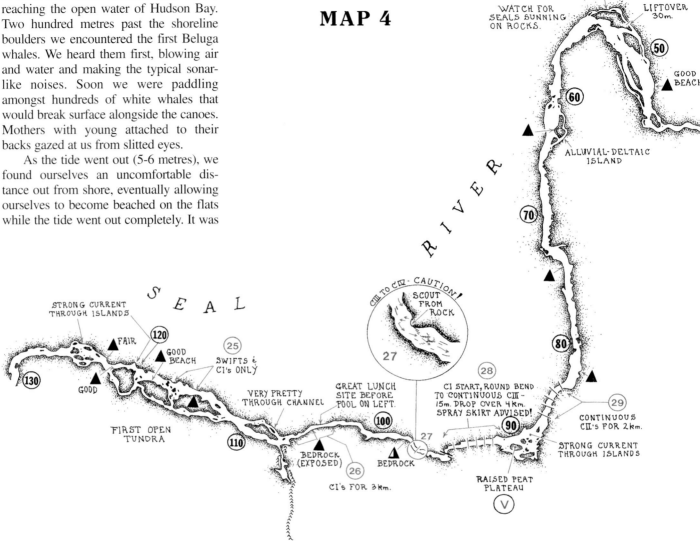

MAP 4

a scene out of a Spielburg movie – a crude sailing vessel dwarfed by the expansive boulder plain. Mud and sand for as far as the eye could see and no visible shoreline! The smoke-filled sky created a mystical ambience in the half-light of a northern night.

The tide came in after midnight, much quicker in fact than it went out, and we were once again afloat with a light breeze to carry us on down the coast. I tied my candle lantern to the mast line in order to shed a friendly glow over the canoes. In a way, it helped to dispel some of the nervousness about the midnight crossing. My compass, at this point, was invaluable since in the dark there were almost no land bearings, except the occasional boulder

that we would get hung up on. Sometimes eider ducks or groups of Canada geese would be surprised by our sudden presence.

Mike wanted to cross Button Bay as the first light from Churchill began showing dimly 18 kilometres to the east. I remembered what Alan had told us about crossing the deep bay and the number of people who had never made it. The decision was unanimous — we would keep the canoes parallel to the coast until we reached the bottom of the wide gut along the Hudson Bay shoreline, swing north and take full advantage of the south wind. For the past several hours we had been paddling the craft with the sail rolled up; now, we once again gained momentum

under the power of wind and sailed the last 20 kilometres past Fort Prince of Wales and into the port town of Churchill.

We had passed by several large pods of Beluga whales. They would often follow us in formation, or come at the canoes from one side or the other, just above the surface, then dive under the canoes within a paddle's reach away. Belugas were once hunted by the Inuit and the Hudson's Bay Company for meat and oil, but are now protected as one the world's most important and largest population of white whales. Today, whale watching, in addition to "Tundra Buggy" polar bear tours, are Churchill's most important tourist attractions.

For us the trip really wasn't over until

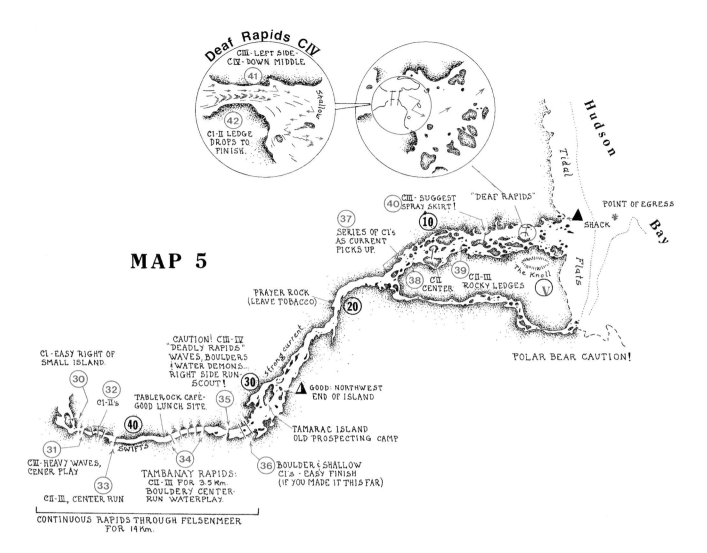

MAP 5

Deaf Rapids CIV
CIII-LEFT SIDE-
CIV-DOWN MIDDLE

41

Shallow

42
CI-II LEDGE
DROPS TO
FINISH.

Hudson

Tidal

CIII- SUGGEST
40 SPRAY SKIRT!

"DEAF RAPIDS"

POINT OF EGRESS

SHACK

37
SERIES OF CI's
AS CURRENT
PICKS UP.

10

Bay

The Knoll

CII
38 CENTER

39 CII-III
ROCKY LEDGES

Flats

V

PRAYER ROCK
(LEAVE TOBACCO)

20

POLAR BEAR CAUTION!

CI - EASY RIGHT OF
SMALL ISLAND.

30

32
CI-II's

CAUTION! CIII-IV
"DEADLY RAPIDS"
WAVES, BOULDERS
& WATER DEMONS...
RIGHT SIDE RUN-
SCOUT!

35

30

GOOD: NORTHWEST
END OF ISLAND

TABLEROCK CAFÉ-
GOOD LUNCH SITE.

40

TAMARAC ISLAND
OLD PROSPECTING CAMP

31

SWIFTS

34

36 BOULDER & SHALLOW
CI's - EASY FINISH
(IF YOU MADE IT THIS FAR)

CIII-HEAVY WAVES,
CENER PLAY

33

CII-III, CENTER RUN

TAMBANAY RAPIDS:
CII-III FOR 3.5 Km.
BOULDERY CENTER-
RUN WATERPLAY.

CONTINUOUS RAPIDS THROUGH FELSENMEER
FOR 14 Km.

we moored the canoes beside an old tug tied up alongside the kilometre-long grain-elevator loading dock, stepped ashore on solid ground, walked into town, and had a cold beer and a greasy hamburger. The 70 kilometre paddle and sail down the Hudson Bay coastline is not recommended for the faint of heart — I do suggest that canoeists doing the Seal should contact the barge operator in Churchill and make preparations to be picked up at the estuary. You will, however, also have to be prepared to deal with polar bears at the mouth of the Seal. I had heard that the Natural Resources game wardens often take rogue bears from the town of Churchill and dump them off near the Seal river estuary! We were lucky...most of the polar bears

were still down the coast to the south, although we would have liked the opportunity to photograph them from a distance. We would now have to wait until another expedition was planned.

We spent two days scouring the countryside around Churchill, visiting the attractions, talking to many of the local outfitters, and then made preparations to take the return train back to Thompson. It was truly an amazing expedition, full of surprises and certainly the added excitement caused by the wildfires and the sail down the coastline at night. The Seal is a place of magic and of a special people who still have their hearts deeply embedded in the golden sands of Sheth tie eye tuay. H.W.

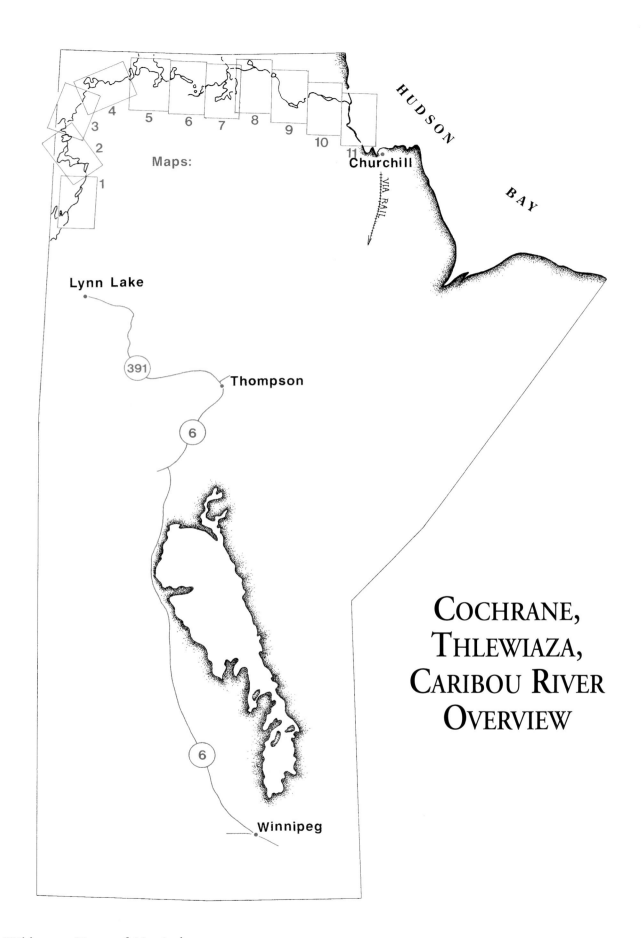

Maps:

HUDSON

BAY

Churchill

VIA RAIL

Lynn Lake

391

Thompson

6

6

Winnipeg

COCHRANE,
THLEWIAZA,
CARIBOU RIVER
OVERVIEW

COCHRANE, THLEWIAZA, CARIBOU RIVERS

NOTE: Because of the complexity of this route the book deals with the specific details of each river segment. There are three geographic divisions: The Cochrane River, upstream to the point of exit over the height of land to gain access to the Thlewiaza; the Thlewiaza River, downstream, from the Cochrane to Nahilin Falls as it enters Nueltin Lake; and the Caribou River, which includes upstream travel on the East River, the chain of lakes joining White Rock Creek, downstream travel on White Rock to Nejanalini Lake, upstream travel on the Wolverine River, downstream travel on Roberts River, and continuing downstream on the Caribou River to Hudson Bay.

COCHRANE RIVER – GENERAL INFORMATION

Classification: Intermediate up or downstream (Information is based on upstream travel). Isolated and difficult lining.

Distance: 210 km. from Lac Brochet village to Height of Land portage.

Elevation Rise: 34 m. (112') or .16 m/km. (.5'/km)

Time: 8-10 days (upstream)

Number of Campsites: 28 or 1 campsite every 7.5 km.

Number of Falls & Rapids: 17 (not numbered) excluding swifts.

Lining & Wading Required: 28 (rapids and swifts. Some can be paddled up).

Portages: 4 (1,010 m.)

Monthly Average Flow (1968-1992): May 186 m³/sec., June 240 m³/sec., July 228 m³/sec., August 205 m³/sec., September 193 m³/sec.

Features: A dramatic mix of boreal Shield topography and fenland shorescapes. As you travel north the appearance of steep esker formations and granite outcrops dominate the landscape. Above Lac Brochet the setting takes on a semi-open "parkland" appearance with scattered spruce and jackpine and a hard-packed moss and lichen forest floor interlaced with caribou trails.

WHITEWATER CHARACTERISTICS AND GENERAL HAZARDS

There are sections of heavy current at the base of rapids and through the narrows, even on the larger lakes where there are several island clusters. Lining and wading may be difficult on some of the bigger volume rapids where shore growth forces you out into deeper water; other rapids can be lined or portaged along the shore. We managed to sail with a southerly wind for almost 100 km., ascending some of the easier sections of current. Add extra time in case of strong west, northwest prevailing winds – you could be windbound on Lac Brochet or any of the other larger lakes en route.

THLEWIAZA RIVER – GENERAL INFORMATION

Classification: Experienced Intermediate
  (isolation and difficult rapids)
Distance: 170 km. from Height of Land portage to Nueltin Lake
Elevation Drop: 84 m. (276') or .6 m/km. (2'/km). From Fort
Hall Lake to Nueltin Lake (140 km.).
Time: 7-8 days
Number of Campsites: 28 or 1 campsite every 6 km.
Number of Falls & Rapids: 23 (not numbered)
Number of Runnable Rapids: 20 (75% CII tech. or greater)
Portages: 14 (5,725 m.)
Features: A transitional landscape of rolling esker formations,
beautiful clearwater lakes, and an exciting ride down the "big
river" as the Dene called the Thlewiaza. As you travel eastward the
forest thins out and exposes glacial erratics and open gravel and
sand-based grassy hummocks. Although sighting caribou during
the summer along this stretch is unlikely, you will see an amazing
maze of well-worn trails and old "kill" sites scattered with bones.

WHITEWATER CHARACTERISTICS AND GENERAL HAZARDS

Portaging can be hard work, particularly if you're carrying several
weeks of provisions. Getting from the Cochrane to the Thlewiaza
is easier now because you have decent maps and you won't waste
time following caribou trails looking for the portage. Whitewater
along the upper Thlewiaza is excellent; but be prepared for fast
manoeuvers through rock gardens when water levels are down, and
you might consider a spray deck for the larger CIII's and IV's. This
is not a river for the novice whitewater paddler.

Ragnar Jonsson

RAGNAR JONSSON

Born in Sweden in 1900, Ragnar Jonsson came to Canada as
a young man. After spending some time around Churchill, Prince
Albert and Reindeer Lake he moved to Nueltin Lake in 1939.

Ragnar spent many summers in his teepee on an island at the
southwestern end of Nueltin Lake and from there travelled and
trapped with only his dogs for company, for 43 years. His grounds
included the Seal, Wolverine and Caribou Rivers, one of his
favourite spots being Twin Falls on White Rock Creek.

The campsite at Twin Falls, where you can still find old tins
and trap chains, has since burned out and is no longer the "paradise" that Ragnar once favoured.

Ragnar lived a quiet and remote life, often disappearing into
the bush for years without human contact. He arrived at the
Brochet Trading Post in 1946 to collect his mail and was completely amazed to learn there had been a second World War while
he was travelling, totally oblivious of a world in chaos.

Ragnar died at 88, leaving behind remnants of his life on the
trail, the occasional axe blaze on the stunted spruce to mark a
portage and rusted traps and chains that can still be found pegged
into the sand, scattered along the crests of the eskers.

CARIBOU RIVER – GENERAL INFORMATION

NOTE: The Caribou is divided into two sections "A" and "B" as indicated.

Section "A" – Nueltin Lake, East River (upstream), White Rock Creek (downstream), Wolverine River (upstream), Roberts River (downstream).

Classification: Experienced Intermediate to Advanced
(Isolation and difficult conditions)
Distance: 265 km.
Elevation Drop: 47 m. (154') overall between Nueltin and the beginning of the Caribou River, although the East River rises to 304 m. at Fediuk Lake at mileage 140, increasing the actual real drop to 74 m. (243') for the downstream portion of the White Rock and Roberts River; (.5 m./km. or 1.7'/km.).
Time: 14-16 days
Number of Campsites: 46, or 1 campsite every 6 km.
Number of Falls & Rapids: 18 (not numbered)
Number of Runnable Rapids: 10 (all CI–CII's along White Rock Creek; shallow and technical).
Portages: 11 (4,665 m.) excluding the Roberts River where an additional 3-4 km. may be necessary from Glover to the Caribou River.
Features: Probably the most diverse topography along this trans-Manitoba adventure, you will travel out of the boreal transitional landscape into the barrens – an almost pastoral, rolling plain, eskers and scattered spruce. Some of the most magnificent beaches can be found throughout with excellent opportunities for hiking along miles of esker formations. Caribou start to frequent the area north and east of Nejanalini Lake and weather can be unpredictable due to the Arctic influence off Hudson Bay.

WHITEWATER CHARACTERISTICS AND GENERAL HAZARDS

Canoeists have the option of following this route as indicated throughout; or taking the Wolverine River south out of Nejanalini Lake, and finishing their trip along the Seal. If water levels are low then this is the suggested route to take to avoid needless misery on the Roberts and upper Caribou. The other option is to fly from Nejanalini Lake Lodge (Little Duck Lake as marked on the map), across to Round Sand Lake on the Caribou.

For canoeists staying on the route, be prepared for a work out! You will have to weigh the benefits of the many wilderness features encountered from Nejanalini to the Caribou, with the obvious difficulty of travel in extreme isolation. Having a herd of caribou file past your tent, silhouetted by a tundra sunset, by far made the hardships worth the effort.

The rapids along White Rock Creek were increasingly more difficult as we neared Nejanalini. The last 2 1/2 km. dropped over 15m. through a series of ledges and boulders which defy description. Running was tedious at times although most of the harder sections can be lined with some difficulty along the often undefined shore. Because of the steep pitch it is probably always shallow, good running channels elusive, and the possibility of broaching is high. Large lake travel and unpredictable weather may add extra days to your travel plans, so be prepared. Wading with the canoe requires sturdy footwear – not sandals; be prepared too for lots of bumps and bruises along this stretch.

Section "B" – The Caribou River

Classification: Advanced (Isolated and difficult)
Distance: 205 km. from Round Sand Lake to Hudson Bay. The upper section was not surveyed due to lack of water in the river.
Elevation Drop: 171 m. (560') or .9m/km. (3'/km.)
Time: 12-14 days
Number of Campsites: 32, or 1 campsite every 6 km.
Number of Falls & Rapids: 114 (not numbered) Note: almost all can be run or lined with occasional lift-overs when necessary depending on water levels.
Portages: 3-5, variable but less than 2,000 m., including the 1 km. portage off-river at point of egress.
Features: Because of its remote nature and difficulty, the Caribou River may very well be one of Canada's most pristine wilderness canoe routes. The beauty of Arctic tundra is unsurpassed; from barrenland blueberries, cranberries and a variegated lichen and moss carpet over a macadam of glacial debris, to a veritable menagerie of wildlife, the explorer is certain to have a memorable adventure.

WHITEWATER CHARACTERISTICS AND GENERAL HAZARDS

If you've gotten this far along this route then the Caribou River will be a breath of fresh air. Even in low water it is a marvellous trip through the tundra and the difficulties manageable on a daily basis. Rapids are tough; often starting in defined channels, then becoming quite rocky and sometimes confusing, ending abruptly at steep pitch-offs or ledges. Be prepared for quick stops, a lot of back paddling and lining around ledges. Use a spotter at critical points and a good repair kit. We almost wore the skid-plates completely off our canoes, not to mention the hull paint.

Weather can be intense, wind ever-present, flies bothersome and top that off with the likelihood of running into a polar bear or two near the coast. It doesn't get any better than this!

Long Trip Logistics:
Access: By air charter from either Thompson or Lynn Lake; floatplane access via Lynn Lake to the Cochrane River, or land-base charter from Thompson to Lac Brochet village (see listing of outfitters). Lynn Lake is accessible by road via hwy #391 northwest of Thompson (road is partially paved). Basic supplies at Lynn Lake.
Egress: By pre-arranged floatplane charter pick-up at the end of the Caribou River (see map) and return to Churchill. Via Rail transport back to Thompson. Boat charter pick-up can also be pre-arranged through Churchill outfitters and barge operators.
Maps Required: 64 F/13 64 F/14 64 K/3, 6, 11, 12, 13 64 N/4, 5, 6, 11 64 N/10, 9, 16 64 O/7, 9, 10, 11, 12, 13, 14 64 P/7, 8, 9, 10, 12, 13, 14, 15 54 M/5, 6, 7, 12
Season: July through August.

Definitely not Kevlar country!

"....awakening in the cold pouring rain, we set out, both of us feeling a little grimly that this could not last forever. Passing our shoals of the night before, we soon became involved in the longest rapid either of us had ever known. It was simply mile after mile of fast water and boulders. At noon we were still in it. We boiled up the kettle at a spot which showed some portage signs. We followed this on foot for a long way. It had been made some time in the past by a white man, for the trees showed white man's blazes. The portage was a very bad one; it twisted on endlessly and crossed several stretches of muskeg into which we sometimes plunged up to the knees in water before touching solid ice. At last it faded out into nothing more but a big swamp.

"Coming back to the smoldering fire hissing and spluttering in the downpour, we sat and watched the seething, rushing water for a long time. Both of us were reluctant to portage everything through the rain and the mosquitoes over such a quagmire. Sitting by the fire and half suspended over it to envelop myself in the

smoke and escape the mosquitoes, I wrote (in my journal). When I snapped the little diary shut, seventeen mosquitoes were caught between the pages.

"After several draughts of good black tea from which the black flies and mosquitoes had been skimmed, our spirits felt stronger. For better or worse, we decided to see if we could make a successful descent with poles.

"Down we went, twisting, dodging, sometimes retracing our course and dropping down a different channel as the way became hopelessly blocked with boulders. Sometimes I would get out and wade a little, leading the canoe down through the more impossible stretches. Hour after hour this went on until the river, as if exhausted in its endless struggle against the rocks, spread out into a delta-like fan and became a congested confusion of boulders with scarce four inches of water to be found. These gray boulders and shattered rocks ranged themselves more and more thickly until they coalesced into a solid wall. Where a trickle of water pierced the wall we slipped through, and

then suddenly we came into a fine large lake full of islands."

From P.G. Downes, *Sleeping Island* 1943 Describing the rapids on the Thlewiaza where it empties into Nahili Lake.

Solitary beach on Nueltin Lake – no houseboats here!

COCHRANE, THLEWIAZA, CARIBOU JOURNAL – "42 DAYS ACROSS THE BARRENS"

"POLAR BEAR!" came the cry from along the gravel beach. We all looked at Jöri, waiting for him to point because the rest of us had no immediate inkling as to where the bear might be.

"ACROSS THE RIVER," he waved his arm for us to look, but by now everyone in the party watched as the Volkswagen size boulder came to life and lumbered towards the shore. It stopped, sniffed the air in a manner peculiar to those who dwell at the top of the food chain, and then slipped soundlessly into the water and began swimming our way. It would take the world's third fastest land mammal about 30 seconds to reach our lunching site. I put down my camera and pulled the Mossberg 12-gauge from its scabbard strapped to the canoe thwart, snapped in the clip loaded with bear scare and stood by the shore. The second clip, loaded with magnum slugs, remained in my left vest pocket; I just hoped that it wouldn't be necessary to use them.

There were several strikes against us undertaking such a trip across the barrens

of northern Manitoba: the length of trip, the perceived hardship, a lack of good information and a limited time frame were only incidental reasons. Cliff Jacobsen, an associate outdoor adventure writer from Minnesota, kindly supplied me with an article he had written two years previous to my anticipated sojourn. He called the Caribou the "River from Hell," intoning doom and gloom from frozen headwaters (in July), to rapids too wild to run and impossible to line from willow entangled shoreways.

And still other reputable canoeists insisted that I listen to the voice of reason. Sir Walter Scott, one of my favourite romantic poets, once said, *"When a man has not a good reason for doing a thing, he has one good reason for letting it alone."* Well, what does a maudlin old minstrel know about the call of the wild? Anyway, I had a good enough reason, perhaps, to dispel any notion of doubt...it was, after all, Manitoba's wildest river.

Not to be easily dissuaded, I continued to research the entire route, coming up

with only scant information at best, and yet more reasons to leave well enough alone. Traditionally, the northern Dene (Den-eh) travelled overland, following sinewy eskers that etched their way across the barren landscape. These served the people and the migrant herds of caribou well as elevated highways. Rivers like the Thlewiaza and Caribou were deemed powerful medicine and dangerous entities to be both respected and avoided. The Dene would often cache canoes or build rafts to cross the rivers whenever an esker was disrupted by water, but they were not people of the canoe like the Cree or Ojibway to the south.

Réal Bérard, who produced a prolific set of canoe maps for the Manitoba government in the early 1970's, had left gaping holes in the information trail along this 850-kilometre route; although depicted with an artistic charm, any usable map data was of little help. To complete the *Wilderness Rivers of Manitoba* inventory, I needed a representative route through the wildest region of the province, to supplement the limited information manifested by Parks Canada. Since few studies had been done along this corridor we figured that whatever else we might contribute would help boost the route to Canadian Heritage River status. The warnings against paddling this route only ignited a deeper passion to explore.

Dates were set and flights were booked. My partner Stephanie and I were joined by Jöri and Walter from Switzerland; both had paddled the Bloodvein with me in '95 and were ably willing to endure the full 42 days in our company. We would take the Twin-Otter from Lynn Lake to Brochet, a Dene village on Reindeer Lake near the Saskatchewan border and paddle upstream on the Cochrane for the first week, jump over to the Thlewiaza and ride its turbulent waters to Nueltin Lake, continue up the East River as far as we could and then pond hop southeast to the White Rock River which would dump us into Nejanalini Lake and the Wolverine River. From the Wolverine we could portage west across the tundra to the Roberts River, thus uniting us with the headwaters of the Caribou, five kilometres south of the NWT border. Here we would join the remainder of our group being flown in from Churchill. It would also be our point of reprovision for the last two weeks on the Caribou ending at *TU-CHO-*Hudson Bay.

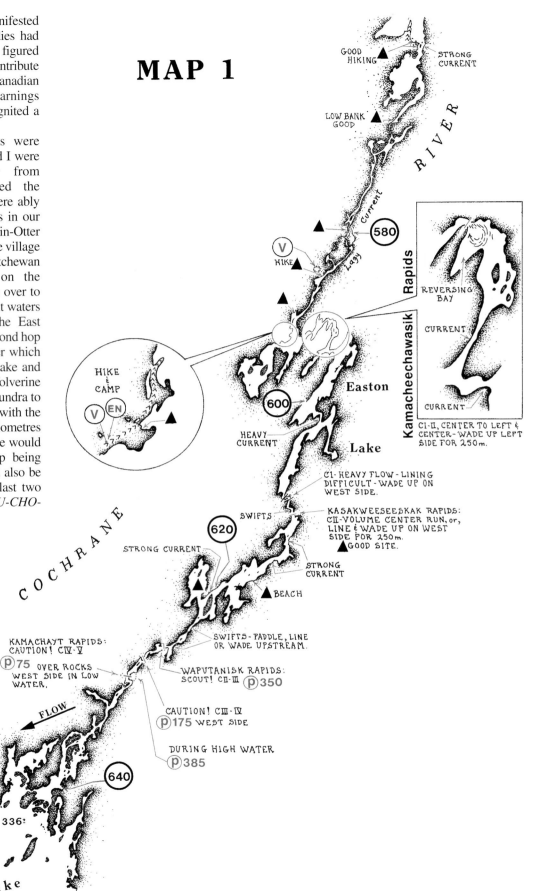

MAP 1

GOOD HIKING

STRONG CURRENT

LOW BANK GOOD

RIVER

Lazy Current

580

V

HIKE

Kamacheechawasik Rapids

REVERSING BAY

CURRENT

CURRENT

Easton

600

HEAVY CURRENT

Lake

C1-II, CENTER TO LEFT & CENTER- WADE UP LEFT SIDE FOR 250 m.

C1- HEAVY FLOW - LINING DIFFICULT - WADE UP ON WEST SIDE.

KASAKWEESEESKAK RAPIDS: CII-VOLUME CENTER RUN, or, LINE & WADE UP ON WEST SIDE FOR 250 m.

SWIFTS

▲ GOOD SITE.

620

STRONG CURRENT

STRONG CURRENT

HIKE & CAMP

V EN

▲ BEACH

SWIFTS - PADDLE, LINE OR WADE UPSTREAM.

COCHRANE

KAMACHAYT RAPIDS: CAUTION! CIV-V

Ⓟ75 OVER ROCKS WEST SIDE IN LOW WATER.

WAPUTANISK RAPIDS: SCOUT! CII-III Ⓟ350

FLOW

CAUTION! CIII-IV Ⓟ175 WEST SIDE

ACCESS

DURING HIGH WATER Ⓟ385

Brochet

640

336'

Reindeer Lake

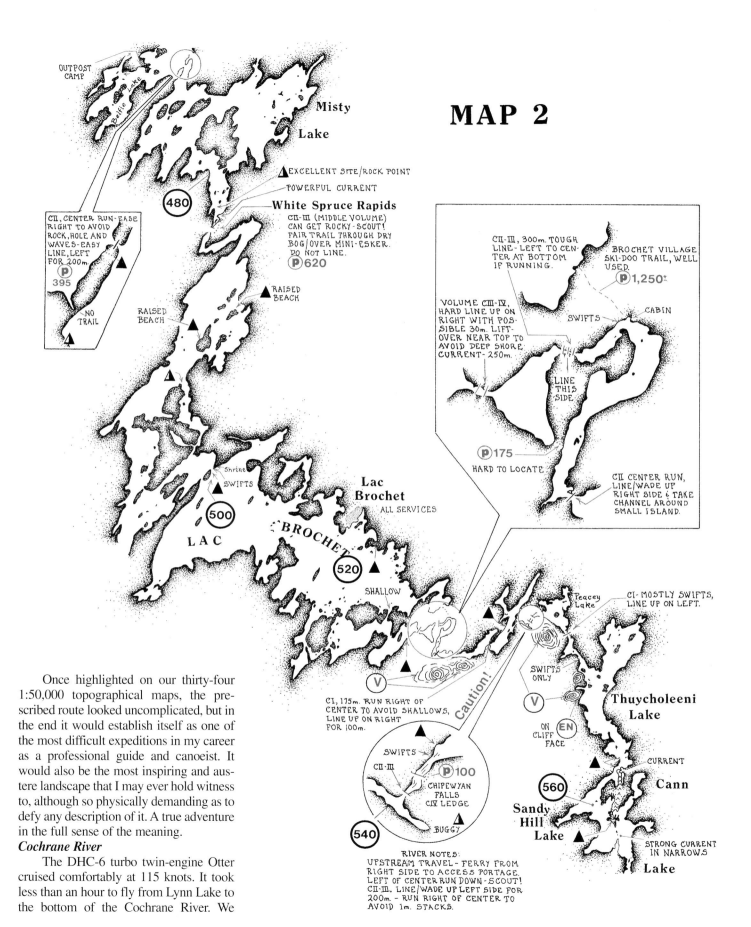

MAP 2

OUTPOST CAMP

Misty Lake

▲ EXCELLENT SITE/ROCK POINT

POWERFUL CURRENT

White Spruce Rapids
CII-III (MIDDLE VOLUME) CAN GET ROCKY-SCOUT! FAIR TRAIL THROUGH DRY BOG/OVER MINI-ESKER. DO NOT LINE.
Ⓟ620

480

CII, CENTER RUN-EASE RIGHT TO AVOID ROCK, HOLE AND WAVES-EASY LINE, LEFT FOR 200m.
Ⓟ395
NO TRAIL
▲
▲

RAISED BEACH

▲ RAISED BEACH

▲

Shrine
▲ SWIFTS

500

LAC

BROCHET

Lac Brochet
ALL SERVICES

520 ▲

SHALLOW

CII-III, 300m. TOUGH LINE - LEFT TO CENTER AT BOTTOM IF RUNNING.

BROCHET VILLAGE SKI-DOO TRAIL, WELL USED
Ⓟ1,250±

VOLUME CIII-IV, HARD LINE UP ON RIGHT WITH POSSIBLE 30m. LIFT-OVER NEAR TOP TO AVOID DEEP SHORE CURRENT- 250m.

CABIN

SWIFTS

LINE THIS SIDE.

Ⓟ175 HARD TO LOCATE

CII CENTER RUN, LINE/WADE UP RIGHT SIDE & TAKE CHANNEL AROUND SMALL ISLAND.

▲ Peacey Lake

CI- MOSTLY SWIFTS, LINE UP ON LEFT.

Ⓥ
CI, 175m. RUN RIGHT OF CENTER TO AVOID SHALLOWS, LINE UP ON RIGHT FOR 100m.

Caution!

SWIFTS ONLY

Ⓥ

ON CLIFF FACE EN

Thuycholeeni Lake

CURRENT

560 **Cann**

▲

SWIFTS
CII-III
Ⓟ100
CHIPEWYAN FALLS CIV LEDGE

▲

540 BUGGY

Sandy Hill Lake

▲

Lake

STRONG CURRENT IN NARROWS

Once highlighted on our thirty-four 1:50,000 topographical maps, the prescribed route looked uncomplicated, but in the end it would establish itself as one of the most difficult expeditions in my career as a professional guide and canoeist. It would also be the most inspiring and austere landscape that I may ever hold witness to, although so physically demanding as to defy any description of it. A true adventure in the full sense of the meaning.

Cochrane River

The DHC-6 turbo twin-engine Otter cruised comfortably at 115 knots. It took less than an hour to fly from Lynn Lake to the bottom of the Cochrane River. We

RIVER NOTES:
UPSTREAM TRAVEL - FERRY FROM RIGHT SIDE TO ACCESS PORTAGE. LEFT OF CENTER RUN DOWN-SCOUT! CII-III, LINE/WADE UP LEFT SIDE FOR 200m - RUN RIGHT OF CENTER TO AVOID 1m. STACKS.

opted to embark from a beach just upstream of the village of Brochet, thus avoiding the open expanse of Reindeer Lake. It was going to prove tough enough plying our paddles against 160 kilometres of swift current to the point of crossover to the Thlewiaza River.

The river bears the name of a surveyor, A.S. Cochrane, who travelled the river in 1881, thirty years after the Hudson's Bay Company erected trade posts at Brochet and Lac Brochet. The Northwest Company first set up shop in 1795 in an attempt to trade with the Nueltin Lake Dene who were then trading at Fort Prince of Wales in Churchill. The Chipewyan Dene began filing to the Brochet posts by way of the Robertson esker, but once a route had been initiated through the Thlewiaza and Cochrane, most travel took place along this corridor.

It took us a week to ascend the Cochrane; luckily, the wind favoured our direction and we were actually able to sail upstream for almost 100 kilometres. The many turbulent rapids, however, proved to be quite challenging, requiring lengthy sessions of wading, lining and vigorous power paddling. The river compromises its directional flow by making an abrupt turn southwest to unite with its headwater lake in Saskatchewan. The entire corridor resides within the Taiga Shield Ecozone, a rolling plain dominated by magnificent rock outcroppings and stunted coniferous forests that showed both recent and regenerative scars from forest fire activity. We camped mostly at what seemed to be traditional Dene hunting sites adjacent to the many eskers along the route and marked by the caribou bones scattered about.

The highlight of the Cochrane was our visit to the Dene village of Lac Brochet early on in our trip. As we arrived at the dock it seemed as if the whole town took a keen interest in our party. Children smiled shyly while youths donning Guns & Roses t-shirts were impatient for any news from the south. They were joined by teams of adults who, it turned out, found it quite interesting that we were paddling all the way to Hudson Bay by way of a river that, to them, would take us to Saskatchewan in the other direction.

At the Band office they seemed honoured that we would take the time to procure the services of a local medicine man so that we could formally ask permission to travel in Dene land. A ceremony was arranged quickly and I was surprised to meet up with the same visiting Navajo healer that I had met at Tadoule in 1994. We were taken by pick-up to a small house in the centre of the village. It is interesting to note that there were far more trucks here than actual kilometres of roads. Others joined in and we all sat in a large circle while preparations were made, smudge-sticks ignited, and the sweetgrass made its round.

We were allowed to talk first, as guests, and with that opportunity thanked the Dene for their hospitality and asked permission to travel through their land with humility and respect. All nodded in compliance and then drum beats and wisps of smoke from the sweetgrass carried the enchanting singing voice of the shaman beyond the realm of the physical place we occupied and a great sense of relief and peace pervaded the room. All trepidation I once had felt about the expedition had been neatly exorcised during the ceremony.

Thlewiaza River

To access the Thlewiaza from the Cochrane we portaged through several small lakes and over the height of land; and no simple explanation can be made of the intrinsic beauty that mixed the heavy toil of the carry with the pleasing grandeur of pristine landscape.

We were leaving any obvious trace of precambria behind, the land now giving precedence to permafrost and thermokarst, heath-rich tundra, polygon peatlands and discontinuous black spruce parkland. Although we had not encountered any caribou, their trails were clearly scribed across the tundra: ancient paths perhaps, etched by the great Kaminuriak caribou herds when they used to migrate this far south and west from the Dubawnt and Yathkyed hinterlands. Any mark upon the fragile turf here would last for centuries.

Scads of sun-bleached caribou bones, intermingling no doubt with those of humans, were scattered haplessly about like pieces of a great terrestrial board game. At one point we stood at the apex of a large esker overlooking Fort Hall Lake, at the narrows before Thanout, and which marked the 1940 burial site of Petit Casimir, chief of the Barren Land Dene. In order to watch his people as they passed by, it is said that Casimir was consigned to the high esker grave in a standing position. Beside a few weathered bones an old leather belt with sheathed knife attached still lay half buried in the sand, no doubt one of the chief's few prized possessions.

Energy here was strong and the wind blew with an unusual fierceness down the lake as if some greater power urged us to move on. The wind was too intense to continue sailing so we separated the canoes here and fastened the spray decks and rolled with the heavy surf and flow of the Thlewiaza – the Big River.

Kasmere Lake was too wild, as it always seems to be windy in these places of the far north, and we had quite a time of it as the shoreline was less than friendly. Waves broke along boulder-strewn shallows much like the tidal flats of Hudson Bay, making it difficult to keep close to shore or even make a safe landing. We did manage to find respite in a quiet beach-lined cove where the weather was sufficiently more peaceful.

The Thlewiaza was every bit as unrestrained and reckless as a summer tornado. And we rode the backs of many frenzied rapids that coursed through bouldery chasms – runs that would surely have swamped an undecked canoe. On Tuninili Lake, while searching for a place to camp amongst a world of boulders and scabrous vegetation, we accidentally fell upon the most amazing tangerine-coloured dolmen stone that must have weighed several tons and was propped ceremoniously in the air by three small rocks.

It was an ancient spiritual site of some significance where huge stones were pre-arranged facing each of the four directions, while two of the dolmens sported an array of primitive projectile points, probably placed there as offerings. The enchanting magic of the tree-lined tundra guided us safely to the immense waters of Nueltin Lake and a much needed rest day. Our schedule was enervating and with the added exploration necessary – we began to fall behind. With the rest, though, rekindled energy could get us back on track; we still had two weeks to go to reach the Caribou River and reprovision – some 300 kilometres to the east, with no prescribed route documentation to guide us.

Nueltin Lake To The Caribou

After sailing a good part of Nueltin Lake, which had only recently shed the last of its ice covering, we headed upstream on the East River. It soon became quite obvious that this was a road less travelled. All canoeists, it seemed, kept strictly to the Thlewiaza, that flowed out of the north end of Nueltin, thus avoiding the sketchy route across the barrens to the Caribou River.

As we ascended creek and river, the waters that tied the lakes together slowly diminished and we found ourselves more often in the water "hauling" than on top of it paddling. The compelling scenery of tundra heath was reminiscent of pastoral Scotland while endless beaches rivalled any found in the Caribbean.

A route was located southeast from Askey Lake through several small lakes that would link us to White Rock River and downstream travel. This obscure route indicated early travel by the Dene people: circles of stone at old camps, well used quartz tooling sites; and more recent axe blazes on the few spruce probably indicated the once travelled trapping route of resident trapper Ragnar Jonsson.

Blunt-leaved pondweed, herb willow and various sedges grew tight to the lake and creek edge, sometimes making portaging difficult. The spongy bog and moss underfoot ensured that our feet would remain wet all day, not to mention the steady rain from the heavens that put Gore-Tex jackets through the ultimate litmus test.

White Rock River took us out to Nejanalini Lake but not without first putting us through a gauntlet of steep, rock-choked rapids full of grayling. There was little room left for water! Taking advantage of the unusual calm on such a large lake we paddled north to the mouth of the Wolverine under the chromatic imagery of a tundra sunset, pitching camp on the flat heath between eskers, in the half-light of an Arctic night.

We began sighting caribou all along the Wolverine. Hardly timid, they stopped to watch us paddle by, or from a secure distance paused in curiosity as we hauled our loads across the tundra between lakes. The Roberts River presented yet a different problem as there was too little water to float the canoes and shore willows were too thick to allow lining or even portaging. For two days we either dragged our canoes over slime-encased river rocks while wading, portaged endlessly along eskers that bordered the Roberts, or skidded our loaded boats across the tundra grass because it was far too windy to carry a canoe over your head.

Exhausted, and only one day from reprovision at the Caribou, the remaining 20 kilometres seemed so very far away. As it was, we had used up our planned rest days sorely needed before meeting with the rest of our group and had little enough energy left to get to the plane the following day. Being somewhat disheartened and argumentative, total peace was restored when a herd of about 200 caribou filed past our campsite just as the sun set.

The next day, upon finally reaching the Caribou, our hearts sank as it became evident that there was no water in the upper reaches of the river. It was necessary to portage the remaining five kilometres to Commonwealth Lake, over the tundra with a strong west wind blowing that made the canoe feel as if you were carrying a sheet of plywood over your head. Exhausted, we were still elevated by the experience of having completed the journey thus far, barely on time. We paid little mind to our blistered and swollen hands or our rock-bruised feet and we slept like babes that night just south of the NWT border.

The Caribou

The rest of our group, including a camera crew from CITY-TV, arrived with fresh food for the last two weeks and 200 kilometres of our trans-Manitoba expedition. I made arrangements with the pilot to jockey us down to Round Sand Lake, 40 kilometres south along the Caribou where I anticipated a better flow, thus avoiding a walk around 50 sets of rapids below Commonwealth.

The Caribou constitutes a rather small drainage basin marked by over 250 steeply-pitched rapids, tumbling 230 metres to Hudson Bay. The barren, almost treeless taiga landscape is erupted by underlying bedrock, forming magnificent mini-canyons and beautifully time-sculptured shelf-rock settings that served well as campsites.

Round Sand Lake was a shallow meteor crater four kilometres across and ringed by extensive beach formations; finding deep water at the river exit was futile and we walked our canoes out of the lake some distance before reaching deep channels. We noticed seals right off so we knew that fishing for grayling wouldn't be that good; with the water levels being so shallow it wouldn't support a concentration of fish where the seals had been land-locked. The caribou herds increased as we progressed downriver and would sometimes stand at the shore, only metres away, while we drifted on.

It took a few days to get everyone accustomed to navigating the rock-garden rapids with any finesse. Although the majority of rapids offered good runs at the top, the terminus was often marked with a steep one to three metre pitch-off that required careful lining. What remained of the Hudson Bay Company post at Caribou Lake was thoroughly enjoyed as part of a rest day. I had brought along a copy of *Trader, Tripper, Trapper, the Life of a Bay*

Portaging across the tundra –
making the Nejanalini/Caribou connection

Hap Wilson

MAP 3

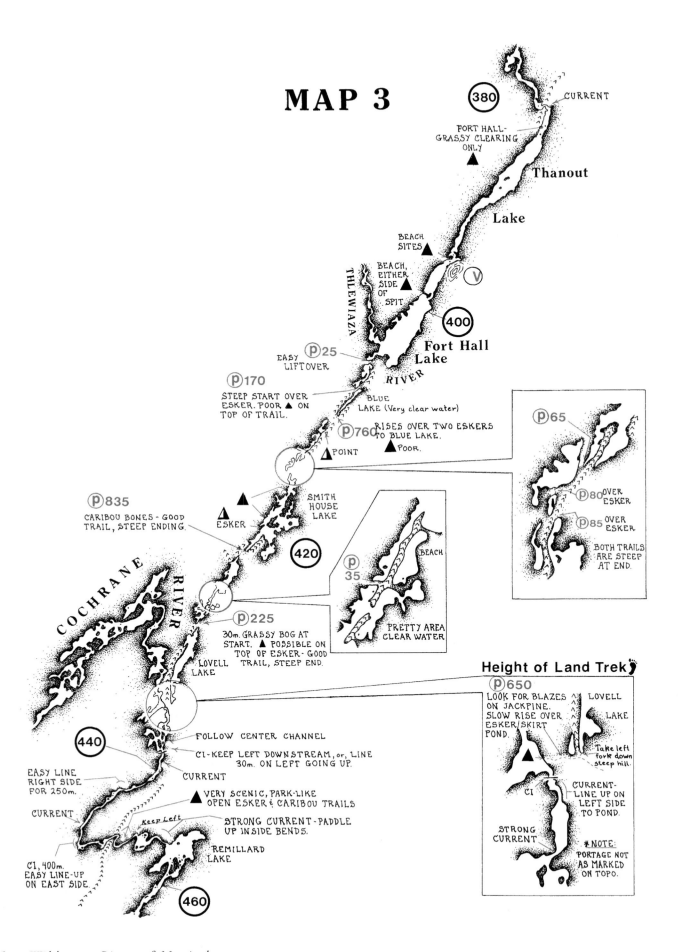

(380)

CURRENT

FORT HALL-
GRASSY CLEARING
ONLY

Thanout

Lake

BEACH
SITES

BEACH,
EITHER
SIDE
OF
SPIT

THLEWIAZA

(V)

(400)

Fort Hall Lake

RIVER

EASY
LIFTOVER

(p)25

(p)170

STEEP START OVER
ESKER. POOR ▲ ON
TOP OF TRAIL.

BLUE
LAKE (Very clear water)

(p)760

RISES OVER TWO ESKERS
TO BLUE LAKE.
▲ POOR.

▲POINT

(p)65

(p)80 OVER
ESKER

(p)85 OVER
ESKER

BOTH TRAILS
ARE STEEP
AT END.

(p)835

CARIBOU BONES - GOOD
TRAIL, STEEP ENDING.

▲

△
ESKER

SMITH
HOUSE
LAKE

(420)

(p)
35

BEACH

PRETTY AREA
CLEAR WATER

COCHRANE

RIVER

(p)225

30m. GRASSY BOG AT
START. ▲ POSSIBLE ON
TOP OF ESKER - GOOD
TRAIL, STEEP END.

LOVELL
LAKE

Height of Land Trek

(p)650

LOOK FOR BLAZES
ON JACKPINE.
SLOW RISE OVER
ESKER/SKIRT
POND.

Lovell
Lake

Take left
fork down
steep hill.

FOLLOW CENTER CHANNEL

CI-KEEP LEFT DOWNSTREAM, or, LINE
30m. ON LEFT GOING UP.

▲

CI

(440)

EASY LINE
RIGHT SIDE
FOR 250m.

CURRENT

CURRENT

VERY SCENIC, PARK-LIKE
OPEN ESKER & CARIBOU TRAILS

CURRENT-
LINE UP ON
LEFT SIDE
TO POND.

Keep Left

STRONG CURRENT-PADDLE
UP INSIDE BENDS.

STRONG
CURRENT

*NOTE:
PORTAGE NOT
AS MARKED
ON TOPO.

CI, 400m.
EASY LINE-UP
ON EAST SIDE.

REMILLARD
LAKE

(460)

MAP 4

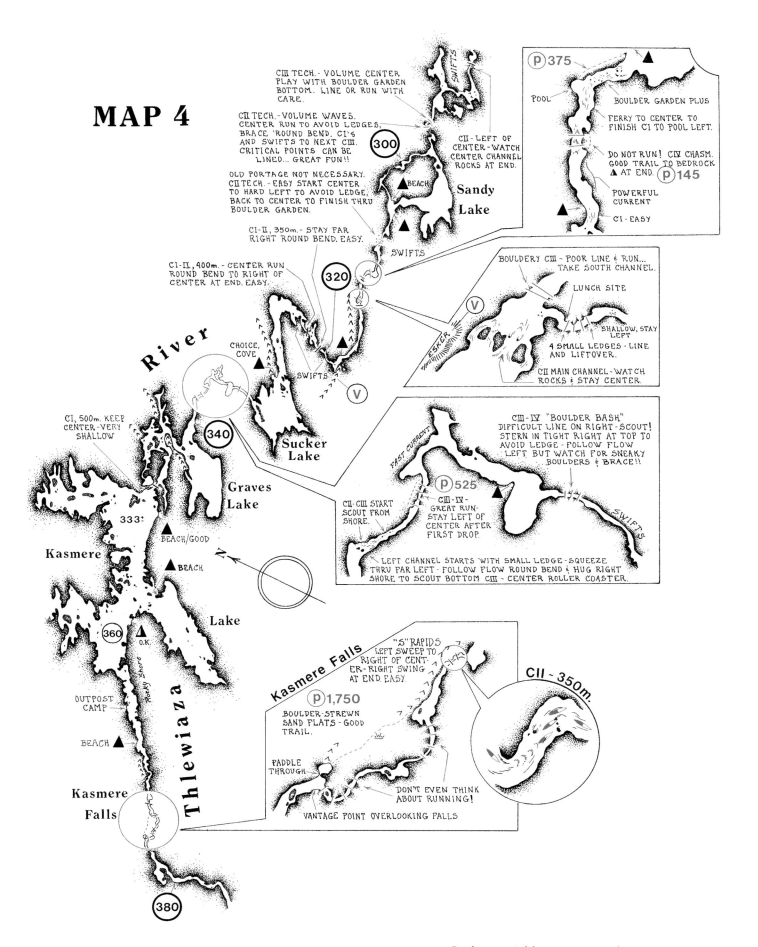

CIII TECH. - VOLUME CENTER PLAY WITH BOULDER GARDEN BOTTOM. LINE OR RUN WITH CARE.

CII TECH. - VOLUME WAVES. CENTER RUN TO AVOID LEDGES, BRACE 'ROUND BEND. CI's AND SWIFTS TO NEXT CIII. CRITICAL POINTS CAN BE LINED... GREAT FUN!!

OLD PORTAGE NOT NECESSARY. CIII TECH. - EASY START CENTER TO HARD LEFT TO AVOID LEDGE, BACK TO CENTER TO FINISH THRU BOULDER GARDEN.

CI-II, 350m. - STAY FAR RIGHT ROUND BEND. EASY.

CI-II, 400m. - CENTER RUN ROUND BEND TO RIGHT OF CENTER AT END. EASY.

(300)

CII - LEFT OF CENTER - WATCH CENTER CHANNEL ROCKS AT END.

SWIFTS

BEACH

Sandy Lake

SWIFTS

(320)

(p)375

POOL

BOULDER GARDEN PLUS

FERRY TO CENTER TO FINISH CI TO POOL LEFT.

DO NOT RUN! CIV CHASM. GOOD TRAIL TO BEDROCK ▲ AT END. (p)145

POWERFUL CURRENT

CI - EASY

River

CHOICE, COVE

SWIFTS

(340)

Sucker Lake

(V)

(V)

ESKER

BOULDERY CIII - POOR LINE & RUN... TAKE SOUTH CHANNEL.

LUNCH SITE

SHALLOW, STAY LEFT

4 SMALL LEDGES - LINE AND LIFTOVER.

CII MAIN CHANNEL - WATCH ROCKS & STAY CENTER.

CI, 500m. KEEP CENTER - VERY SHALLOW

Graves Lake

333'

Kasmere

BEACH/GOOD

▲ BEACH

N

(360)

O.K.

Lake

OUTPOST CAMP

Rocky Shore

BEACH ▲

Thlewiaza

Kasmere Falls

FAST CURRENT

(p)525

CII-CIII START SCOUT FROM SHORE.

CIII-IV GREAT RUN - STAY LEFT OF CENTER AFTER FIRST DROP.

CIII-IV "BOULDER BASH" DIFFICULT LINE ON RIGHT - SCOUT! STERN IN TIGHT RIGHT AT TOP TO AVOID LEDGE - FOLLOW FLOW LEFT BUT WATCH FOR SNEAKY BOULDERS & BRACE!!

SWIFTS

LEFT CHANNEL STARTS WITH SMALL LEDGE - SQUEEZE THRU FAR LEFT - FOLLOW FLOW ROUND BEND & HUG RIGHT SHORE TO SCOUT BOTTOM CIII - CENTER ROLLER COASTER.

Kasmere Falls

"S" RAPIDS LEFT SWEEP TO RIGHT OF CENTER - RIGHT SWING AT END. EASY.

(p)1,750

BOULDER-STREWN SAND FLATS - GOOD TRAIL.

PADDLE THROUGH

CII ~ 350m.

DON'T EVEN THINK ABOUT RUNNING!

VANTAGE POINT OVERLOOKING FALLS

(380)

Trans-Manitoba team; from left to right: Hap Wilson, Stephanie Aykroyd, Walter Von Ballmoos, Jöri Von Ballmoos

Man, the story of S.A. Keighley who had manned the post in the 1930's. By sheer accident, we again located the old trading post graveyard that offered the only frost-free soil in which to bury the dead. Here, we found time-worn picket fence markers, hand hewn and scribed tomb epitaphs, stone cairns and even the head of a Hudson's Bay Company standard issue axe. We left these sites intact, as always, and no souvenirs were pocketed.

The Taiga Shield Ecozone along the Caribou sports the only Manitoba population of hairgrass and is mixed congenially with typical species such as alpine sweetgrass, wiry sedge and diapensia. As we entered the Hudson Plain Arctic Tundra, the assemblage of flora consisted of more coastal species such as sea-purslane, blue heather and nodding saxifrage.

At Long Lake we camped at a busy caribou crossing and watched for two days while small groups swam the narrows of the lake and marched past our tents, seemingly disinterested but mildly curious as to our presence. Near Sac Rapids, while run-

ning a particularly gnarly class III rapid, one canoe happened to unceremoniously unload its passengers. After extricating the canoe and paddlers from the cold water we elected to pitch camp high up on the river bank along the heath plateau. This gave us a panoramic view of the river and an accidental look at a strange barn-size boulder that lay on the tundra about one kilometre away. Upon closer inspection of the monolithic stone – a vivid face appeared to be naturally contoured into the rock, as if a giant head had been plopped upon the ground. It was perhaps a deity, or spirit rock to the travelling Dene who once passed this way; certainly of some significance because a quarter-ton dolmen was hoisted and placed on the crown of the head. No archaeological studies had been carried out on the river to date, although this particular find may constitute one of Manitoba's most unique petroform sites.

The following day we had the polar bear encounter, 20 kilometres inland from the Bay. As the bear started to swim toward us, he suddenly changed his mind

midstream just as I had picked up the rifle. Seeing the bear certainly increased the pace and excitement of the group. Nobody lagged behind.

The river widened near Hudson Bay and it was increasingly difficult to find deep channels. We were forced to make rather lengthy portages over boulder flats; the canoes took quite a beating.

Our rendezvous plane from Churchill was designated to land at a goose camp just off-river on a shallow lake, which we had to make a pilgrimage of 1.5 kilometres across boggy tundra to access. Very tired, somewhat humbled by the vastness of the tundra and in total elation for having arrived intact, all of us had few words to share as we sat in the small plywood shack on the edge of the Arctic Ocean. For some of us who had endured the entire trip across the province, not once encountering any other travellers, it was a soulful journey; only simple expletives could betray the full meaning of it all. Awesome will have to suffice. H.W.

MAP 5

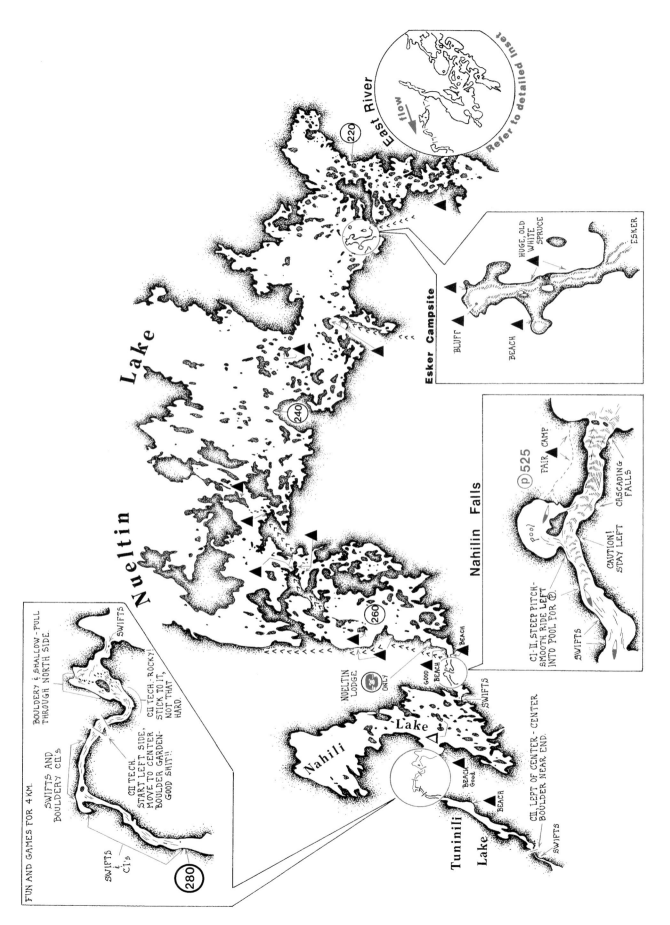

East River

220

Refer to detailed inset

flow

Lake

Nueltin

Esker Campsite

HUGE, OLD WHITE SPRUCE

ESKER

BLUFF

BEACH

240

Nahilin Falls

P 525

FAIR CAMP

CASCADING FALLS

POOL

CAUTION! STAY LEFT

CI-II STEEP PITCH - SMOOTH RIDE LEFT INTO POOL FOR P.

SWIFTS

260

BEACH

GOOD

BEACH

SWIFTS

NUELTIN LODGE

ONLY

FUN AND GAMES FOR 4 KM.

BOULDERY & SHALLOW - PULL THROUGH NORTH SIDE.

SWIFTS

SWIFTS AND BOULDERY CII's

CII TECH. START LEFT SIDE, MOVE TO CENTER BOULDER GARDEN- GOOD SHIT!!

CII TECH.- ROCKY! STICK TO IT, NOT THAT HARD.

SWIFTS & CI's

280

Nahili

Lake

BEACH Good

CII LEFT OF CENTER - CENTER BOULDER NEAR END.

BEACH

Tuninili Lake

SWIFTS

East River Detail

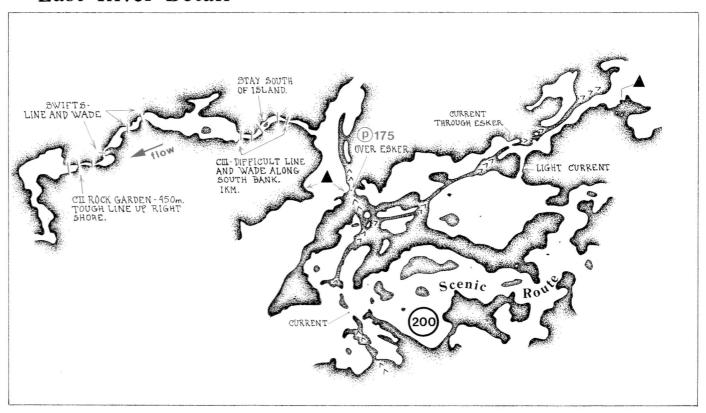

SWIFTS - LINE AND WADE

STAY SOUTH OF ISLAND.

CURRENT THROUGH ESKER

flow

Ⓟ175 OVER ESKER

CIII-DIFFICULT LINE AND WADE ALONG SOUTH BANK. 1KM.

LIGHT CURRENT

CII ROCK GARDEN - 450m. TOUGH LINE UP RIGHT SHORE.

Scenic Route

CURRENT

200

Morning camp on the East River

MAP 6

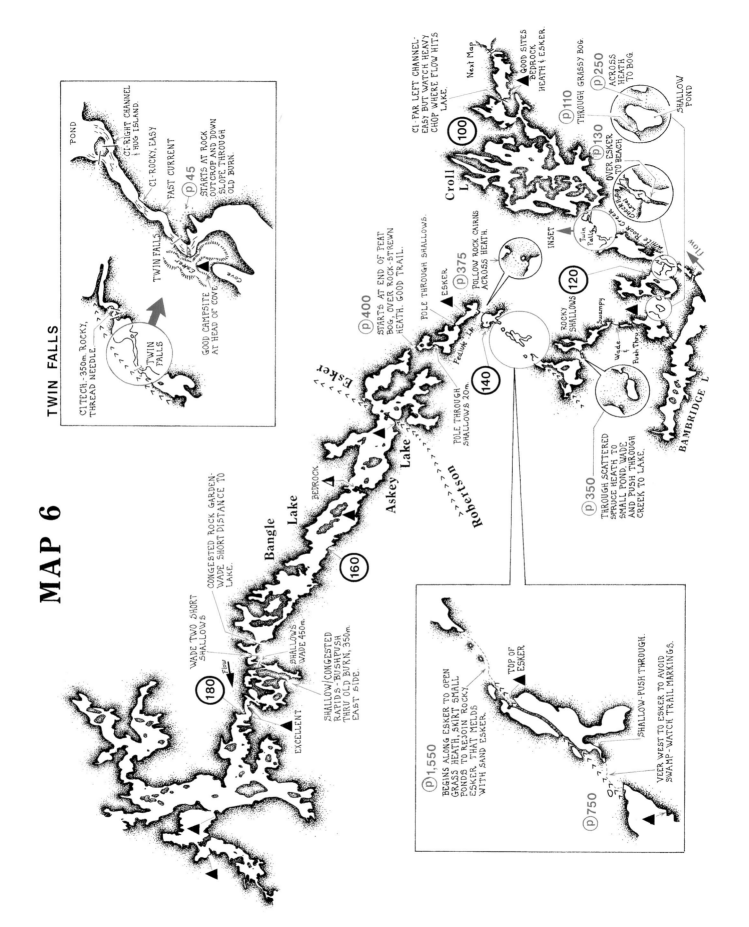

TWIN FALLS

C1 TECH.- 350m. ROCKY, THREAD NEEDLE.

TWIN FALLS

POND

C1-RIGHT CHANNEL & HUG ISLAND.

C1-ROCKY, EASY

FAST CURRENT

STARTS AT ROCK OUTCROP AND DOWN SLOPE THROUGH OLD BURN.

Ⓟ45

GOOD CAMPSITE AT HEAD OF COVE

TWIN FALLS

COVE

Esker

Bangle

Lake

BEDROCK.

CONGESTED ROCK GARDEN - WADE SHORT DISTANCE TO LAKE.

Ⓟ160

Askey

Lake

WADE TWO SHORT SHALLOWS

SHALLOWS WADE 450m.

Ⓟ180

Flow

SHALLOW/CONGESTED RAPIDS - BUSHPUSH THRU OLD BURN, 350m. EAST SIDE.

EXCELLENT

Esker

Robertson

STARTS AT END OF PEAT BOG, OVER ROCK-STREWN HEATH. GOOD TRAIL.

Ⓟ400

POLE THROUGH SHALLOWS.

Ⓟ375

ESKER.

FOLLOW ROCK CAIRNS ACROSS HEATH.

POLE THROUGH SHALLOWS 20m.

Pedlar Lk.

Ⓟ140

C1-FAR LEFT CHANNEL - EASY BUT WATCH HEAVY CHOP WHERE FLOW HITS LAKE.

Next Map

GOOD SITES BEDROCK HEATH & ESKER.

Croll L.

Ⓟ100

Ⓟ110

THROUGH GRASSY BOG.

Ⓟ130

Ⓟ250

ACROSS HEATH TO BOG.

OVER ESKER TO BEACH

SHALLOW POND

CHICKEN CREEK

Little Thode Creek

Twin Falls

INSET

Ⓟ120

ROCKY SHALLOWS

SWAMPY

Wade & Push Thru

Flow

BAMBRIDGE L.

Ⓟ350

THROUGH SCATTERED SPRUCE HEATH TO SMALL POND. WADE AND PUSH THROUGH CREEK TO LAKE.

Ⓟ1,550

BEGINS ALONG ESKER TO OPEN GRASS HEATH, SKIRT SMALL PONDS TO REJOIN ROCKY ESKER THAT MELDS WITH SAND ESKER.

TOP OF ESKER

SHALLOW - PUSH THROUGH.

Ⓟ750

VEER WEST TO ESKER TO AVOID SWAMP - WATCH TRAIL MARKINGS.

MAP 7

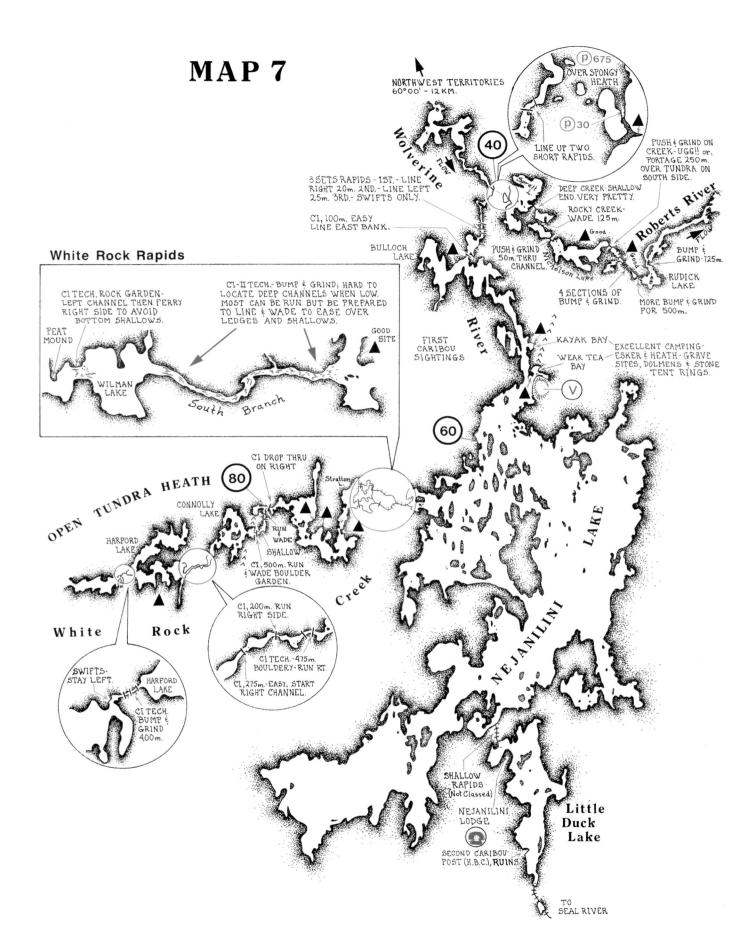

NORTHWEST TERRITORIES
60°00' - 12 KM.

Wolverine

FLOW

③ 675
OVER SPONGY
HEATH

⑫ 30
LINE UP TWO
SHORT RAPIDS.

40

PUSH & GRIND ON
CREEK - UGG!! or,
PORTAGE 250m.
OVER TUNDRA ON
SOUTH SIDE.

3 SETS RAPIDS - 1ST. - LINE
RIGHT 20m. 2ND. - LINE LEFT
25m. 3RD. - SWIFTS ONLY.

DEEP CREEK - SHALLOW
END. VERY PRETTY.

Roberts River

C1, 100m. EASY
LINE EAST BANK.

ROCKY CREEK -
WADE 125m.

FLOW

BULLOCH
LAKE

PUSH & GRIND
50m. THRU
CHANNEL

Good

BUMP &
GRIND - 125m.

Nicholson Lake

RUDICK
LAKE

Good

4 SECTIONS OF
BUMP & GRIND.

MORE BUMP & GRIND
FOR 500m.

White Rock Rapids

C1 TECH. ROCK GARDEN -
LEFT CHANNEL THEN FERRY
RIGHT SIDE TO AVOID
BOTTOM SHALLOWS.

C1-II TECH. - BUMP & GRIND; HARD TO
LOCATE DEEP CHANNELS WHEN LOW.
MOST CAN BE RUN BUT BE PREPARED
TO LINE & WADE TO EASE OVER
LEDGES AND SHALLOWS.

PEAT
MOUND

GOOD
SITE

FIRST
CARIBOU
SIGHTINGS

River

KAYAK BAY

EXCELLENT CAMPING -
ESKER & HEATH - GRAVE
SITES, DOLMENS & STONE
TENT RINGS.

WEAK TEA
BAY

WILMAN
LAKE

South Branch

V

60

C1 DROP THRU.
ON RIGHT

Stratton
L.

OPEN TUNDRA HEATH

80

CONNOLLY
LAKE

RUN &
WADE

SHALLOW.

C1, 500m. RUN
& WADE BOULDER
GARDEN.

NEJANILINI LAKE

HARFORD
LAKE

Creek

C1, 200m. RUN
RIGHT SIDE.

White   Rock

C1 TECH. - 475m.
BOULDERY - RUN RT.

C1, 275m. - EASY, START
RIGHT CHANNEL.

SWIFTS -
STAY LEFT.

HARFORD
LAKE

C1 TECH.
BUMP &
GRIND
400m.

SHALLOW RAPIDS -
(Not Classed)

NEJANILINI
LODGE

Little
Duck
Lake

SECOND CARIBOU
POST (H.B.C.), RUINS

TO
SEAL RIVER

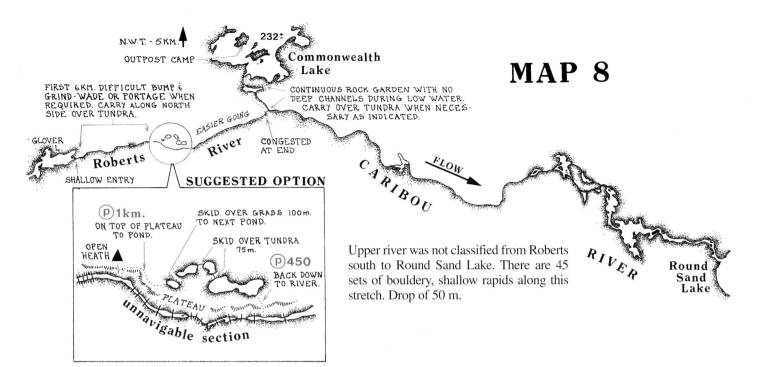

MAP 8

N.W.T. - 5KM.

OUTPOST CAMP

232?

Commonwealth Lake

FIRST 6KM. DIFFICULT BUMP & GRIND-WADE OR PORTAGE WHEN REQUIRED. CARRY ALONG NORTH SIDE OVER TUNDRA.

CONTINUOUS ROCK GARDEN WITH NO DEEP CHANNELS DURING LOW WATER. CARRY OVER TUNDRA WHEN NECESSARY AS INDICATED.

EASIER GOING

GLOVER L.

Roberts River

CONGESTED AT END

SHALLOW ENTRY

SUGGESTED OPTION

Ⓟ **1km.**
ON TOP OF PLATEAU TO POND.

SKID OVER GRASS 100m. TO NEXT POND.

SKID OVER TUNDRA 75m.

OPEN HEATH ▲

Ⓟ **450**
BACK DOWN TO RIVER.

PLATEAU

unnavigable section

CARIBOU

FLOW

RIVER

Round Sand Lake

Upper river was not classified from Roberts south to Round Sand Lake. There are 45 sets of bouldery, shallow rapids along this stretch. Drop of 50 m.

Scouting rapids on the Caribou River

Stephanie Aykroyd

MAP 9

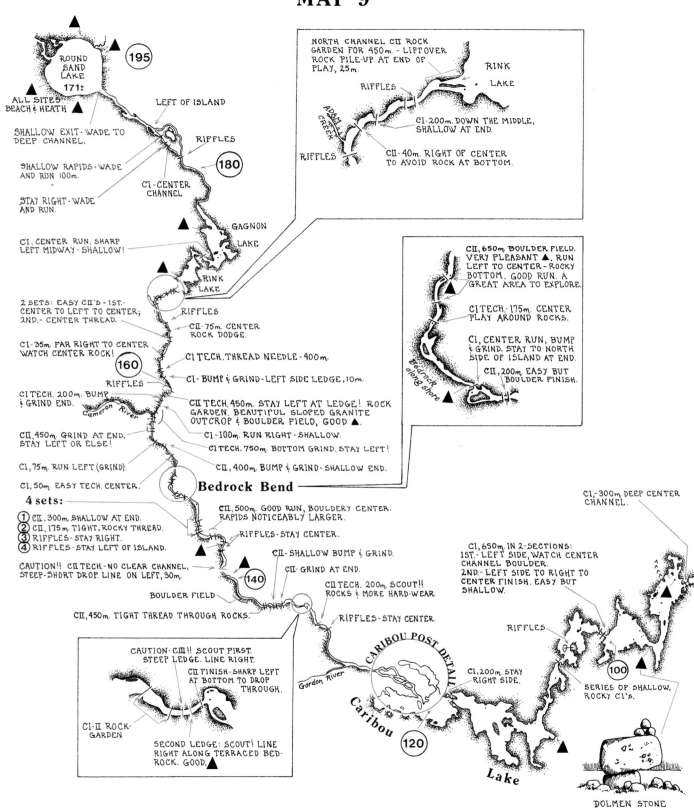

ROUND SAND LAKE 171±

195

ALL SITES BEACH & HEATH

SHALLOW EXIT - WADE TO DEEP CHANNEL.

LEFT OF ISLAND

SHALLOW RAPIDS - WADE AND RUN 100m.

RIFFLES

STAY RIGHT - WADE AND RUN.

180

C1 - CENTER CHANNEL

C1, CENTER RUN, SHARP LEFT MIDWAY - SHALLOW!

GAGNON LAKE

RINK LAKE

2 SETS: EASY C1I's - 1ST. - CENTER TO LEFT TO CENTER; 2ND. - CENTER THREAD.

RIFFLES

C1 - 35m. FAR RIGHT TO CENTER WATCH CENTER ROCK!

CII - 75m. CENTER ROCK DODGE.

160

RIFFLES

C1 TECH. THREAD NEEDLE - 400m.

C1 - BUMP & GRIND - LEFT SIDE LEDGE, 10m.

C1 TECH. 200m. BUMP & GRIND END.

Cameron River

CII TECH. 450m. STAY LEFT AT LEDGE! ROCK GARDEN. BEAUTIFUL SLOPED GRANITE OUTCROP & BOULDER FIELD, GOOD ▲.

CII, 450m. GRIND AT END, STAY LEFT OR ELSE!

C1 - 100m. RUN RIGHT - SHALLOW.

C1 TECH. 750m. BOTTOM GRIND, STAY LEFT!

C1, 75m. RUN LEFT (GRIND).

CII, 400m. BUMP & GRIND - SHALLOW END.

C1, 50m. EASY TECH. CENTER.

4 sets:

① CII, 300m. SHALLOW AT END.
② CII, 175m. TIGHT, ROCKY THREAD.
③ RIFFLES - STAY RIGHT.
④ RIFFLES - STAY LEFT OF ISLAND.

CAUTION!! CII TECH. - NO CLEAR CHANNEL, STEEP - SHORT DROP. LINE ON LEFT, 30m.

Bedrock Bend

CII, 500m. GOOD RUN, BOULDERY CENTER. RAPIDS NOTICEABLY LARGER.

RIFFLES - STAY CENTER.

CII - SHALLOW BUMP & GRIND.

CII - GRIND AT END.

140

BOULDER FIELD

CII TECH. 200m. SCOUT!! ROCKS & MORE HARD-WEAR.

CII, 450m. TIGHT THREAD THROUGH ROCKS.

RIFFLES - STAY CENTER.

CAUTION - CIII!! SCOUT FIRST. STEEP LEDGE. LINE RIGHT.

CII FINISH - SHARP LEFT AT BOTTOM TO DROP THROUGH.

CI-II ROCK GARDEN

SECOND LEDGE: SCOUT! LINE RIGHT ALONG TERRACED BEDROCK. GOOD. ▲

Gordon River

CARIBOU POST DETAIL

Caribou

120

Lake

NORTH CHANNEL CII ROCK GARDEN FOR 450m. - LIFTOVER ROCK PILE-UP AT END OF PLAY, 25m.

RIFFLES

RINK LAKE

ADAM CREEK

RIFFLES

C1 - 200m. DOWN THE MIDDLE, SHALLOW AT END.

CII - 40m. RIGHT OF CENTER TO AVOID ROCK AT BOTTOM.

CII, 650m. BOULDER FIELD, VERY PLEASANT ▲. RUN LEFT TO CENTER - ROCKY BOTTOM. GOOD RUN. A GREAT AREA TO EXPLORE.

C1 TECH. - 175m. CENTER PLAY AROUND ROCKS.

C1, CENTER RUN, BUMP & GRIND. STAY TO NORTH SIDE OF ISLAND AT END.

bedrock along shore

CII, 200m. EASY BUT BOULDER FINISH.

C1 - 300m. DEEP CENTER CHANNEL.

C1, 650m. IN 2-SECTIONS: 1ST. - LEFT SIDE, WATCH CENTER CHANNEL BOULDER. 2ND. - LEFT SIDE TO RIGHT TO CENTER FINISH. EASY BUT SHALLOW.

RIFFLES

100

SERIES OF SHALLOW, ROCKY C1's.

C1, 200m. STAY RIGHT SIDE.

DOLMEN STONE

Caribou Post Detail

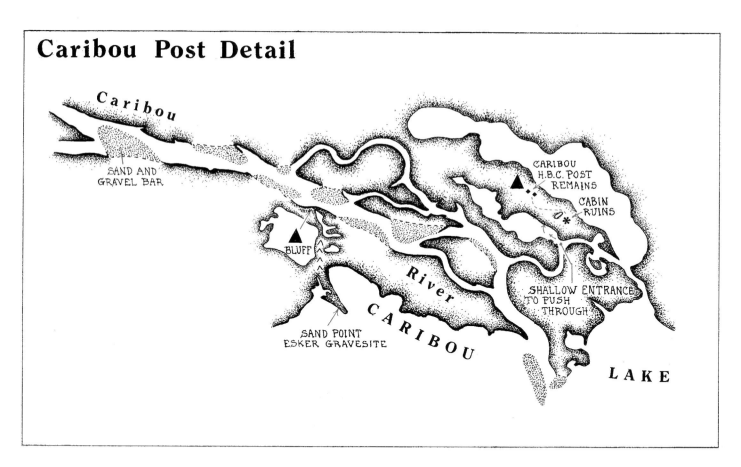

Caribou

SAND AND GRAVEL BAR

CARIBOU H.B.C. POST REMAINS

CABIN RUINS

BLUFF

River

SHALLOW ENTRANCE TO PUSH THROUGH

SAND POINT ESKER GRAVESITE

CARIBOU

LAKE

Stephanie Aykroyd

H.B.C. Post, Caribou Lake, Caribou River

MAP 10

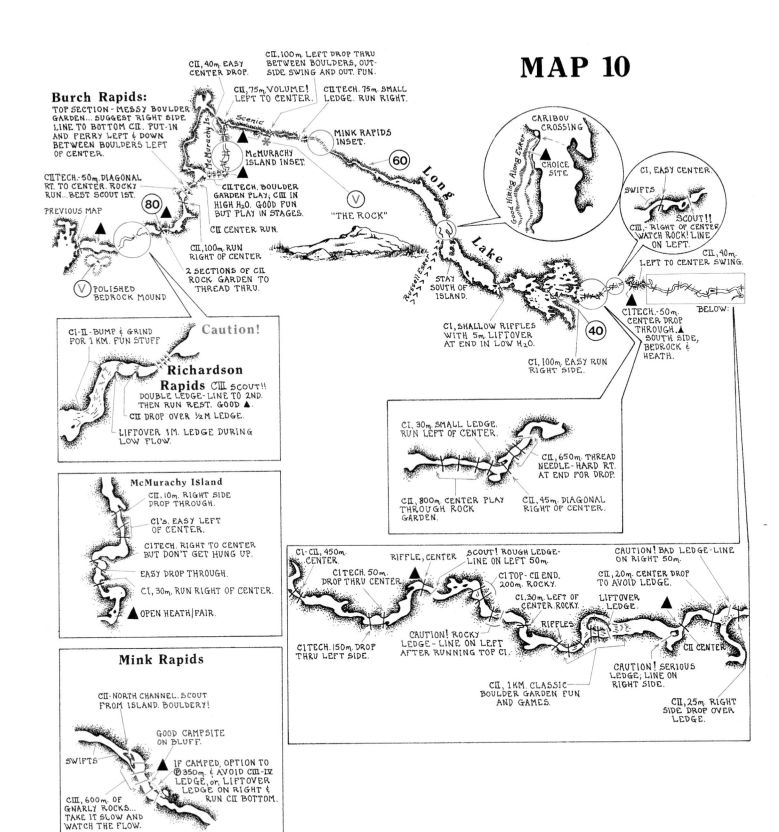

Burch Rapids:
TOP SECTION - MESSY BOULDER GARDEN... SUGGEST RIGHT SIDE LINE TO BOTTOM CII. PUT-IN AND FERRY LEFT & DOWN BETWEEN BOULDERS LEFT OF CENTER.

CII, 40m. EASY CENTER DROP.

CII, 75m. VOLUME! LEFT TO CENTER.

CII, 100m. LEFT DROP THRU BETWEEN BOULDERS, OUTSIDE SWING AND OUT. FUN.

CII TECH. 75m. SMALL LEDGE. RUN RIGHT.

Scenic

McMurachy Is.

McMURACHY ISLAND INSET.

MINK RAPIDS INSET.

CIITECH.- 50m. DIAGONAL RT. TO CENTER. ROCKY RUN... BEST SCOUT 1ST.

CIITECH. BOULDER GARDEN PLAY; CIII IN HIGH H₂O. GOOD FUN BUT PLAY IN STAGES.

CII CENTER RUN.

CII, 100m. RUN RIGHT OF CENTER.

2 SECTIONS OF CII ROCK GARDEN TO THREAD THRU.

PREVIOUS MAP

80

V POLISHED BEDROCK MOUND

"THE ROCK"

60

V

Long Lake

STAY SOUTH OF ISLAND.

Russell Esker

CARIBOU CROSSING

Good Hiking Along Esker

CHOICE SITE

CI, EASY CENTER.

SWIFTS

SCOUT!!

CIII, - RIGHT OF CENTER. WATCH ROCK! LINE ON LEFT.

CII, 40m. LEFT TO CENTER SWING.

CIITECH.- 50m. CENTER DROP THROUGH. SOUTH SIDE, BEDROCK & HEATH.

BELOW:

40

CI, SHALLOW RIFFLES WITH 5m. LIFTOVER AT END IN LOW H₂O.

CI, 100m. EASY RUN RIGHT SIDE.

Caution!

CI-II - BUMP & GRIND FOR 1 KM. FUN STUFF

Richardson Rapids CIII SCOUT!! DOUBLE LEDGE - LINE TO 2ND. THEN RUN REST. GOOD ▲.

CII DROP OVER ½ M. LEDGE.

LIFTOVER 1M. LEDGE DURING LOW FLOW.

CI, 30m. SMALL LEDGE. RUN LEFT OF CENTER.

CII, 650m. THREAD NEEDLE - HARD RT. AT END FOR DROP.

CII, 800m. CENTER PLAY THROUGH ROCK GARDEN.

CII, 45m. DIAGONAL RIGHT OF CENTER.

McMurachy Island

CII, 10m. RIGHT SIDE DROP THROUGH.

CI's, EASY LEFT OF CENTER.

CIITECH. RIGHT TO CENTER BUT DON'T GET HUNG UP.

EASY DROP THROUGH.

CI, 30m. RUN RIGHT OF CENTER.

▲ OPEN HEATH/FAIR.

CI-CII, 450m. CENTER.

CITECH. 50m. DROP THRU CENTER.

RIFFLE, CENTER

SCOUT! ROUGH LEDGE - LINE ON LEFT 50m.

CI TOP - CII END. 200m. ROCKY.

CI, 30m. LEFT OF CENTER. ROCKY.

RIFFLES

CAUTION! BAD LEDGE - LINE ON RIGHT 50m.

CII, 20m. CENTER DROP TO AVOID LEDGE.

LIFTOVER LEDGE.

CITECH. 150m. DROP THRU LEFT SIDE.

CAUTION! ROCKY LEDGE - LINE ON LEFT AFTER RUNNING TOP CI.

CII, 1KM. CLASSIC BOULDER GARDEN FUN AND GAMES.

CAUTION! SERIOUS LEDGE; LINE ON RIGHT SIDE.

CII, 25m. RIGHT SIDE DROP OVER LEDGE.

CII CENTER

Mink Rapids

CII - NORTH CHANNEL. SCOUT FROM ISLAND. BOULDERY!

GOOD CAMPSITE ON BLUFF.

SWIFTS

▲ IF CAMPED, OPTION TO ℗ 350m. & AVOID CIII-IV LEDGE, or, LIFTOVER LEDGE ON RIGHT & RUN CII BOTTOM.

CIII, 600m. OF GNARLY ROCKS... TAKE IT SLOW AND WATCH THE FLOW.

MAP 11

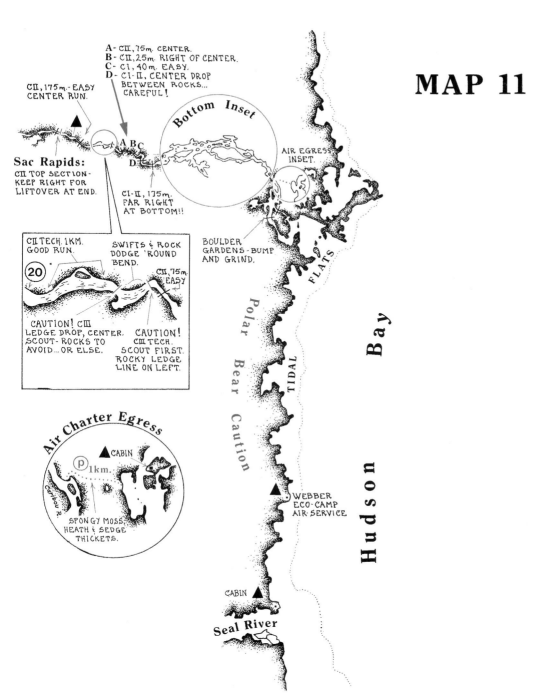

CII, 175m.- EASY CENTER RUN.

A- CII, 75m. CENTER.
B- CII, 25m. RIGHT OF CENTER.
C- CI, 40m. EASY.
D- CI-II, CENTER DROP BETWEEN ROCKS... CAREFUL!

Bottom Inset

A B C
D

AIR EGRESS INSET.

Sac Rapids:
CII TOP SECTION-KEEP RIGHT FOR LIFTOVER AT END.

CI-II, 175m. FAR RIGHT AT BOTTOM!!

BOULDER GARDENS- BUMP AND GRIND.

CII TECH. 1KM. GOOD RUN.

(20)

SWIFTS & ROCK DODGE 'ROUND BEND.

CII, 75m. EASY

CAUTION! CIII LEDGE DROP, CENTER. SCOUT- ROCKS TO AVOID... OR ELSE.

CAUTION! CIII TECH. SCOUT FIRST. ROCKY LEDGE LINE ON LEFT.

Polar Bear Caution

TIDAL FLATS

Air Charter Egress

(p) 1km.

▲ CABIN

Caribou R.

SPONGY MOSS, HEATH & SEDGE THICKETS.

Hudson Bay

▲ WEBBER ECO-CAMP AIR·SERVICE

CABIN ▲

Seal River

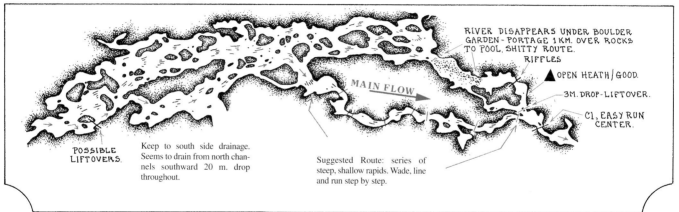

RIVER DISAPPEARS UNDER BOULDER GARDEN- PORTAGE 1KM. OVER ROCKS TO POOL. SHITTY ROUTE.

RIFFLES

▲ OPEN HEATH / GOOD.

3M. DROP- LIFTOVER.

CI, EASY RUN CENTER.

MAIN FLOW

POSSIBLE LIFTOVERS.

Keep to south side drainage. Seems to drain from north channels southward 20 m. drop throughout.

Suggested Route: series of steep, shallow rapids. Wade, line and run step by step.

Nueltin Lake beach

SECTION V

AFTERNOTES

*"To inquire into the intricacies of a distant landscape,
then, is to provoke thoughts about one's own interior
landscape, and the familiar landscapes of memory.
The land urges us to come around to an
understanding of ourselves."*

Barry Lopez

Hap Wilson

RIVER CONSERVATION – THE POLITICS OF WILDERNESS

Bridge over the Leyond that was to be removed in 1994 – still creating its own environmental problem

How we perceive wilderness is a state of mind; it is wholly dependent upon lifestyle, knowledge of the way Nature works, our own personal experiences in the outdoors or opinion consecrated by political fervour.

Our reverence for wild places, regardless of politics, should embrace the spiritual or philosophical, rather than the economic foundation of belief. As a wilderness advocate and activist for three decades I have endured the changes taking place within my own camp, where mainstream environmentalism has taken on a new role – a movement, that I believe, has been modified and destructured by both internal conflict and, political will. Instead of concentrating and acting upon root problems, most mainstream groups are now directing policy that actually encourages technological development, or industrialism that is perceived to be safe for the environment and human life. This has evolved at a time when we are suffering the loss of Canadian wilderness at a breakneck speed. Emphasis should instead be placed on the preservation of "roadless wilderness" and undeveloped water resources.

Canadians, and those organizations charged with the duty of wise resource stewardship and environmental protection, have become complacent, easily swayed by Faustian and myopic politics, and, rendered ineffective when it comes to sparring with the policy makers. This sedateness fashions itself from two angles; distance from the root issue, molded by inexperience in the field and a willingness to make quick compromises.

Not to discredit reform-environmentalism completely, the changes have evolved slowly, through battle, defeat and compromise, and have shifted from radical or "anarcho-environmentalism" whereby policy allows development to happen through various economic justifications.

The Administration, generally, deals only with the tangible, dollar value of natural resources – be they wildlife (fish and game), rivers, or public land (wilderness). To communicate the importance of saving wilderness to the bureaucrats, environmentalists have been forced to adopt a new front or economic philosophy. This meant a quick divorce from the emotional and spiritual plea to save wilderness, and a new foundation in favour of the economic rationale (economics of aesthetics, ie; eco-tourism for instance). Holistic beliefs that praise a healthy environment for reasons of spiritual well-being, have, effectively been locked out of the boardroom where policy, and the state of the environment, is being formulated. Governments continue to re-define wilderness in order to lend itself to a quickly depleting natural resource, and where policy adopts a "multiple-use" paradigm for management.

Aldo Leopold said it best;

"We abuse land because we regard it as a commodity belonging to us. When we see land as a community to which we belong, we may begin to use it with love and respect,"

But there is hope. Changes and awareness evolve slowly; much quicker if we ratify a healthy eco-spiritual view of Nature, the sacredness of the river environment, and our place within the scheme of things. On an individual basis, those who do usurp wilderness must adhere to responsible codes and practice conscientious tripping ethics. River conservation and wilderness protection also demand a respect for the inherent cultural character or identity of place.

Responsibility, as good trippers and responsible citizens, should also include political action when it comes to river conservation.

Canoeists who insist on accessing rivers by way of intrusive logging roads, in political terms, support the creation of yet more roads from the industrial point of view, at a time when "roadless wilderness" should be emphasized. In this book we have been careful not to illustrate these obtrusive access points.

The building of Inukshuks, Inuit waymarkers, within Dene territory by white travellers, is a direct insult to the Chipewyan sites, and the despoiling of wilderness with garbage left behind, are all by-products of ignorance to the traditional ways of the trail.

River conservation and the protection of wild places depends upon us, our actions, our strength of voice, and our involvement within the machinations of the political morass. Manitoba rivers...by getting out there and experiencing them is certainly one way to guide policy in the right direction.   Hap Wilson

Manitoba Hydro – a continued threat to some rivers. How much power is necessary?

CHECKLIST

BASIC

_____ Menu completed (calculated per person/day plus 2 extra days)

_____ All food packed in waterproofed & labelled dry bags

_____ Two sets of maps/map case and this book

_____ Fishing/travel licences purchased

_____ Medical/dental check-up

_____ Itinerary/trip schedule left with family or friend

_____ Outfitter services double-checked & verified

_____ Toilet seat up and kibble left for dog/cat

_____ Note to spouse

SPECIFIC LISTS

PERSONAL SAFETY ITEMS:

First Aid Kit – A good one must include various adhesive-strips, gauze and tape, butterfly closures, antiseptic cream or ointment, pain medication such as Advil, antihistamine such as Benadryl for allergic reactions, antacid tablets (almonds, dried papaya, and fennel tea also work well), scissors, tweezers, razor & new blades, burn cream, lip balm & sunscreen, eye patch & eye flush, finger splint, 2 tensor bandages, blister patches, foot powder, aluminized rescue blanket, and first aid manual. Suggested reading: _"Official Wilderness First-Aid Guide"_ by Wayne Merry/St. John Ambulance.

CEREMONY:

Pouch or plug of tobacco. A gift offering of money & tobacco is often standard etiquette required to secure the services of a medicine healer or shaman for personal ceremony. Tobacco offerings should be done at the beginning of your trip and at places of special prominence such as rock-art sites.

RESCUE AND SAFETY:

_____ PLB/ELT: Cell Phones will soon make these obsolete

_____ GPS unit & waterproof case

_____ Rescue Throw-bag for each canoe

_____ Extra rope: 2 painters per canoe plus 100-150 ft. of climbing rope

_____ Handy prussik lines & carabiners

_____ for quick Z-drag set-up

_____ Bear Scare: 12-gauge with slugs & poppers for Polar Bear country; or flares, air-horn, pepper spray (or just make sure that you can run faster than anyone else in your party!)

_____ Good Insurance Policy if none of the above works

EQUIPMENT PARTICULARS

_____ Paddles (plus one spare per canoe)

_____ Appropriate canoe(s)

_____ Knee pads (affixed or slip-on type)

_____ Padding for yoke(s)

_____ Bailer & sponge per canoe

_____ Flotation bags and/or spray-deck

_____ Quality tent(s)

_____ Kitchen fly and/or bug canopy

_____ Rope bag for tarps

_____ Ground-sheet for tent(s)

_____ Stove, fuel, funnel, fire-irons or grill (for open fire cooking)

_____ Reflector-oven (optional for baking)

_____ Pots, dishes, cups & cutlery

_____ Dishtowel, scrubber, bio-degradable soap & wash basin

_____ Compass, whistle per person

_____ Water purifier or tablets

_____ Dromedary bag or water bucket (collapsible)

_____ Sleeping-bag(s) & therma-rest

_____ Toilet paper

_____ Day-pack with water bottle & goodies

_____ Waterproof matches/lighter

_____ Folding saw and axe (no hatchets)

_____ Garbage bags & zip-lock bags

_____ Gear packs, dry-bags, kitchen wannigan checked out

PERSONAL ITEMS:

_____ PFD (personal flotation device)

_____ Clothing: 2-piece Gore-Tex rain suit, paddling gloves, bug-jacket/headnet, hat or bandanna, canoe shoes & boots, wool socks, long underwear, briefs, T-shirts, fleece or wool sweater, baggy pants & shirts (quick-dry), bathing suit

_____ Sunglasses & skin protection

_____ Belt knife

_____ Whistle

_____ Toiletries, towel & face cloth

_____ Personal medication/vitamins

_____ Insect repellent (avoid DEET and use natural types)

_____ Cards/games for rainy days

_____ Mouth harp/musical instrument

_____ Diary or Journal pad & pens

_____ Camera, waterproof case, extra battery & film

_____ Compact fishing kit & lure box *NOTE: barbless hook regulation in Manitoba

EMERGENCY REPAIR KIT

- Roll of quality duct tape
- Mutli-tool
- Tent-screen patch kit/Therma-rest patch kit
- Sewing kit/extra buttons & heavy-duty waxed thread
- Self-tapping screws for quick canoe repairs
- Extra Snap-X fasteners for packs
- Waterproof adhesive
- Roll of copper wire

PLEASE NOTE:

These are only suggested basic checklists; you may wish to add or delete items listed according to personal preferences.

Menu Chart – 2 Weeks

BREAKFAST	LUNCH	DINNER

DAY 1

BREAKFAST	LUNCH	DINNER

DAY 8

BREAKFAST	LUNCH	DINNER

DAY 2

BREAKFAST	LUNCH	DINNER

DAY 9

BREAKFAST	LUNCH	DINNER

DAY 3

BREAKFAST	LUNCH	DINNER

DAY 10

BREAKFAST	LUNCH	DINNER

DAY 4

BREAKFAST	LUNCH	DINNER

DAY 11

BREAKFAST	LUNCH	DINNER

DAY 5

BREAKFAST	LUNCH	DINNER

DAY 12

BREAKFAST	LUNCH	DINNER

DAY 6

BREAKFAST	LUNCH	DINNER

DAY 13

BREAKFAST	LUNCH	DINNER

DAY 7

BREAKFAST	LUNCH	DINNER

DAY 14

River Notes

_____

_____

_____

_____

_____

_____

_____

_____

_____

_____

_____

_____

_____

_____

_____

_____

_____

_____

_____

_____

_____

_____

BIBLIOGRAPHY AND SUGGESTED READINGS

RESOURCE MATERIAL

Brandson, Lorraine E.
1981 *From Tundra to Forest – A Chipewyan Resource Manual,* Manitoba Museum of Man & Nature.

Hallowell, A. Irving
1992 *The Ojibwa of Berens River Manitoba – Ethnography into History,* Jennifer S.H. Brown editor, Holt, Reinhart and Winston

Woodland Caribou Provincial Park – Background Information, 1986, Queen's Printer for Ontario, OMNR document. Copies available from the Red Lake District Office, P.O. Box 5003, Red Lake, Ontario, P0V 2M0

Lytwyn, Victor
1986 *The Fur Trade of the Bloodvein River,* Technical Report #5, OMNR document.

Steinbring, Jack H.
1981 *Saulteaux of Lake Winnipeg – Handbook of North American Indians,* Subarctic, vol. 9, Smithsonian Institute, Washington

Kor, Philip S.G.
1986 *A Brief Geology and Geomorphology of Woodland Caribou Prov. Park,* Technical Report, OMNR document

Brunton, Daniel F.
1986 *A Reconnaissance Life Science Inventory of Woodland Caribou Prov. Park,* Technical Report, OMNR document

Walshe, S.
1980 *Plants of Quetico and the Ontario Shield,* University of Toronto Press

Wepruk, Randy L.
1986 Woodland Caribou Investigation of Woodland Caribou Prov. Park/1985, Technical Report, OMNR document

McDonald, Archibald
1872 *Peace River: A Canoe Voyage from Hudson Bay to the Pacific Ocean by the late Sir George Simpson,* 1828, archives

Thompson, David
1971 Travels in Western North America 1784-1812, edited by Victor G. Hopwood, MacMillan of Canada

Morse, Eric W. 1969
Fur Trade Canoe Routes of Canada: Then and Now, Queen's Printer, Ottawa.

Lanken, Dane
1996 "Home of the White Bear," *Canadian Geographic,* Nov./Dec. issue pp.26-34

Dodds, Graham
1990 *Towards a Management Plan for the Seal Heritage River,* CHRS/Manitoba Natural Resources, Technical document

Weir, Thomas
1983 Manitoba Atlas, Surveys and Mapping Branch

Kurt, Donna
1992 *Bloodvein River Trip Report,* Manitoba Recreational Canoeing Association

Manitoba Canadian Heritage River Site Surveys, Background documents, Parks Canada

SUGGESTED READING

Rajnovich, Grace
1994 *Reading Rock Art – Interpreting the Indian Rock Paintings of the Canadian Shield,* Natural Heritage, Toronto

Blondin, George
1997 *Yamoria – The Lawmaker, Stories of the Dene,* Newest Press

Warren, William W.
1984 *History of the Ojibway People,* (first published 1885), Minnesota Historical Society Press.

Keighley, Sydney Augustus
1989 *Trader, Tripper, Trapper – The Life of a Bay Man,* Watson and Dwyer Publishing Ltd.

Beardy, Flore/Coutts, Robert
1996 *Voices from Hudson Bay – Cree Stories from York Factory,* McGill-Queen's University Press.

Downes, P.G.
1943 *Sleeping Island, The Story of One Man's Travels in the Great Barren Lands of the Canadian North,* Western Prairie Books

Franklin, John
1970 *Narrative of a Journey to the Shores of the Polar Sea in the Years 1819,* 20, 21, 22, Charles F. Tuttle editor.

Gahlinger, Paul M.
1995 *Northern Manitoba From Forest to Tundra, A Canoeing Guide and Wilderness Companion,* G.B. Communications.

Johnston, Basil
1976 *Ojibway Heritage,* McClelland and Stewart.

Walbridge, Charles/Sundmacher, Wayne A. Sr.
1995 *Whitewater Rescue Manual, New Techniques for Canoeists, Kayakers, and Rafters,* Ragged Mountain Press

Buchanan, John 1997
Canoeing Manitoba Rivers, Rocky Mountain Books

Merry, Wayne 1994 *Official Wilderness First-Aid Guide,* St. John Ambulance, McClelland and Stewart.

DIRECTORY OF SERVICES

CANADAMAPSALES.COM
MANITOBA CONSERVATION
PRODUCT DISTRIBUTION
MAP SALES OFFICE

Canadamapsales.com offers a wide variety of mapping products and services for across Canada, for both the outdoor and recreational enthusiast. Topographic maps, canoe route maps, hydrographic/aeronautical charts and angling maps are only a sample of the wide range of products available.

Manitoba Conservation
Canadamapsales.com
Product Distribution
1007 Century
Winnipeg, MB R3H 0W4
Toll free call: 1-877-627-7226
Fax: 1-204-945-1365
Email: mapsales@gov.mb.ca

NORTHERN SOUL WILDERNESS
ADVENTURES

Breathe the pine scented air, feel the spray of the rapids, or dip your paddle into adventure. Northern Soul is your specialist for guided canoe adventures on the wilderness lakes and rivers of Manitoba. Custom tours, CRCA certified instruction, rentals, wilderness food catering, shuttle services and route consultation.

Northern Soul Wilderness
Adventures
67 Cunnington Ave.
Winnipeg, MB R2M 0W4
Toll free call: 1-866-284-4072
Tel: 204-284-4072
Fax: 204-477-5525
Email:
adventure@northernsoul.ca

WAVE TRACK CANOES
& KAYAKS

Wave Track is Winnipeg's largest specialty canoe and kayak store. We sell and rent from a large number of manufacturers such as Old Town, Wenonah, Western Clipper, Grumman, Clearwater, Dimension, Necky, Ally and more. We also sell topo maps, paddles, life jackets, tents, sleeping bags, water filters and everything else needed to enjoy your canoe or kayak trip. We are always happy to answer any questions on trips or equipment.

Wave Track Ltd.
42-C Speers Rd.
Winnipeg, MB R2J 1M3
Tel: 204-231-8226
Fax: 204-231-8227
Email: wavetrak@mts.net

DYMOND LAKE OUTFITTERS

Servicing northern Manitoba and Nunavut rivers — including the Seal, Knife, Caribou, Churchill and many others. Complete fly-in service, canoe rentals, outfitting, pick-up & drop-off and shuttle service. Accommodations/food service at one of our lodges for pre & post trip can be arranged in advance.

Dymond Lake Outfitters Ltd.
P.O. Box 304
Churchill, MB R0B 0E0
Toll Free call: 1-888-932-2377
Fax: 204-675-2386
Email: info@webberslodges.com

HORIZON'S UNLIMITED

Horizon's Unlimited is located on the Churchill River in northern Saskatchewan. We offer guided canoe trips on most Saskatchewan Rivers and many rivers in northern Manitoba and eastern Nunuvat. Horizon's also offers extensive canoe courses in whitewater, canoe camping and river rescue. We also have canoes and canoeing equipment for rent, shuttle services, maps, route information and overnight cabins.

Horizon's Unlimited
Box 1110
LaRonge, Sask, S0J 1L0
Tel/Fax: 306-635-4420
Email: ric.crco@sasktel.net

NORTHWAY AVIATION LTD.

The most affordable fly-in, canoe out access to the Bloodvein River from our base at Pine Dock. For over 40 years Northway has flown to the Bloodvein, Berens, Pigeon, Gammon, Leyond and Sasaginnigak rivers. We have Cessna 180, Cessna 185, Beaver and Otter aircraft on floats. Canoe rentals are available.

Northway Aviation Ltd.
Pine Dock, Manitoba
Tel: 1-888-536-5353
or 204-276-2084
Email: info@biscuitharbour.com

WAMAIR SERVICE &
OUTFITTING INC.

Providing air service, canoe rentals (Nova Craft ABS), shuttles and outfitting to Manitoba's Bloodvein, Berens, Pigeon, Poplar and many other wilderness river. As one of Manitoba's most respected fly-in and outfitting services, we use Cessna 180, 185, Beaver and Otter aircraft. Visit our website for more information. Open year round.

Wamair Service and
Outfitting Inc.
General delivery
Matheson Island, MB, R0C 2A0
Tel: 204-276-2410
Fax: 204-276-2101
Email: kmowat@escape.ca

MANITOBA PIONEER CAMP

Offering canoeing instruction and canoe trips ranging from three day lake trips to ten day whitewater trips for people of all ages and abilities (or disabilities). Spring and fall programs. Our mission is to provide world class wilderness-based recreation and education that promotes integration, interdependence, environmental awareness and personal challenge in a Christian setting.

Manitoba Pioneer Camp
230 Sherbrook St.
Winnipeg, MB, R3C 2B6
Tel: 204-788-1070
Fax: 204-788-1001
Email: pioneercamp@mts.net

SOURIS RIVER CANOES

Manufacturer of lightweight, high quality Kevlar/Epoxy and Duralite canoes (including the stable, tough, lightweight Quetico 17). Souris River Canoes are the number one choice of the finest outfitters in North America.

Souris River Canoes
104 Reid St. Box 1116
Atikokan, Ontario, P0T 1C0
Tel: 807-597-1292
Fax: 807-597-1292
Toll free: 1-888-CANOE-86
Email: keith@sourisriver.com

PADDLING MANITOBA.COM

We are an amalgamation of industry-leading Manitoba-based, eco and adventure tourism operators that specialize in paddling programs. The respected members of PaddlingManitoba.com, set the highest standards for safe, professional and environmentally respon-sible experiences on Manitoba's waterways. Introductory programs to extended wilderness whitewater adventures.

PaddlingManitoba.com
P. O. Box 2384
Winnipeg, MB, R3C 4A6
Toll free: 1-877-432-6868
Email:
info@PaddlingManitoba.com

SUNRISE ADVENTURES

Thirty years experience in wilderness education and adventure tours. Hap Wilson and Stephanie Aykroyd offer challenging and environmentally oriented eco-tours throughout most of Canada. Check our website for more information.

Sunrise Adventures
1141 Crawford St.
Rosseau, Ontario, P0C 1J0
Tel: 705-732-8254
Fax: 705-732-8255
Email: sunrise@vianet.on.ca

WILDERNESS SPIRIT
CANOEING ADVENTURES

We offer guided canoeing adventures in the pristine Canadian Shield and arctic wilderness of Manitoba and Nunavut Territory. Specializing in customized adventures, trips range from 4-16 days and include the Bloodvein, Hayes, Seal, Thelon (Heritage Rivers) and many others. Fully outfitted and professionally guided wilderness trips.

Wilderness Spirit
696 McMillan Ave.
Winnipeg, MB, R3M 0V1
Tel: 204-452-7049
Toll free: 1-866-287-1591
Email:
info@WildernessSpirit.com